Qigong Theory

混元整體理論

Hou Hee Chan

Based on the teachings & writings of Dr. Pang Ming

Disclaimer

To reduce the risk of injury, consult your doctor before beginning this or any exercise program. The instructions and advice presented are in no way intended as a substitute for medical counseling. The author, the editors, Chilel Qìgōng, Inc., producers, participants and distributors of this book are not liable for any inadvertent errors or for misinterpretation or misuse of information presented here. The author, the editors, Chilel Qigong, Inc., producers, participants and distributors of this book disclaim any liability or loss in connection with exercise and advice herein.

Published by: Chilel Qìgōng, Inc.
PO Box 2097
Rocklin, CA 95677

Website: www.chilelwellness.com
www.chilel.com

Email: info@chilelwellness.com

ISBN: 978-1-893104-16-7

SPECIAL THANKS TO DR. PÁNG MÍNG

Zhìnéng Qìgōng Founder：Páng Míng

智能氣功編創人：龐明

Páng (family name) Míng, also known as Páng Hè Míng (龐鶴明), was born in September 1940 in Hébĕi (河北), China. He is the founder of *the Huáxià Zhìnéng Qìgōng Clinic & Training Center (華夏智能氣功培訓中心),* He was an associate editor of the "Eastern Qìgōng" Magazine ("東方氣功" 雜誌常務副主編), and chairman of the Advisory Committee of Beijing Qìgōng Research Association (北京氣功研究會顧問委員會主任).

After graduating from the Beijing Physician School (北京醫士學校) in 1958, he worked as a Clinical Internist from 1958 to 1962. During that period of time, he studied Traditional Chinese Medicine at the Beijing Physician Association (北京醫師會) and has worked as a Traditional Chinese Medicine doctor since 1963.

From an early age, Dr. Páng has had a keen interest in Traditional Chinese Medicine (especially Acupuncture), Qìgōng and the Martial Arts. He has studied with nineteen teachers, beginning with teachers of Buddhist Qìgōng, and then Martial Art Qìgōng. In the 1970s, he began to study and did research on Dàoist Qìgōng and Folk Qìgōng.

With his unique knowledge of both Western and Traditional Chinese Medicine and Qìgōng, he started the movement for the establishment of the first Qìgōng research organization for the general public—the Beijing Qìgōng Research Association (北京氣功研究會) in 1979, and became one of its founders. He was one of the organizers for the first National Qìgōng Conference (全中國氣功匯報會), July 1979.

In the 1980s, he began to reform Traditional Qìgōng. With innovative applications to Qìgōng, he created Zhìnéng Qìgōng in the early 80's, and in 1989, he opened the first Zhìnéng Qìgōng school in Shíjiāzhuāng, Hébĕi Province (河北省石家莊). Later, he moved the school to Qínhuángdăo (秦皇島), and renamed it "*the Huáxià Zhìnéng Qìgōng Clinic & Training Center*." From 1989 to 1993, the school trained more than sixty thousand students. Dr. Páng has written many articles and has published over fifteen books on Qìgōng.

ACKNOWLEDGMENTS

When I was studying at *the Huáxià Zhìnéng Qìgōng Clinic & Training Center* in the early 90s, during one of his lectures, Dr. Páng Míng mentioned that some of us (the audience) may have difficulties in comprehending the concept of *the Hùn Yuán Wholistic Theory*. It was an understatement; to understand the theory vaguely in Chinese is one thing, to interpret it into English needs team efforts.

I want to thank Fàn Bǎo Zhēn 范寶珍 Lǎoshī of New Zealand for sharing with me her collections of Zhìnéng Qìgōng literature; her collections of Dr. Páng Míng's lectures on the Hùn Yuán Wholistic Theory are the main source materials I used for this book. I owe a special debt of gratitude to my colleagues and editors B. J. Kish Irvine, Ph.D. and Barbara Benson, J.D. They spent a considerable number of hours editing and clarifying each sentence of this book. Although their efforts were hindered by the poor written materials presented to them, their editing and suggestions helped to refine the presentation of this book and are the main reasons that the message in this book is easily understood. In this book, I follow the accepted practice used by organizations such as Associated Press, the Washington Post and the American Dialect Society to use singular they as a gender-neutral singular pronoun. To maintain the original style of Dr. Páng's writing as much as possible, I may not follow my editors' recommendations in some of the writings. Any mistakes in the book are mine, not my editors'. Finally, I owe my deepest debt to my wife, Eva Lew, M.D. This book would not have been possible had it not been for her support and encouragement.

Most of all, I am indebted to all my students. By teaching them, I gained many insights into the art of Qìgōng. They are not only my students; they are my colleagues and teachers.

Please note that this book is based on the writings and teachings of Dr. Páng. It is not a direct translation of his work.

Table of Contents

SERIES PREFACE

After helping Guō Lín Lǎoshī (郭林老師) establish the theoretical aspects of the Xīn Qìgōng (新氣功), Dr. Páng Míng began to reform Traditional Qìgōng in the 1980s. With innovative applications to Qìgōng, he created his own system and called it Zhìnéng Qìgōng (智能氣功); Zhìnéng means intelligent. In 1989, he opened the first Zhìnéng Qìgōng school in Shíjiāzhuāng, Hébĕi Province (河北省石家莊). Later, he established the first research and training center dedicated to exploring human potential through the ancient art of Qìgōng in the city of Qínhuángdǎo (秦皇島). He named it *the Huáxià Zhìnéng Qìgōng Clinic & Training Center (華夏智能氣功培訓中心).* Zhìnéng Qìgōng has become one of the most popular forms of Qìgōng which has ever been created.

In 1995, in order to introduce Zhìnéng Qìgōng to non-Chinese, Dr. Páng gave approval for my brother, Luke, and me to teach Zhìnéng Qìgōng as Chilel Qìgōng in the Americas and in Europe. Throughout the years, we have shared the arts of Chilel Qìgōng with thousands of people. Although Luke has written a book titled *101 Miracles of Natural Healing* documenting some of the healing powers of Chilel Qìgōng, we do not use teaching manuals in our teachings. Basically, we tailor our teaching to each individual class/workshop. As our students and other teachers began to teach the methods outside of China, standardized non-Chinese text books became necessary. With the support and encouragement from my colleagues and students, I took on the challenges to translate and interpret some of Dr. Páng's writings.

Dr. Páng Míng has written extensively on Qìgōng including a nine-book series on Zhìnéng Qìgōng. The challenges facing me and my colleagues who have translated some of his work into other languages are that he wrote for an audience with a very specific background and his Zhìnéng Qìgōng books in the series are related to one another. A reader who does not have sufficient knowledge in Dàoism, Buddhism, Confucianism and Tàijí Quán may have a difficult time understanding a direct translation of his work. To translate just one book of the Zhìnéng Qìgōng series does not make for easy reading either, because some of the background information is in another book. No one can translate Dr. Páng's books as they are written; all one can do is to interpret them as close to the original as is possible.

The project started out as teaching manuals for instructors in Chilel Qìgōng and has evolved into a series translating some of Dr. Páng's writings. To follow the Chinese tradition of honoring and respecting the teacher, Zhìnéng Qìgōng (known as *Chilel Qìgōng* in the Western world) will be used in the series.

The series, "Guides to Zhìnéng (Chilel) Qìgōng," is an ongoing project; initially, it will consist of three books. The first book in the series is *Zhìnéng (Chilel) Qìgōng: Overview and Foundation Methods,* and it covers the basic information about Zhìnéng Qìgōng and its foundation methods, which work on External Qì for health and vitality. The second book is *Zhìnéng (Chilel) Qìgōng: The Body & Mind Method,* and it covers Zhìnéng Qìgōng's Second Step Gong (intermediate level), which works on the integration of the physical body and mental activities. The third book: *Qìgōng Theory* covers some of the traditional Qìgōng theories and the theories developed and compiled by Dr. Páng Míng.

Although some words such as Qigong and Taiji are accepted as common English words, for continuity, I will use only Pīnyīn (official English translations of Chinese words) throughout the series. Because there are no set rules in Pīnyīn to guide whether a certain term should be in one word or two words, for standardization and reference purposes, I will use one word for technical names and two or more words for general terms; for example, 氣功 is a technical name, so Qìgōng will be used, 科學 (science)—a general term, will be kē xué. Also, I will put both Chinese characters and/or Pīnyīn next to the quotations and technical terms in the main text or as a footnote when they first appear. When necessary, I also include "Translator's note" to explain some of the terms or concepts that may be new to some readers. To stay within the context of the original writing, the information in these "Notes" is very brief. Readers interested in in-depth explanations need to do some research on their own or ask their teachers for more information.

Chinese writing is very different from English; for example, in English, the "Translator's note" would be inserted as an endnote or a footnote, but in Chinese, it would be in the main text. Since the series is either a direct translation or interpretation of Dr. Páng's writings, I have maintained the original style of his writing as much as possible. This approach may not agree with standard publishing practices. Any mistakes in the series are mine, not my editor's.

Qìgōng is a living art. It will keep on evolving. As a Qìgōng practitioner, my understanding of Qìgōng will evolve with time. The interpretation presented in the series is my understanding of Zhìnéng Qìgōng at this time. By no means is it the final interpretation or only interpretation. There is a Chinese Proverb that says, "To initiate a discussion, show a brick (your work), someone may answer with a Jade (抛磚引玉)." I hope this series will inspire some of my colleagues to translate some of Dr. Páng's work into not just English, but also other languages.

Hou Hee (Frank) Chan

Roseville, CA

PREFACE

With his innovative approach to Qìgōng, Dr. Páng Míng has helped to introduce and popularize Qìgōng to the general public for over 30 years. Nowadays, Qìgōng has become a part of wellness programs for millions of people. With all his accomplishments, I consider the Hùn Yuán Wholistic Theory to be one of his biggest contributions to Qìgōng. Although there are many writings on Qì theories in classical manuscripts, to the best of my knowledge, most of them are very fragmented and limited to their particular school's point of view. Dr. Páng Míng incorporated the essence of various Qìgōng schools' Qì theories and modern science to form the Hùn Yuán Wholistic Theory which consists of Hùn Yuán Theory, Wholistic Entity Theory, Human Hùn Yuán Qì Theory, Yìshí Theory, Ethic Theory, and Optimization (Life) Theory. Whether one agrees with him or not, I find his theory is the most comprehensive in the coverage of various topics. He coined the name Yì Yuán Tǐ to describe Upper Dāntián Qì which is very revolutionary.

This book is not a translation, it is my interpretation of Dr. Páng's teachings; it is based on his lectures and follows the format of his Hùn Yuán Wholistic Theory book. Dr. Páng's Hùn Yuán Wholistic Theory book has seven chapters: Introduction, Hùn Yuán Theory, Wholistic Entity Theory, Human Hùn Yuán Qì, Yìshí Theory, Ethic Theory, and Optimization (Life) Theory. In this book, I mainly focused on subjects related to Qìgōng and left out most of the social and communist philosophy which are not related to Qìgōng practice but are backgrounds for the formation of the theories. Also, I omitted the last two chapters (Ethic Theory and Optimization (Life) Theory). Ethical concepts change with time and different cultures have different standards. Dr. Páng's book is written for the Chinese audience; it is inappropriate to use Chinese ethical standards for the rest of the world. Dr. Páng's book was written in the early 90s, the science he described in his Optimization (Life) Theory is obsolete. I will leave that chapter for others to translate. In the Optimization (Life) Theory chapter, Dr. Páng very briefly mentioned Qìgōng Theories of Illness. I believe it is such an important subject that it should be explained in detail in a book by itself. Since I omitted the Ethic Theory and the Optimization (Life) Theory in this book, I can no longer call it the Hùn Yuán Wholistic Theory; therefore, I named this book "Qigong Theory."

第一章：绪論

Chapter One: Introduction

I. The concept of the Hùn Yuán Wholistic Entity

The Hùn Yuán Wholistic Theory is a special theory developed by Dr. Pang Ming in the 1980s. It is the foundation theory that guides all Zhìnéng Qìgōng practice. This theory describes/explains the wholistic characteristics of an entity, the formation of the wholistic entity, and how to understand/recognize and use/apply the special characteristics of the wholistic entity. The Hùn Yuán Wholistic Theory states that an entity is not the sum of all parts, it is the transmutation of the entity's space and time—it is called the Hùn Yuán Wholistic Entity. The Hùn Yuán Wholistic Entity is different from the whole entity as described in science.

In our daily life, when sensory organs interact with a substance, each sensory organ receives some (partial) information such as color, shape and smell from the substance. After all this information is summarized, processed and analyzed by the consciousness (mental activity), this information will be conceptualized to form a "whole entity" concept. An old fashioned non-digital reel projector will be used to explain how the normal "whole entity" concept is formed.

To understand/know what a projector is, the sensory organs must be used. A person sees and touches the projector, then turns the power on and inserts the reel in order to see the projected image on the screen. Only after repeating the process many times can one have some understanding of the projector. Seeing the projector only reveals its parts and not its function. To truly understand the projector, one must know how it operates. An understanding of the functions of a projector involve knowing how the parts work and the assembly sequences. In order to operate the projector, it must be switched on with the film properly loaded. By experiencing the functions and operation of a projector through information gained through different sensory organs, the brain can then summarize, process, analyze and finally abstract the information into a concept of the projector as a whole entity

In science, an entity has many levels/layers and each level is a "whole entity" that consists of sub-levels. Each higher level consists of systems built with components belonging to the immediately prior sub-level. These levels form a system (entity). For example, the earth is an entity that consists of organic and inorganic materials. Inorganic materials such as water consist of compounds which consist of atoms—protons—neutrons—electrons—quarks. Organic material such as an animal is an entity that consists of systems such as organs, tissues, and cells. In science, a "whole entity" is a substance's structure that is unified with its functions. Functions are the end results of arrangements of the structural components. Certain structures (arrangements) will have certain functions.

The Hùn Yuán Wholistic Theory describes a Hùn Yuán wholistic entity as an entity in which space and time are transmuted as one. This entity is a structural entity that occupies space and follows time. When a person picks up something using their hand, this action is the embodiment of the space functions; the space changes (hand moves from point A to point B) are the movement of time. The processes of space changes are completed during the time movements, and the time movement process is called integrated time. The entity that is formed by integrated time merging with the space changes is called the Hùn Yuán Wholistic Entity. Therefore, a Hùn Yuán Wholistic Entity has both space and time characteristics. When the hand rests on point B, normally, a person is not aware of the hidden time information—the hand moving from point A to point B. All one is aware of is the space characteristics, not the time characteristics. To understand the space and time characteristics of Hùn Yuán Wholistic Entity, a plant (organic) and a kitchen mixer (inorganic) can be used as examples.

A plant is a Hùn Yuán Wholistic Entity. The plant starts as a seed, and then goes through the process of sprouting, seedling, young plant, flowering and finally producing seeds. This process fully shows the plant's space and time characteristics. When do the wholistic characteristics appear? It is when the plant matures that the process of space and time becomes reality. When the plant matures, it has all the physical components—roots, stems, leaves and flowers; it is the expression of Hùn Yuán Wholistic Entity showing the space and time characteristics from seed to maturity. Once it has seeds, the space and time information will store inside the seed and becomes part of the seed. From seed to seed, it is a repeating cycle with added-on information with each successive cycle.

Hùn Yuán Wholistic entity can be described as the relationship between the matter inside the substance, including structural components of the substance and other factors not directly related to structure. Besides the physical components (trunk, branches and leaves), a plant has many other components that cannot be sensed, such as vitality. Vitality cannot be seen or touched, but it is part of the plant. In Qìgōng, it is called Qì. If the plant's vitality is gone, the plant's wholistic feature will be gone. The physical structure and appearance maybe the same in a dead plant, but its vitality and life are gone. Qì inside the plant is no longer the live-plant Qì; the original Hùn Yuán Wholistic Entity no longer exists.

A Hùn Yuán Wholistic Entity is an entity with its structures and functions (produced by the structures) merged as one. In a plant, the physical structures and activities/functions (metabolism) which are produced by the structures (roots, leaves, etc.) are integrated. A plant has life and vitality and its activities/functions are expressed through vitality. This vitality-structures integrated entity is a Hùn Yuán Wholistic Entity.

A kitchen mixer is a structure/entity with many components. But structures alone cannot make it a Hùn Yuán Wholistic Entity. Besides structures, it must have functions, and more important, it must be able to express/perform these functions. Only when the functions are expressed can it be called a Hùn Yuán Wholistic Entity. Therefore, the mixer must have three components to be a Hùn Yuán Wholistic Entity.

- Correct components (structures).
- Functions of each component.
- Power to express the overall functions.

Even if the mixer has the right components and all components function well, it must have electricity to express its overall functions. If the sequences of the structure are incorrect or the parts are damaged, even with electricity, it still would not express its overall functions. Therefore, only when the correct components and interactive functions plus power in the form of electricity merge as one will the mixer show its overall functions.

Even when the mixer is functioning correctly, it will not show its value without some flour in the bowl. The definition of an entity's characteristic includes the entity's existing value. The existing value is expressed during the process of the entity's interactions with external substances. Without the flour, the value (mixing the flour) of the mixer would not show; only when mixing the flour does the value (wholistic feature) of the mixer show. When the mixer is not working properly, a regular technician would take it apart and check the components. This is a structural approach. An expert would be able to diagnose the problem by just listening to the sound or seeing how it turns. It is not a structural approach but a merged structure and functions approach known as a wholistic approach in Qìgōng.

From another angle, the value of the mixer as a complete entity can refer to the physical body. The mixer is no more than an assembly of plastic and metals. In a few years, the plastic will become brittle and the metal will rust. The structure of the mixer may still be intact, but its value is gone because it can no longer express its functions; the value of the mixer is in its wholistic functions.

In conclusion, a Hùn Yuán Wholistic Entity is an entity in which physical structures and functions are merged as one. Physical structures and functions are the two sides of the Wholistic Entity; they cannot be separated. The Hùn Yuán Wholistic Theory is a theory that explores the Wholistic Entity's formation, characteristics and laws that govern its changes.

II. Origins of the Hùn Yuán Wholistic Theory

All new knowledge is based on existing knowledge and every new theory has its roots and continuity of history and culture. Hùn Yuán Wholistic Theory is no exception. Although Qìgōng theories and methods, Traditional Chinese Medicine and Western Medicine, and modern science and philosophy all play a very important rule in the formation of the Hùn Yuán Wholistic Theory, the Hùn Yuán Wholistic Theory is mainly based on Traditional Qìgōng's Wholistic Theories and Qì Theories. To understand the Hùn Yuán Wholistic Theory, one must understand Traditional Qìgōng's Wholistic View (Theory) and Qì View (Theory) first.

A. Traditional Wholistic Theory in Qìgōng

Wholistic Theory is a modern term. In Traditional Qìgōng, human beings and Nature are considered one entity and called "Humans and Nature Merged as One (天人合一)." There are three components:

- Universe View.
- Human Wholistic View.
- Humans and Nature Wholistic View.

1. The Universe (Yǔ Zhòu 宇宙) View

In Chinese culture, Yǔ Zhòu 宇宙 (Universe) means space and time. The classical manuscript Shīzi (尸子) says, "up, down and four directions are Yǔ (宇), past and future are Zhòu (宙)." In a more common way, the Universe is referred to as "Heaven and Earth." Basically, the Yǔ Zhōu is not empty, it has substance and is dynamic.

a) The Substances of the Universe

Yǔ Zhòu is divided into two categories: the one with form/shape is called Xī (器 substance with form, the correct Pīnyīn is Qì); the one without form is call Dào (道). Furthermore, Yǔ Zhòu is divided into five levels: Dào, Tàijí, Yīn-Yáng, Sān (三 Three) and Wànwù (萬物 Ten-Thousand Things). The first four levels are formless, they belong to Dào; Wànwù level has form/shape, it belongs to Xī (器 Qì).

(1) The First Level

This is the most basic level of the Universe. Dàoism calls it Dào, Confucianism calls it Wújí (無极) or Yì (易) and Traditional Chinese Medicine calls it Tàixū (太虛). The most common name for this level is Dào. Dào is described as "the root of the Universe" and cannot be divided any further. All things in the Universe are evolved from this level.

What is Dào/Wújí?

Dào Dé Jīng (道德經 common English translation is Tao Te Ching) describes Dào as:

In chaos, a thing is formed before Heaven and Earth;
It is silent and formless; unique and unchanging;
Revolving and inexhaustible, it can be the mother of all things;
I do not know its name; I just call it Dào; reluctantly, I describe it as "Big."
"Big" means it is (goes) everywhere; everywhere means it is infinite; infinite means it is returning.
有物混成,先天地生,寂兮寥兮,独立而不改,周行而不殆,可以为天下母,吾不知其名,字之曰道.强为之名曰大.大曰逝,逝曰远,远曰返.

As a substance, Dào is entirely elusive and invisible.
It is invisible and elusive, yet it has images.
It is elusive and invisible, and it has matter.
Oh, it is profound and obscured,
and it gives rise to energy Jīng.
The energy Jīng is very real,
and it is evident in all things.
道之为物, 惟恍惟惚. 惚兮恍兮, 其中有象; 恍兮惚兮, 其中有物; 窈兮冥兮, 其中有精; 其精甚真, 其中有信.

The classical Qìgōng book Xīn Chuánshù Zhèng Lù (心傳述證錄) describes Wújí as:

The truth of Wújí is that it is neither "have/substantial" nor "have-not/empty." It has all the information for all imagines and existences, but it does not have forms/shapes. It is neither empty nor substantial. It is "empty," yet it can fill-up/nourish everything. It is the origin of Dàoism, Buddhism and Confucianism; its substances and their functions are hidden; it has no boundary (within or without) and it connects all directions (up, down, dark and bright); it has no mental activities (thinking and worry, etc.) nor has smell nor sound; it is soundless and still, and both inside and outside are secured and alert; it covers both Heaven and Earth (Universe). Dào's motion is never aimless.
無極之真, 非空非有, 萬象具備,有理無形, 無無不有, 虛而能盈,三教之祖,體用未呈, 無內無外, 通幽通明,何思何慮,希臭希聲,寂然不動,表裡鞏靈,範圍天地,道不虛行.

The Origin is an undefined (chaotic) state; Yīn and Yáng have not been separated; Qì and information are within one another. It is called Wújí.
先天混混沌沌,陰陽未分,氣與理附,乃無極也.

In today's language, Dào is a substance, but it is very elusive. It cannot be seen, yet it is real and has images. It can be listened to, but cannot be heard. It can be grasped at, but cannot be touched. It exists before space and time. All things in the Universe are begotten from Dào. Dào is not only the special substance that permeates/occupies the whole Universe and can beget Wànwù (Ten-Thousand Things), Dào is also the natural characteristics and functions of every particular substance in the Universe. In other words, the natural characteristics and functions of a particular substance is its Dào. Therefore, in a narrow sense, Dào (of a substance) is the sum of the substance, its functions, and the behavioral patterns express by the functions.

From a physical/material point of view, as a substance, Dào is so small, it is beyond imagination and it is infinite and inexhaustible. From space and time's point of view, the space has no boundary and it is permeated with Dào; therefore, Dào has no boundary. Dào's body (space) and space are the same, and space is Dào's body. Time has no beginning nor ending. As an entity, time is the movement (behavioral pattern) of the substance/entity, and is an expression of the function of the movement (change). Time is Dào's function. When changes occur within Dào's substance and functions, they will express through space and time. Unlike the space and time in science which is relative, Dào's space and time is absolute. It is an objective substance, which does not exist nor cannot be extinguished.

(2) The Second Level

This level is the level above Dào. It has the same attributes as Dào. Compared to Dào, this level is more specific and complex. Confucianism calls this level Tàijí (太極), Dàoist calls it Yī (One 一) or Tàiyī (太一) and Traditional Chinese Medicine calls it Yuán Qì (元氣). Normally, this level is referred to as Tàijí.

What is Tàijí? In his manuscript, Zhōuyì Zhèngyì (周易正義), Kǒngyǐngdá (孔穎達 574-648) says, "Before it is separated into Heaven and Earth, the transmuted Yuán Qì is called Tàijí." Yuán Qì is evolved from Dào. Yuán Qì is very vague, and it is also entirely elusive and invisible. Yuán Qì permeates the whole universe and gives vitalities to all things.

Yuán Qì has movement. Ancient people described it as "Yuán Qì moves/flows 一氣流行." When there is movement, things will be created. The movement of Yuán Qì is not the same as the common understanding of movement. Commonly, a movement is described as the dynamic state of a substance related to its static state or the location of a substance as it moves from point A to Point B. Yuán Qì's movement is not the change of locations. It is called "Pulsation 脈動" in ancient manuscripts. Pulsation occurs in Yuán Qì when it is in an unimaginably small state.

Although the pulsation is extremely weak, it is very easy to create things when it happens in an unimaginably small state. In Dào level, the pulses are not obvious, but they are attributes of Tàijí.

(3) The Third Level

With the movements of Tàijí, the third level is born. Dàoism calls it Èr (二 two), Confucianism calls it Liǎng Yí (兩儀). Traditional Chinese Medicine calls it Yīn Yáng (陰陽). It is commonly known as Yīn Yáng. Normally, Yīn Yáng refers to the opposite attributes of a substance. In this level, Yīn Yáng means Yīn Qì and Yáng Qì and the attributes of Yīn and Yáng. The characteristic of Yīn is static and concentrating, Yáng is dynamic and dispersing. Yīn Qì and Yáng Qì are relative to each other, depending on the context, interchangeable. Life and Death as an example, from Life's point of view, "life" is Yáng and "death" is Yīn. But from Death's point of view, "death" is Yáng and "life" is Yīn. When "life" is gone, "death" is born; and "death" is the mother of "life." Therefore, Tàijí is neither Yīn nor Yáng. Only when a substance's Tàijí moves/separates, does it create Yīn and Yáng.

(4) The Fourth Level

Dàoism calls this level Sān (三 three), Confucianism calls it Sìxiàng (四象). When Yīn (Qì) and Yáng (Qì) interact, they create three categories: pure Yīn, pure Yáng, and Yīn-Yáng mix. Confucianism defines this level in four categories: Tàiyīn 太陰 (pure Yīn), Tàiyáng 太陽 (pure Yáng), Shǎoyīn 少陰 (more Yīn than Yáng) and Shǎoyáng 少陽 (more Yáng than Yīn).

Pure Yīn has the attribute of cohesion, it is the origin of substances with forms. Pure Yáng has the attribute of developing functions, it is the origin of substance's functions. Yīn-Yáng mix (Shǎoyīn and Shǎoyáng) remains as Qì. Therefore, Xíng 形 (form), Qì and Zhì 質(function) will be formed. In human beings, it is called Jīng, Qì, Shén 精氣神. Shén has the highest functions. Substance that has form is called Xíng; Xíng and Zhì (function) that merge as one is called Qì. This level is the origin of Xíng, Qì and Zhì, but the physical substance is not formed yet; Xíng, Qì and Zhì are still transmuted together in a formless state.

(5) The Fifth Level

Dàoism calls it Bāguà (八卦 the eight trigrams). All substance, including subatomic particles, which has matter/form belong to this level. All these substances are the results of interactions/transmutations within Sān/Sìxiàng (Fourth Level). The ancient manuscript Sù Wèn (素問) says, "Dynamic and Static react to each other; Above and Below complement each other; Yīn and Yáng transmute each other. The changes give birth to all things 动静相召,上下相临, 陰陽相錯, 而變由生也" Furthermore, it says, "Above/Heaven it forms Qì, Below/Earth it forms substances (with forms); as Qì and substances interact, ten-thousand things are born. 在天為氣，在地成形，形氣相感而化生萬物矣."

The interactions/transmutations within Sān/Sìxiàng (Fourth Level) give birth to the physical substances; the thousand things give birth to ten-thousand things; simple substances evolve into complex substances, and complex substances disintegrate into simple substances; the physical world is born.

The evolution of the five levels is from Level one to Level Five in succession, and each lower level can permeate and exist in higher level(s); therefore, the four formless levels all exist in Wànwù level.

b) The Dynamics of the Universe

In order to evolve from First Level (Dào) to the Fifth Level (Wànwù), substances must have movements. These movements occur in both Dào (formless substance) and Xī (器 Qì substance with form).

(1) The movements/changes in the Dào (formless) Levels

Although there are movements within each level and between different levels, these movements, such as the electron movements within the atoms, are very small and subtle. Therefore, classic manuscripts mainly describe the substance's changes in the Universe, not the changes within the substance. Ancient people focused on the movements/changes between the Dào (Formless) and Qì (Form), and considered these movements/changes to be crucial and important. They called these movements Yǒu (有 Have/existing) gives birth to Wú (無 non-existing) and Wú gives birth to Yǒu (無中生有,有無相生). In other words, formless substance begets (changes into) substances with form, and vice versa. For example, mass is Yǒu, energy is Wú; they are interchangeable ($E=mc^2$). They (Yǒu / Wú interchange) are the most basic and essential movements in the Universe.

In Chinese culture, Yǒu "有 Have/existing" refers to physical substances or substances that have form/shape. Wú "無 non-existing" refers to substance that cannot be seen, such as electricity, sound waves. Wú does not mean nothingness. There are different stages of Yǒu and Wú. Zhuāngzi (庄子 369 – 286 BC) divided Yǒu and Wú into four stages/categories:

- substance without Qì (the most basic stage; it is very vague, elusive and cannot be described and belongs to Dào).
- substance with Qì.
- substance with physical form.
- substance with life.

The transformation, from one stage to another, is Qì's concentrating and dispersing motion that enables Wú (non-existing) to beget Yǒu (Have/existing) and vice versa. Classic manuscripts describing whether a substance has form or not depended on Qì's appearance/state. Substance with a form is Qì in a concentrated state, without a form it is Qì in a dispersed state. The transformation process is very complicated and is continuous. Ancient people called it "Form and Qì are connected successively" (形氣相續). When Form disappears, it disintegrated into Qì; when Qì accumulates, it condenses into Form. The processes are repeated constantly, they are the fundamental movement of Nature. Classic manuscripts mainly describe the substance's changes in Nature, not the changes within the substance.

(2) The movements/changes in Xī (器 substance with form) State

There are two types of movements in Xī State, one is the interaction between substances and the other is the transformation within the substance.

All substances in the Universe interact with substances in the surrounding area; these interactions are called movements. When there are movements, there will be changes. All changes occur in and are dictated by their natural environment. In the past, Chinese used Bāguà (八卦): 乾 Qiàn (天 Tiān Space), 兌 Duì (澤 Zé Lake), 離 Lí (火 Huǒ Fire), 震 Zhèn (雷 Léi Thunder & Lighting), 巽 Xùn (風 Fēng Wind), 坎 Kǎn (水 Shuǐ Water), 艮 Gèn (山 Shān Mountain), 坤 Kūn (地 Dì Land)), to represent the essential functions/ elements of the natural environment. The interactions between these natural elements create ten-thousand things and give them vitality.

How does it work? A tree can be used to illustrate the point. In the natural environment, a tree interacts with the basic elements to maintain vitality. When the tree dies, it will fall down and disintegrate back to basic elements. These basic elements will become the source of vitality when they interact with other elements. Death gives vitality to Life, and Life gives vitality to Death. Nature creates all vitalities because the eight elements (Bāguà) interact with one other and these interactions are limitless. Humans are the product of Nature, and absorb Nature's vitality to maintain vitality. Practicing Qìgōng is to follow and rely on the changes in Nature to strengthen one's vitality; Qìgōng manuscripts call this *"take/steal the essence/Qì from the Universe" (盜天地之精氣)*.

Besides the interaction between substances, there are changes/transformations within the substance itself. These changes include the substance's internal changes that lead to its integration and disintegration, and the changes inside the substance when it is still in a relatively stable condition. These two are interrelated. When changes/transformation inside the substances reaches a certain point, balance will be broken, and integration and disintegration will take place. The duration of the substance's external stable condition is related to its internal change process. The changes within the substance is *called "Qì Huà (transmutation) 氣化"* in Qìgōng.

According to Qìgōng theory, substance has Up-Down, Open-Close, and In-Out movements. These movements include motions within the substance and motions between the substance and the external environment. For example, in human beings, there are In-Out movements between the body and the external environment, and In-Out movements between different organs/cells/systems. Generally speaking, "Up-Down" refers to the Up and Down of Nature Qì that enable the substances in Nature to have the "live, growth, transmutation, absorbing/collecting and storage" functions. "In-Out" refers to Internal Qì in and out of a substance (especially human beings) that enable "birth, growth, health, aging and death" functions.

2. The Human Body Wholistic Theory

The concept of the human body as a wholistic entity is part of Chinese culture and the foundation of Traditional Chinese Medicine (TCM) and Qìgōng. Normally, the wholistic characteristics are described in three different views/angles: body and mind; body; and parts of the body.

a) Xīn (心 mind with emotion) or Shén (神 mind) and Xíng (形 body) Wholistic View

Human beings are wholistic entities consisting of the formless Shén and the physical Xíng. But Xíng is not just the physical body, it includes the Qì inside the body. In some manuscripts, a human being is referred to as a Shén-Qì entity; in this context, Xíng is included (part of) in Qì. Therefore, human beings are called "Xíng-Qì-Shén wholistic entities." In Qìgōng, Xíng is also called Jīng, and physical subsistence is also called Jīng. Jīng-Qì-Shén and Xíng-Qì-Shén are the same.

No matter whether it is called Jīng-Qì-Shén or Xīn-Xíng, this entity (human) is a Shén controlling Xíng entity. The Xīn-Xíng wholistic view emphases the importance of Xīn. Old manuscripts have very detailed descriptions on the relationship between Shén and Xíng. For example, Huáinán Zi Yuán Dào Xùn 淮南子.原道訓 says:

> *Jīng is the physical structure of all activities relied on, Qì is the special substance that permeates the whole body and unites Jīng and Shén, Shén is the controller of life activities.*
> *夫形者,生之舍也;氣者,生之充也;神者,生之製也.*

Huáinán Zi Yuán Dào Xùn also says that:

Xīn is the manager of the five inner organs (heart, liver, spleen, lung, and kidney) and the emotions associated with them (happiness, anger, worry, sadness and fear). Xīn can direct/control the limbs' movements such as walking, movements, picking up things. It can circulate Qì and blood (Qì and blood movements are affected by mind and emotions). It can distinguish the good and the bad; it can control one's emotions, manage oneself, and enable one to move freely in the society. Xīn can manage all sorts of things in the external world and navigates the human relationship. If one tries to manage all kinds of Qì before one can master/control the Xīn, it is like tuning the music instruments while one cannot hear, love to read and yet one is blind. These cannot be done.
夫心者,五臟之主也. 所以製使四肢, 流行血氣, 馳騁於是非之境, 而出入於百事之門戶者也. 是故不得於心, 而有經天下之氣, 是猶無耳而欲調鐘鼓, 无目而欲喜文章也, 亦必不勝其任矣.

淮南子.原道訓

b) Human Body Wholistic Entity View

The human body is a wholistic entity. Every part of the body, from the inner organs to the limbs, is related to, nurtures and restrains each other. According to Qìgōng and TCM, the core of the human entity is the five solid internal organs and the six hollow internal organs. The core connects the bones and extremities via meridians to form an interrelated entity. Traditionally, the relationship between the solid organs is explained in Five-Element Theory, the relationship between the solid and hollow organs is explained in Yīn-Yáng Theory.

Note: The five solid organs are the heart, spleen, liver, lungs and kidneys. The six hollow organs are the stomach, large intestine, small intestine, bladder and Sānjiāo 三焦. Technically, Sānjiāo is not an organ, it is the three sections of cavity within the trunk of the human body.

(1) Between solid organs

The relationship between the elements are both to nurture and to restrain (regulate). According to the Five-Element Theory, liver belongs to wood, heart belongs to fire, spleen belongs to soil, lung belongs to metal and kidney belongs to water. Fig. 1-1. Five-Element Theory states that.

To nurture:
Wood (liver) → Fire (heart) → Earth/Soil (spleen) → Metal (lung) → Water (kidney) → Wood (liver)

To restrain (regulate):

Wood (liver) → Earth/Soil (spleen) → Water (kidney) → Fire (heart) → Metal (lung) → Wood (liver)

The five organs nurture each other; therefore, the organs maintain/strengthen their vitality. Since they are also restraining/regulating each other, they maintain balance.

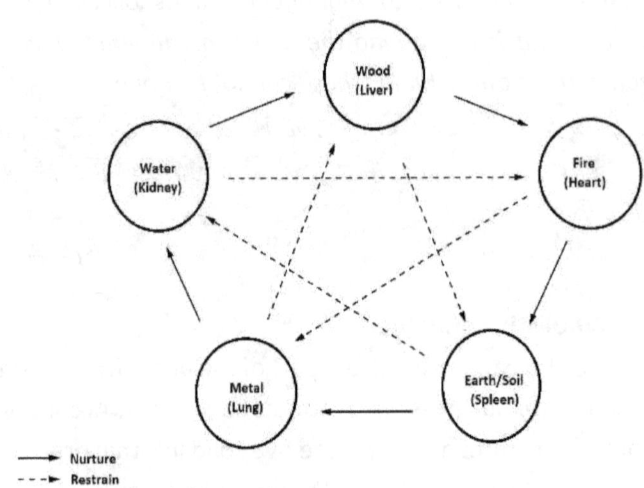

Fig. 1-1 The Relationship between the Elements

(2) Between solid and hollow organs

The relationships between solid and hollow organs can be summarized as Yīn-Yáng, inner layer-outer layer, and corresponding solid-hollow organs. Solid organ is Yáng and inner layer; hollow organ is Yīn and outer layer. Liver corresponds to gallbladder, heart corresponds to small intestine, spleen corresponds to stomach, lung corresponds to large intestine, kidney corresponds to bladder and pericardium corresponds to Sānjiāo.

(3) Between the organs and different parts of the body

According to the Yellow Emperor's Classic of Internal Medicine (黃帝內經), not only every part of the body, but also the physiological and pathological functions of humans, and up to a certain point, the complex phenomena of Nature are all related/connected to the five organs.

How is this human body wholistic entity connected/formed? The key is the Meridian Qì. According to Qìgōng and TCM, Qì in the Meridians connects the inner organs with the bones and the extremities to form an entity. Qì regulates the entity's functions; all the human physiological and pathological functions are the results of Qì movements. Basically, Qìgōng and TCM have the same wholistic theory, but their focus is different. TCM's focus is on the entity. TCM considers the human being as an entity whose inner organs are connected with the extremities by the meridians; the core of the human entity is the inner organs (both solid and hollow). TCM uses this view to explain the human physiological and pathological functions and to develop treatments. Many of the treatment methods evolved to become part of traditional Medical Qìgōng. Regular Qìgōng emphasizes maintaining health. Therefore, it does not focus on inner organs and meridians, it emphasizes the wholistic characteristics of Jīng Qì Shén. Practitioners use Qìgōng methods to strengthen the Xīn (mind) and Xíng (body) connections.

c) Part of the body reflects the wholistic entity

The human body is a wholistic entity and every part of the body, by itself, is a wholistic entity. This entity not only contains its own information, it also contains and is able to reflect the whole body information. Because meridians connect the inner organs with the bones and the extremities to form an entity, Qì circulates and permeates the whole body; therefore, Qì contains all the information. Under certain circumstances, the body information can be shown in a particular part of the body. TCM utilizes this wholistic characteristic and develops techniques that become the cornerstone of TCM diagnosis. For example, in TCM, there is a diagnosis technique called "Observing Diagnosis 望診" where a doctor would look at a certain part of the patient's body and be able to diagnose the health condition of the patient. The face can represent and reflect the organs, body/trunk and limbs. Fig. 1-2. The Human Face and Related Organs and Body Parts.

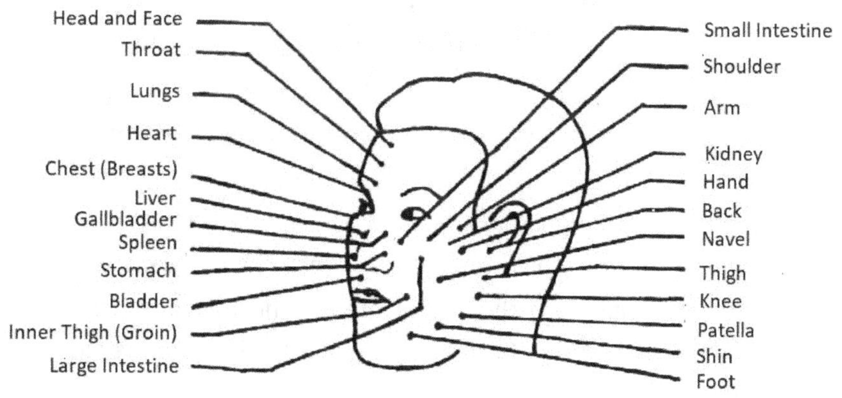

Fig. 1-2 The Human Face and Related Organs and Body Parts

The eye also represents the whole body, it is called "Five Wheels and Eight Octagons 五輪八廓." The five areas that reflect the solid organs are called "Five Wheels" and the areas the reflect the hollow organs and meridians are called "Eight Octagons." Fig. 1-3 Five Wheels, Fig. 1-4 Eight Octagons.

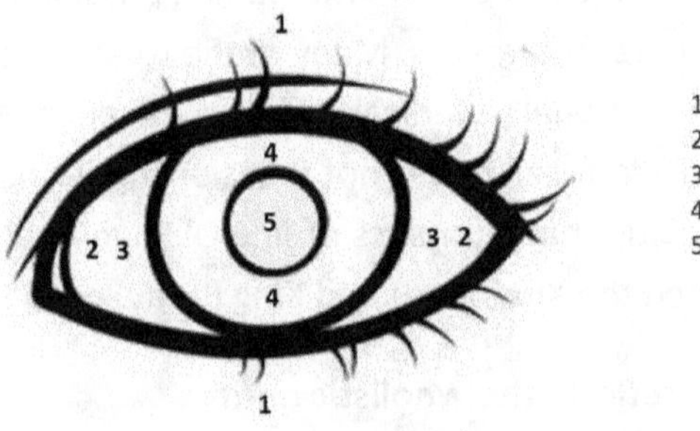

Fig. 1-3 Five Wheels

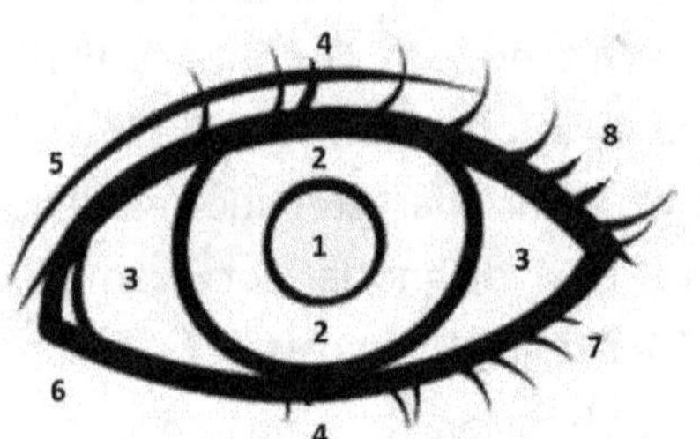

Fig. 1-4 Eight Octagons

Each of the twelve meridians in the body contains not only the information of its corresponding organ, it also reflects the whole-body information. Each meridian has five Yú xué 俞穴 (metal, wood, water, fire and earth) and each Yú xué represents an organ (metal - lung, wood - liver, water - kidney, fire - heart, earth - spleen). For example, the five Yú xué in the Lung Meridian are Shǎo shāng xué 少商穴 which represents liver, Yú jì xué 魚際穴 which represents heart, Tài yuān xué 太淵穴 which represents spleen, Jīng qú xué 經渠穴 which represents itself (lung) and Chǐ zé xué 尺澤穴 which represents kidney. Therefore, the Lung Meridian contains the information of the five elements which include the five organs as expressed through different Yú xué. In acupuncture, the penetration depth of the needle is also related to the five elements (skin-lung, muscle-spleen, tendon-liver, vein-heart and bone-kidney).

Although the wholistic characteristics are described in three different ways, they are the same except in different levels (body and mind level; body level; and parts of the body level).

3. Humans and Nature Wholistic View

Humans and Nature Wholistic View mainly focuses on the relationship between human beings and Nature. The ancient Chinese believed the reason humans are alive is because Human Qì is connected with Nature Qì. Manuscript Sù wèn 素问 says:

"Heaven Qì connects with lung, Earth Qì connects with stomach, Wind Qì connects with liver, Thunder Qì connects with heart, Grain (food) Qì connects with spleen, and Rain Qì connects with kidney."
天氣通於肺, 地氣通於咽, 風氣通於肝, 雷氣通於心, 谷氣通於脾,雨氣通於腎.

Human life activities and Nature are inter-connected. This connection can be explained in three ways:

a) Heaven, Earth and Humans originated from the same Qì

Nature (Heaven, Earth, Humans) belongs to Wànwù Level Qì, which evolved from Dào. For simplicity, most manuscripts call this Qì Yuán Qì. Depending on the location of Yuán Qì, it is called Heaven, Earth or Humans. According to Manuscript Sù wèn 素问,

> *Qì locates above and below, Humans live in the midst (where Qì connects). Above the midst, Heaven Qì controls; below the midst, Earth Qì controls; the midst, where Heaven Qì and Earth Qì connect, Human Qì follows and Wànwù (Ten-Thousand Things) originate.*
> *上下之位, 氣交之中, 人之居也, 故曰: 天樞之上, 天氣主之: 天樞之下, 地氣主之:氣交之分, 人氣從之, 萬物由之, 此之謂也.*
>
> *Note: Heaven and Earth are the areas above and below Wànwù. Earth carries Wànwù which have physical forms.*

Humans are between Heaven and Earth. To humans, Heaven and Earth are the environment. Heaven, Earth and Humans (Wànwù) are part of Nature, and all are nourished by Yuán Qì. The human obtains Qì from Heaven and Earth, Wànwù obtain Qì from humans, and Heaven and Earth obtain Qì from Wànwù. This is an endless cycle that creates/enables the continuous changes in Nature. One of the main goals of Qìgōng practice is to maintain vitality; therefore, besides protecting one's own Qì, one must obtain Qì from Heaven and Earth and Nature.

b) Humans and Wànwù are inseparable and closely interconnected by Xī 息 (breath/Qì)

Life in Nature needs Xī to power its functions and activities. Xī can be either breath/air and/or Qì. Zhuāngzi 庄子 (369-286 BC) said *"living creatures breathe Xī (air/Qì) to each other 生物之以息相吹也."* It means organisms receive and maintain their vitality by sending and receiving Qì to each other via breathing. Qì and information follow the living creatures' breath to move in and out of the bodies and unite together to form a field (it is called Qì Field in Qìgōng), so you are in me and I am in you. We are all connected and inseparable in the Qì Field. It is very easy to witness this phenomenon in nature. For example, if one stands on a higher ground and looks at a field (e.g., rice field), besides the water vapor, one can see the dense Qì Field, which is created by plants. Due to the fact that plants breathe, the plant's Qì would form a field and move like gentle waves even without the presence of wind. When lying down on the ground, one can see the Earth Qì. How the Earth Qì interacts with the environment is very important in Fèng Shuǐ 風水, a major branch of Chinese Metaphysics.

Lǎozi 老子 described Heaven and Earth as a big bellows. The force that moves the bellows is from within, it is created by ten-thousand things' breathing. The air and Qì's in-out, open-close and up-down movements will power the movement of the bellows. This is called: when inhale, Heaven and Earth inhale with Humans (Wànwù); when exhale, Heaven and Earth exhale with Humans.

c) Heaven, Earth, Humans and Wànwù are one Wholistic Entity

Human beings live among Heaven, Earth and Wànwù, together, they form an entity. From the human's point of view, a human being, surrounded by Heaven and Earth, is the center of this entity. Because a human being utilizes the resources of Nature for its survival, a human being must be aware of the laws of Nature and follow and obey the laws of Nature in daily activities to strengthen vitality.

Manuscript Sù wèn says:

> *Four seasons and Yīn/Yáng are the root/foundation of Wànwù (Ten-Thousand Things). In order to adhere to the laws of Nature and follow the root, sages nourish Yáng in Spring and Summer, nourish Yīn in Autumn and Winter. Therefore, they can synchronize life and death with Wànwù in Nature. If one goes against the root (laws), it is to destroy the foundation and damage the essence.*
>
> *夫四時陰陽者, 萬物之根本也, 所以聖人春夏養陽, 秋冬養陰, 以從其根. 故與萬物浮沉於生長之門. 逆其根則伐其本, 壞其真也.*
>
> *素問.四氣調神大論*

In other words, the changes of seasons and the adjustment of Yīn and Yáng are the foundation upon which all life activities are based. Spring and Summer are the seasons of growth, one should cultivate Yáng Qì to meet the demand; Autumn and Winter are the seasons of harvest, one should cultivate Yīn Qì for nourishment. If one adheres to the laws of Nature (changes of seasons and adjustment of Yīn/Yáng), one will be able to follow the life process (birth, growth, harvest and store) of ten-thousand things. Deviating from the laws of Nature will cut into one's vitality and damage one's Zhēn Qì 真氣 (Prenatal and Postnatal Qì transmuted as one is called Zhēn Qì).

Another concept of the human and Nature Wholistic View is that humans and Nature are similar. In Chinese culture, Qiánkūn 乾坤 is another name for Heaven and Earth. When a thing is created/born, it has a body, within the body, there is a Qiánkūn. A human body is a small Qiánkūn, Heaven and Earth is a big Qiánkūn. As mentioned before, part of the human body can reflect/contain the whole-body information, similarly, part of the Nature can reflect/contain the whole Nature information. Because the human is part of Nature, by studying the human, one can understand Nature. The human is the concentration of Nature (Wànwù) Qì. The human being contains information from the beginning of evolution through every stage of evolution. Nature is also described as a Tàijí or a Yīn/Yáng; a human being is also a Tàijí or a Yīn/Yáng. Manuscript Sùwèn 素問. 金匱真言論 describes the similarity between Nature and Humans as the following:

> *In Nature, there are Yīn within Yīn and Yáng within Yáng. From sunrise to mid-day, it is Heaven's Yáng, and is Yáng within Yáng. From mid-day to sunset, it is Heaven's Yáng, and is Yīn within Yáng. From evening to approximately 3 a.m. (rooster crows), it is Heaven's Yīn, and is Yīn within Yīn. From rooster crows to sunrise, it is Heaven's Yīn, and is Yīn within Yīn. Therefore, humans should correspond to Nature. For humans, the exterior is Yáng, interior is Yīn. For the body, the back is Yáng, abdomen is Yīn. For the organs, solid organs are Yīn, hollow organs are Yáng. When the back is Yáng, the heart is the Yáng within Yáng, and the lung is Yīn within Yáng. In the abdomen is Yīn, the spleen is the utmost Yīn, the kidney is Yīn within Yīn, and liver is Yáng within Yīn. All these are the correspondences of Yīn-Yáng, exterior-interior, internal-external and male-female. They are corresponding to Nature's Yīn-Yáng.*
>
> *故曰: 陰中有陰, 陽中有陽. 平旦至日中, 天之陽, 陽中之陽也; 日中至黃昏, 天之陽, 陽中之陰也; 合夜至雞鳴, 天之陰, 陰中之陰也; 雞鳴至平旦, 天之陰, 陰中之陽也. 故人亦應之. 夫言人之陰陽, 則外為陽, 內為陰. 言人身之陰陽, 則背為陽, 腹為陰. 言人身之藏府中陰陽, 則藏者為陰, 府者為陽. 故背為陽, 陽中之陽, 心也; 背為陽, 陽中之陰, 肺也;為陰, 陰中之陰腎也; 腹為陰, 陰中之陽, 肝也腹為陰, 陰中之至陰, 脾也. 此皆陰陽表裏內外雌雄相輸應也, 故以應天之陰陽也.*

Based on the similarities between humans and Nature, many Qìgōng branches develop practice methods based on the Yīn/Yáng characteristics of Nature. For example, when one cultivates a particular organ Qì, depending on the Yīn/Yáng characteristics of that organ, one would practice during a certain time of the day that would correspond to the Yīn/Yáng characteristics of Nature. Also, one would focus on Yáng Qì cultivation in Spring and Summer and Yīn Qì in Autumn and Winter. Some of the TCM treatments are based on the four seasons' Yīn/Yáng characteristics. For example, TCM considers illness in Winter and Spring is mainly caused by Yīn (functions); illness in Summer and Autumn is caused by Yáng (functions) and they treat the person accordingly.

B. Traditional Qìgōng's Qì Theory

Qì Theory has two components, Qì and Qì Huà 氣化. It describes Qì and Qì's functions and changes.

1. Qì

Both Qìgōng Theories and Chinese classical philosophy consider Qì to be a physical substance and is the material that makes up the Universe. One of the first manuscripts that used the name Qì was written by Guǎnzi 管子 (approximate 471-211 B.C.). Before him, all writing used Dào. When mentioning Qì, Guǎnzi combined Qì and Jīng together. He says, *"What is Jīng? Jīng is the essence of Qì; the Qì that can change is called Jīng."* It means Qì and Jīng are the same substance. He also says, "Jīng begets Heaven above, Wànwù (Ten-Thousand Things) below, and all living things in between."

Although some say it is Dào and some say it is Yuán Qì (Primal Qì) that is the building block of the Universe, they do not contradict each other. Dào is the most basic substance of the invisible Universe; Yuán Qì is the most basic substance of the physical Universe. Depending on its location, Yuán Qì has different names; above is Heaven, below is Earth and in between are Humans and Wànwù. Depending on its functions, Yuán Qì is divided into Nature (Heaven, Earth and Wànwù) Yuán Qì and Human Yuán Qì.

a) Nature Yuán Qì

Manuscript Tàipíng Jīng 太平經 (？－200) says, "Dào is One, Yuán Qì is One, Nature is One." What is One? One is the original Qì; it is the origin of ten-thousand things. One is formless and invisible; it does not have a name; things with form and visibility have names. Yuán Qì is very big, it contains everything, therefore, it can beget all kinds of substances. The container (Yuán Qì) does not have form, it is the original Qì and is called Yuán. Names are given to ten-thousand things with form which are located in different areas to differentiate them from one another. Therefore, nameless is the beginning of Heaven and Earth, name is the mother of ten-thousand things.

Ten-thousand things must contain One to exist; without One, things will disappear. Therefore, One cannot be absent. One is called Tàiyī 太一, Tàiyī separates into Heaven and Earth, Heaven and Earth is called Èryí 二儀; Èryí separates and establishes Sāncái 三才, Heaven, Earth and Humans is called Sāncái .

The passage quoted above means Dào and Yuán Qì are the same substance that forms the universe; it is the source material for all existence. As Yuán Qì evolves, the finer Qì becomes Heaven, the coarse Qì becomes Earth, and Heaven Qì and Earth Qì merge to beget Humans (Wànwù). Although it is very similar to previous description of Tàijí begets Yīn-Yáng or One begets Two, what Manuscript Tàipíng Jīng described is the process of Yuán Qì evolving from one to many. Finer Qì means the substance we cannot see, coarse Qì means the elements that form the physical substances, and ten-thousand things are the product of merging finer and coarse Qì. Ancient people did not know about the evolution, they believed Yuán Qì begets all existences; therefore, once Yuán Qì separated into Heaven and Earth, Humans (Wànwù) were created. Because Yuán Qì is so vague, Confucianism uses two sentences to describe/summarize Nature Yuán Qì: *"Substance without form is called Dào, with form is called Xī 器 (the correct Pīnyīn is Qì)."*

b) Human Yuán Qì

Manuscript Nánjīng 難經 (206-220 BC) says, *Yuán Qì is the power source for all life activities, it originated from between the kidneys (Mìngmén area); it is the foundation of inner organs, the root of the twelve Meridians, the door for prenatal breathing, the origin of Sānjiāo.*
谓肾间动氣也, 此五 脏六腑之本, 十二经脉之根, 呼吸之门, 三焦之原.

The Yuán Q is also called the protector guarding against abnormalities. When a tree is used as example, Yuán Qì is the root. The organs, tendons and blood vessels are the branches and leaves, if the root is rotten, branches will die.

For human beings, Yuán Qì is the most important and basic substance. It is the primal source for all life activities, it facilitates growth and development, activates organs' functions and circulates blood. Therefore, Yuán Qì is the essence/root of humans. Yuán Qì is the combination of Prenatal Qì which is stored in the Mìngmén (between Kidneys) area and Postnatal Qì which is the physical body and the nutrition from food one eats and the air one breathes.

Life activities have prenatal and postnatal processes; Prenatal Qì forms the entity, and the entity needs Postnatal Qì to continue its existence. Sānjiāo (the three trunk cavities) move and spread Yuán Qì.

In describing the relationship between the human and Yuán Qì, Manuscript Tàipíng says Yuán Qì maintains the root of human life activities. What is the root of life activities? It is the Shén (mind activities). It says Yuán Qì is the food for Shén. When Yuán Qì is absent or insufficient, Shén would not be able to function. When one is too tired, one's Yuán Qì is overused and becomes insufficient or damaged, Shén will not be able to function normally. Qìgōng practice is to cultivate Yuán Qì and to maintain its sufficiency of nourishing the body. Manuscript Nánjīng describes the way to cultivate Yuán Qì as:

> *Concentrating on stabilizing the Shén and harmonizing the Qì. When the Shén is stable and Qì is harmonized, Yuán Qì will come automatically; with Yuán Qì, inner organs will be nourished; with nourished organs, all meridians and blood vessels open; with opened meridians and blood vessels, body fluid from organs will be sufficient and one would not crave for smells, food nor water. When the three Dāntiáns have accumulated enough Yuán Qì, one's body will be full of energy and organs will be strong, countenance will be youthful and have long longevity.*
> *神定氣和, 則元氣自至, 元氣自至, 則五臟通潤, 五臟通潤, 則百脈流行, 百脈流行, 則津液上應, 而不思五味飢渴, 永絕三田, 道成則體滿藏實, 童顏長春矣.*

Huángdì Nèijīng 黃帝內經 (Yellow Emperor's Classic of Internal Medicine) describes all things as Qì and there are many kinds of Qì in the human body. For example, there are Zhēn Qì 真氣, Yíng Qì 營氣, Wèi Qì 衛氣, Zōng Qì 宗氣, Organ Qì 臟腑之氣, Meridian Qì 經絡之氣. According to Huángdì Nèijīng, human life activities depend on Zhēn Qì. Zhēn Qì is a collective name for many types of Qì. The most common definition of Zhēn Qì is: "Zhēn Qì is the combination of Nature Qì and food Qì to nourish the body." It means the Qì that combines Nature Qì (air we breathe), Prenatal Qì and Postnatal Qì (food we eat) to use for nourishing the body is called Zhēn Qì.

Yíng Qì is finer Postnatal Qì (Qì from food we eat). It circulates continuously and ceaselessly among the five solid organs, and spreads all over the six hollow organs and circulates inside the blood vessels; therefore, it follows the blood vessels to connect the organs.

Wèi Qì is a coarse Postnatal Qì (Qì from food we eat). It is aggressive and its mobility is strong and swift. It cannot enter the blood vessels; it circulates in the skin and between the muscles (membranes). It immerses in the spaces between the organs and between the muscles, and disperses/spreads in the chest and abdomen.

Zōng Qì is the air from Nature that transmutes with Postnatal Qì (Qì from food digested by stomach and spleen. The formation of Zōng Qì is similar to Zhēn Qì; some consider Zhēn Qì and Zōng Qì to be the same Qì). Zōng Qì is formed in the lung and stored in the chest. The strength of breathing and blood circulation is related to Zōng Qì.

c) Qì Huà

Qì Huà means Qì's functions. It is a technical name in Qìgōng and TCM, and it means all changes in the Universe are the result of Qì's functions/ movements. As long as there is Qì, there will be changes/transformation which can be external or internal. Qì is invisible and formless; once it transforms, it creates substances with forms and images. The process of creating ten-thousand things from nothing is External Qì Huà. Once a substance has a physical form/shape, change/ transformation of Qì within the substance is Internal Qì Huà. Qì Huà is the collective name for all changes in the Universe.

The brief discussion on Qì Huà (from nothing to something) in the previous Wholistic View section is from the physical appearance point of view. It mainly discusses the changes of physical appearance from nothing to something with form or image. A different approach will be taken in this section. Qì Huà will be discussed from the point of view of the changes within Qì.

Huángdì Nèijīng has the most detailed description of Qì Huà, it says:

> *Tài Xū 太虛 (the origin or Dào) is unimaginably big and soundless; it is formless and imageless, it is the foundation of Qì Huà, the beginning of Qì movement and the origin of all substances. Once Qì moves, it creates Wǔ Yùn 五運 (wind, heat, humidity, dryness and cold; or wood, fire, soil, metal and water) and there is weather and nature. With Wǔ Yùn's movements, Yuán Qì spreads and covers the earth and becomes the foundation for ten-thousand things to grow. With Nine Stars (Big Dipper plus two small stars next to handle star Alkaid) shining above and Seven Yàos (Sun, Moon, Venus, Jupiter, Mercury, Mars and Saturn) rotating and orbiting, they create Yīn and Yáng, soft and hard, places with brightness or darkness, day and night, and hot and cold. With these changes, the earth evolves to have ten thousand things; and give them vitality.*

太虚寥廓,肇基化元,万物资始,五运终天,布氣真灵,总统坤元,九星悬朗,七曜周旋,曰阴曰阳,曰柔曰刚,幽显既位,寒暑弛张,生生化化.品物咸章.

Note. Tài means extreme (big). Xū 虛 is a special Chinese word with no equivalent in English. The closest translation is "nebulous." It has a meaning of existing yet not existing—empty yet not empty. It describes something that does not have a physical form nor occupies space. For example, although one can see and walk around in an empty room which is filled with light smoke, one cannot say the room is empty, because it is not, it is xū. Tài Xū normally refers to space/universe.

Wǔ Yùn 五運 also called Wǔ Qì (Wǔ means five), it can be Wood, Fire, Soil, Metal and Water, or Wind, Heat, Humidity, Dryness and Cold. To distinguish the two, Fire is added to the latter five and it is called Liù Qì (six Qìs). Instead of just using Wǔ Yùn, it is common to use Wǔ Yùn (Wood, Fire, Soil, Metal and Water) and Liù Qì (Wind, Fire, Heat, Humidity, Dryness and Cold) together to describe the functions of Wǔ Yùn. Wǔ Qì and Liù Qì are the same.

The Qì Huà process is normally described as: at the beginning, there is Tài Xū or Yuán Qì. Yuán Qì is a transmuted state in which Wǔ Yùn 五運 (wood, fire, soil, metal and water) have not been formed; Sāncái 三才 (Heaven, Earth and Man) have not separated and Yīn and Yáng have not been established. With pulsation (脉动), Yuán Qì separates and creates Wǔ Qì (Wood, Fire, Soil, Metal and Water). Each Qì has a shape/image, Water is round (•), Wood is straight (l), Fire is point (Λ), Soil is square (L), and Metal is thin surface (ロ). With the five shapes, Heaven and Earth are created. Heaven is round and is engulfed by Qì, and Earth is square and solid. As Wǔ Yùn evolves to Wǔ Yùn and Wǔ Qì, they create Yīn and Yáng, soft and hard, places with brightness or darkness, day and night, and hot and cold. When Wǔ Yùn and Wǔ Qì interact, weather appears, and ten-thousand things evolve. In conclusion, the evolution from Yuán Qì to ten-thousand things is a Qì Huà process. Yuán Qì huà (transmute) into Wǔ Qì (Wood, Fire, Soil, Metal and Water). The five shapes of Qì form the foundation for all existences. The transmutation of Wǔ Qì creates weather and enables the creation of ten-thousand things.

Note: The shape/image of each Qì is a concept, not a fixed image. Round is not a circle, it is not straight but curved; straight is not a straight line, it is not bend; point is not a point, it is two straights intersected in an angle; square is two straights perpendicular to each other; thin surface is not a surface, it consists of two squares.

The way Yuán Qì affects ten-thousand things' Qì Huà (transmutation) is through the movements of Wǔ Yùn and Liù Qì. Basically, Qì has four movements: up (upward) and down (downward), and in and out. Each living thing has Shén Jī 神机 and Qì Lì 氣立. Qì Lì depends on the movements of Qì. Exchanging matter, energy and information are "in and out" movements; the Qì Huà within an organism are up/upward and down/downward movements.

Note: Shén Jī 神机 is the root of life and the life activities controlling mechanism, equivalent to DNA. Qì Lì 氣立 is the exchange and transmutation of Qì between the living thing and Nature. It is the activity that living things depend on to survive. It is the activity in which the organism exchanges matter, energy and information with Nature.

When Yuán Qì changes (evolves), the first outcome is Yīn and Yáng. Yīn and Yáng is the fundamental law of the Universe. All substances' Qì Huà (changes) are based on and start with Yīn and Yáng. The changes within the human body and the changes between humans and Nature must integrate with Yīn and Yáng. Therefore, Qì must be involved in any change within the body; Qì Huà is part of the metabolic process.

TCM considers that all changes and functions of the human body rely on Qì. A substance without Qì is a dead substance and cannot transmute. Qì Huà needs the participation of Qì. The functions of the bladder can be used as an example. The bladder is the storage area for urine before it is discharged. But TCM does not consider urine to be a waste, it considers urine to be a body fluid. When urine (body fluid) is transmuted by Qì (Qì Huà), the useful part of the body fluid will be transmuted and absorbed into the body; the waste (urine) will be discharged. Without the transmutation, the urine cannot be discharged.

Huángdì Nèijīng (Yellow Emperor's Classic of Internal Medicine) describes the relationship between metabolism and Qì Huà as the following:

Water is Yīn, Fire is Yáng; Yáng is Qì, Yīn is Wèi (taste/flavor). Wèi belongs to Xíng (physical body), Xíng belongs to Qì, Qì belongs to Jīng (essence), Jīng belongs to Shén (mind activity). Jīng consumes Qì, Xíng consumes Wèi. Shén begets Jīng, Qì begets Xíng. Wèi hurts Xíng, Qì hurts Jīng.... Jīng transmutes to Qì.
水為陰, 火為陽, 陽為氣, 陰為味, 味歸形, 形歸氣, 氣歸精, 精歸化, 精食氣形食味, 化生精, 氣生形. . . . 精化為氣.

TCM considers a physical substance to have two parts, one Yīn and one Yáng. The physical body or structure is Yīn; physical substance has taste/flavor/odor; the taste/flavor/odor is Yīn and its function is Yáng. For example, an apple has one Yīn and one Yáng. Yáng is its Qì, Yīn is its Wèi (taste/flavor, physical structure). When an apple is eaten, its Yīn and Yáng will go separate ways. Its Yáng (Qì) will directly merge with human Qì; but its Yīn (physical structure) cannot become Qì directly, it must go through a series of Qì Huà processes. It is the process of metabolism. The apple is digested, absorbed into the body and becomes part of the body. It is "Wèi belongs to Xíng (physical body)." When the body (energy) metabolizes, it becomes Qì. It is "Xíng belongs to Qì." Qì concentrates (Qì Huà) to become Jīng. Jīng is a physical substance, but this Jīng is not Wèi, it is essence. TCM considers the essence of the inner organs and the reproductive sperms and eggs as Jīng. Jīng is the nucleus of a cell. It is "Qì belongs to Jīng." Jīng Qì Huà to become Shén (mind activity). It is "Jīng belongs to Shén."

In summary, metabolism requires the activation and participation of Qì to finish the Qì Huà process. At the same time, the Qì required for life activities is generated in the metabolism process. The Qì Huà process from external to internal is: Wèi (external substance) → Xíng → Qì → Jīng → Huà; the internal Qì Huà process is the interactions among the above five steps. Fig. 1-5. The Qì Huà Process.

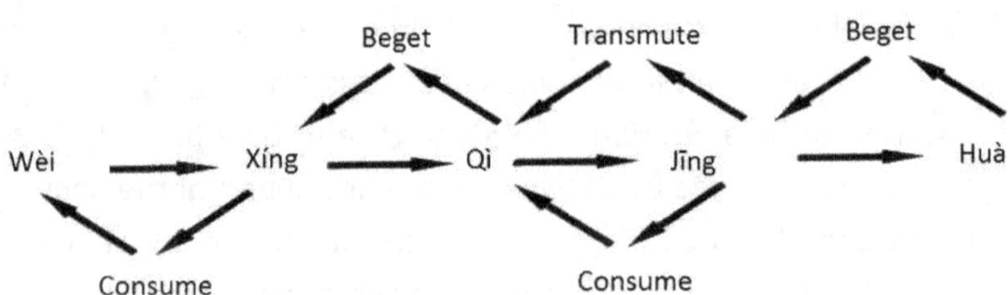

Fig. 1-5 The Qì Huà Process

3. Hùn Yuán Qì

Unlike Qì and Qì Huà, there are very few writings on Hùn Yuán Qì in Qìgōng books. There is no established theory on Hùn Yuán Qì and it is not an important part of the traditional Qìgōng theories. But Zhìnéng Qìgōng's Hùn Yuán Qì Theory is based on Hùn Yuán Qì; therefore, the author will use some of the available writings on it to discuss it in detail.

Hùn Yuán Qì has many names, the most common are Hùn Yuán Yī Qì 混元一氣, Innate Hùn Yuán Yī Qì 先天混元一氣, Hùndùn 混沌 (Nebulous state), Yuán Qì 元

氣, Kōngdòng 空洞 (Empty hole), Hùnlùn 混論 (Transmuted state). Depending upon the name (context), Hùn Yuán Qì can be a form of nebulous state or a form of Hùn Yuán Qì. Generally speaking, Hùn Yuán Qì is divided into two major categories. One is Human Hùn Yuán Qì, and the other is Nature Hùn Yuán Qì. In writing, if Qì is part of the name, such as Hùn Yuán Yī Qì, it refers to Human Hùn Yuán Qì; if Qì is not part of the name, then it refers to Nature Hùn Yuán Qì.

Nature Hùn Yuán Qì has the following names: Hùn Yuán, Hùndùn, Kōngdòng and Hùndòng. The following are some of the writings in ancient Chinese manuscripts describing Nature Hùn Yuán Qì.

What is Hùndùn 混沌 (Nebulous state)?

Manuscript Yún Jí Qī Qiān 雲笈七籤 says:

> *Hùn Yuán is before Hùndùn (Nebulous state), and is the beginning of Yuán Qì (Primal Qì). Before Yuán Qì is formed, it is a vast silent space without any existence. With pulsation, Yuán Qì is formed. With Yuán Qì movements, Heaven and Earth are established. As Yuán Qì circulates and spreads, it becomes the material for ten-thousand things to use. Hùndùn is something that is Xū (empty yet not empty) inside and empty outside; it is extremely big and cannot be named.*
> *混元者, 記事於混沌之前, 元氣之始也. 元氣未形, 寂寥何有？至精感激而真一生焉, 元氣運行而天地立焉, 造化施張而萬物用焉. 混沌者, 厥中惟虛, 厥外惟無, 浩浩蕩蕩, 不可名也.*

Manuscript Yuán Qì Lùn 元氣論 says:

> *The state which Wǔ Qì (Wood, Fire, Soil, Metal and Water) have not been formed, Sāncái 三才 (Heaven, Earth and Man) have not been separated and Yīn and Yáng have not been established is called Hùndùn; and it is also called Hùn Yuán.*
> *五氣未形, 三才未分, 二儀未立, 謂之混沌, 亦謂混元.*

From the above descriptions, one can conclude that Hùn Yuán and Hùndùn are both Primal (Yuán) Qì. But Hùn Yuán exists slightly before Hùndùn, Hùn Yuán is close to Dào level and before One. Where does Primal (Yuán) Qì come from? It is from Kōngdòng (Empty Hole). What is Kōngdòng? Manuscript Yún Jí Qī Qiān 雲笈七籤 says that:

Primal (Yuán) Qì is inside a very vast and fuzzy unclear appearance place; and it is outside of a dark and faraway place. It is born inside the Kōngdòng.
元氣於眇莽之內, 幽冥之外, 生乎空洞.

Nine Qìs exist before the universe, and they are hidden inside the Kōngdòng, which is no light, no image, no form, no name, no color and no sound.
九氣出乎太空之先, 隱乎空洞之中. 無光無象, 無形無名, 無色無緒, 無音無聲.

Note: When the emptiness inside the Kōngdòng moves, it begets three Qìs, Upper Qì is called Shǐ 始, Middle Qì is called Yuán 元 and Lower Qì is called Xuán 玄. When the Qìs interact, they become nine Qìs, three upper, three middle and three lower.

The Primal (Yuán) Qì originates and begins its existence inside Kōngdòng. Kōngdòng is very similar to the Black Hole in in today's origin of the universe theories.

What is Hùnlùn 混論? The Manuscript Lièzǐ 列子 says that:

If formless/invisible substances beget substances with form, then what begets the Heaven and Earth? Therefore, there are Tàiyì 太易, Tàichū 太初, Tàishǐ 太始, and Tàisù 太素. Tàiyì is the state before Qì 氣 is formed, Tàichū is the state Qì begins, Tàishǐ is the state Xíng 形 (Form) begins and Tàisù is the state Zhì 質 (Essence) begins. When Qì, Form and Substance are present but have not been separated is called Hùnlùn. Hùnlùn means that substances are transmuted together and have not been separated, it is "look at but cannot be seen; listen to but cannot be heard; it cannot be followed."
夫有形者生於無形,則天地安從生? 故日有太易,有太初,有太始,有太素,太易者未見氣地,太初者,氣之始也;太始者,形之始也;太素者,質之始也.氣,形質具而未相離,故曰渾沦.浑沦者,言万物相浑沦而未相离也.视之不见,听之不闻,循之不得.

Note: In today's language, Qì 氣 means energy, Xíng 形 (Form) means mass and Zhì 質 means information.

From the information gathered from various manuscripts, Hùn Yuán (Hùndùn, Kōngdòng or Hùndòng) can be a process or Qì. The Universe is formed in two stages. The first stage is Tàiyì 太易, in this stage, Qì has not been formed, it is "look at, but cannot be seen; listen to, but cannot be heard; it cannot be followed" stage. Some manuscripts consider Tàiyì similar to Dào. The second stage is divided into three steps, forming Tàichū 太初(energy), Tàishǐ 太始 (mass), and Tàisù 太素

(information); although Tàichū, Tàishǐ and Tàisù are formed in this stage, they are not separated, they are transmuted as a nebulous One. Some manuscripts call this stage Tàijí. As Qì, it is collectively called Nature Hùn Yuán Qì for both stages.

What is Human Hùn Yuán Qì?

Manuscript Bào hùn yuán xiān shù 抱混元仙術 says: *What is Hùn Yuán (Qì)? It is Yuán (prenatal) Jīng 精, Yuán Qì 氣 and Yuán Shén 神.* It means the transmuted state of prenatal Jīng, Qì and Shén is called Hùn Yuán (Qì). The prenatal Jīng is not the reproductive Jīng (postnatal Jīng is sperm and egg), it is the essence from Yuán Shén. The prenatal Qì is not the air we breathe, it is vague, smoke like, and able to circulate inside the body Qì. The prenatal Shén is not the logical reasoning Shén, it is the highest-level of mind activity Yuán Shén. Chinese Buddhism called Yuán Shén *"Fú Xìng 佛性."* Fú means be conscious of inwardness/inherent quality, and Xìng means constant/ unchanging. Chinese Buddhism considers that everyone has Fú Xìng, it is an innate, inherent quality. It says, *"the regular person does not have less (Fú Xìng), the sage does not have more. 在凡不減, 在聖不增."*

Yuán (prenatal) Jīng, Yuán Qì and Yuán Shén are innate human qualities, not acquired after birth. According to ancient Chinese, before there is a body, there must be Hùn Yuán Qì. With Hùn Yuán Qì present, the body and information are formed (from non-existence to existence). The sperm and egg contain Yuán (prenatal) Jīng, Yuán Qì and Yuán Shén. Once the egg is fertilized, Hùn Yuán Qì is formed. In today's language, Hùn Yuán Qì is one's genetic marker or DNA, which would not exist unless an egg is fertilized. A fertilized egg contains Jīng, Qì and Shén (genetic marker). When Jīng, Qì and Shén are still merged as one, it is Hùn Yuán Qì; when Hùn Yuán Qì is separated into three, they are Jīng, Qì and Shén. One is Three, and Three is One. Hùn Yuán Qì is the substance/structure, Jīng, Qì and Shén are the functions. The function of Shén is mental activities, the function of Qì is to circulate and cultivate blood, and the function of Jīng is to provide a physical body which Qì and Shén can depend and attach.

Some of the teachings on Hùn Yuán Qì are only in the form of verbal instruction from teacher to student and not in written form. For example, there is verbal teaching that says the following:

> *Hùn Yuán is a (one) Five-Element, it can be a form or formless; it contains Yīn and Yáng and the keys to evolution; with Open-Close and Concentration-Dispersion, it gives birth to ten-thousand things.*
> *混元一五行, 有形亦無形. 中寓阴阳造化机. 开合聚散万物生.*

It means Hùn Yuán is a Wǔháng 五行 which can be Five-Elements (Wood, Fire, Soil, Metal and Water) or five shapes (round, straight, point, square and thin surface). When the elements interact with one another, Hùn Yuán can have form or be formless. It contains Yīn and Yáng and the key to evolution. The key is Yuán Shén; Yuán Shén is also the key to life. Hùn Yuán's Open-Close and Concentration-Dispersion movements beget all existences.

Another example is the following:

> *Hùn Yuán Qì, can be permeated by Shén, can concentrate into physical form, physical form can disperse to nothingness.*
> *混元氣,神貫通,聚則成形,散則成風.*

It means Shén can permeate and control Hùn Yuán Qì. Once Shén permeates Hùn Yuán Qì, Shén concentrates, and Hùn Yuán Qì will be concentrated to become physical substance; Shén disperses, physical substance will become nothingness.

In addition to the old manuscripts' writings on Hùn Yuán Qì, Zhìnéng Qìgōng's Hùn Yuán Qì Theory also relied on the teachings/writings of Chinese Buddhism, specially the Eight Faculties of Consciousness Theory and the Transcendence into Wisdom Theory 八識心王理論轉識成智理論. Philosophy and sociology, specially the writings of Karl Marx and Friedrich Von Engels are an important part of the Wholistic Entity Theory and the Ethics Theory. Modern science, specially Quantum theory, the theory of relativity and Systems theory, is also part of the foundation.

第二章：混元論

Chapter Two: Hùn Yuán Theory

The Hùn Yuán Theory is an important component of the Hùn Yuán Wholistic Theory and consists of Hùn Yuán Qì Theory and Hùn Huà Theory

I. The Hùn Yuán Qì Theory

There are many writings on Hùn Yuán Qì in Qìgōng literature, but there is no theoretical system. The Hùn Yuán Qì Theory is intended to organize the writings into a theory. Although the commonly accepted term "Hùn Yuán Qì" is used here, due to the increased knowledge of Qì, the Hùn Yuán Qì described in the theory is much more complex than the classical descriptions. The definition of Hùn Yuán will be discussed first.

A. The definition of Hùn Yuán

In Traditional Qìgōng manuscripts, "Hùn" (混) is described as "Yīn and Yáng, Wǔ Xíng (five Elements) are formed but their individual characteristic has not evolved yet 二五合凝而未兆." Yuán (元) is described as one. Together, Hùn Yuán means some things are transmuted into one. What are the things that are transmuted into one? According to Dào Dé Jīng (道德經 common English translation is Tao Te Ching), they are Yí, Xī and Wēi (夷, 希, 微).

視而不見曰夷; 聽而不聞曰希; 搏而不得曰微; 三者不可致詰; 故混而為一

Looked at, but cannot be seen; it is called Yí.
Listened to, but cannot be heard; it is called Xī.
Grasped at, but cannot be touched; it is called Wēi.
These three things cannot be used to reach the end of inquiry.
Because they are Hùn (transmuted/blended) as Yuán (One).

Translated by Luke Chan.
Luke Chan (2015). *8 Secrets of Tao Te Ching.* Roseville, CA. Benefactor Press

Interpretation:

Yí has no color and therefore it can be looked at but can't be seen.
Xī has no sound and therefore it can be listened to but can't be heard.
Wēi has no form and therefore it can be grasped at but can't be felt.
These three things are colorless, soundless and formless; therefore, they cannot be told through the mouth and transmitted through writing. They are Hùn (transmuted) as Yuán (One).

By Dào Dé Jīng's definition, the formation of Dào is the transmutation of Yí, Xī and Wēi. The process is called Hùn Yuán. Dào (One) is a Hùn Yuán Entity consists of Yí, Xī and Wēi.

Note: Dào Dé Jīng has 81 Chapters, Chapter 14 describes the formation and appearance of Dào (One).

Hùn Yuán can be a noun or a verb. As a noun, it implies nothing in the universe is singular. Everything is a Hùn Yuán (Entity), which is the result of the transmutation of two or more things. For example, the Universe is a Hùn Yuán Entity that consists of visible matter and invisible energy; a human being is a Hùn Yuán Entity that consists of Jīng, Qì and Shén.

As a verb, Hùn Yuán can be divided into Hùn Hé (混合)and Hùn Huà (混化). The process of two or more things transmuting together to form an entity is called Hùn Hé. For purposes of simplicity, this new entity is called "Hùn Yuán Qì (Entity)." The process of dissolving (transmuting) a thing into something that can transmute with other things to form a new entity is called Hùn Huà. These two concepts will be explained as "Hùn Yuán Qì Theory" and "Hùn Huà Theory" in the following sections.

Yuán can also mean Qì. In this context, Hùn Yuán means transmuted as Hùn Yuán Qì. In most cases, Hùn Yuán and Hùn Yuán Qì are interchangeable. Although Hùn Yuán has many names such as Hùndùn (混沌), Húnyuán (渾元) and Kōngdòng (空洞), in classical Chinese Qìgōng manuscripts, they are all within the category of Primal Qì. Depending on the context of the writing, Hùn Yuán Qì can be either Nature Primal Hùn Yuán Qì or Human Prenatal Hùn Yuán Qì.

In Zhìnéng Qìgōng, Hùn Yuán is a special term used to describe the wholistic existence of an entity. In fact, Hùn Yuán is a concept in Zhìnéng Qìgōng; it is an awareness of the innate (wholistic) characters of an objective substance. Normally when one touches a substance, one is only aware of the substance's physical phenomenon, not its innate (wholistic) characters. To be aware of the wholistic characters of the substance, one must use logical reasoning. A thermal cup will be used as an example. The concept of "thermal cup" is the collective information of the cup's characteristics. The phase "thermal cup" is a concept, not an object; therefore, no one can feel it. When one sees an object called "thermal cup" whose function is to hold and maintain water temperature for some time; through logical reasoning, gradually, the concept of "thermal cup" is formed. When the phrase "thermal cup" is mentioned, the wholistic characters of the substance will automatically register in one's mind. This wholistic information is called Hùn Yuán in Zhìnéng Qìgōng.

All things in the universe are Hùn Yuán Entities, which are transmuted together by two or more elements. For example, the Universe is a Hùn Yuán Entity that consists of substances with and without physical appearance; these substances beget each other, from form to formless, and from formless to form. The formless substance is a Hùn Yuán Entity of energy and information. The physical (with form) substance is a Hùn Yuán Entity of mass (Xíng 形), energy (Qì 氣) and information (Zhí 質). Hùn Yuán consists of two parts. One is the process of transmuting two or more elements to a new wholistic entity, it is called Hùn Huà (混化); the other is the transmuted wholistic entity, it is called Hùn Yuán Qì (混元氣). Therefore, in Zhìnéng Qìgōng, there are Hùn Yuán Qì Theory and Hùn Huà Theory. The Hùn Yuán Qì Theory discusses the essence/innate characteristics of a substance. The Hùn Huà Theory discusses the physical characteristics of a substance.

B. Hùn Yuán Qì Theory

Unlike traditional Qìgōng, which considers Hùn Yuán and Hùn Yuán Qì as one thing with different names, Zhìnéng Qìgōng considers Hùn Yuán as broader than Hùn Yuán Qì. Hùn Yuán has two parts, Hùn Yuán Qì and Hùn Huà (transmutation). There are also External Hùn Yuán, Internal Hùn Yuán and Central Hùn Yuán in Zhìnéng Qìgōng practice methods. Therefore, in Zhìnéng Qìgōng, Hùn Yuán and Hùn Yuán Qì are not the same. In the practice methods, Hùn Yuán means transmutation; it is the mind intent and Qì transmuting process. Depending on where the transmutation takes place, it can be External Hùn Yuán, Internal Hùn Yuán or Central Hùn Yuán. For this text, focus will be on the Hùn Yuán Qì Theory, not the Hùn Yuán in practice methods.

1. What is Hùn Yuán Qì?

According to traditional Qìgōng, Hùn Yuán Qì is the transmuted state of Xíng, Qì and Zhí. Zhí is also called Shén as in Xíng, Qì and Shén in traditional Qìgōng. Xíng, Qì and Zhí are interdependent, one exists, all exist. When Xíng, Qì and Shén are transmuted as one, it is called Hùn Yuán Qì. Xíng, Qì and Zhí are similar to how mass, energy, and information describe a substance in science. Xíng corresponds to mass, Qì to energy and Zhí to information. Although Xíng, Qì and Zhí are similar to mass, energy and information, they are not the same. For example, energy can be in an expressed state or in a hidden state. The power (energy) of an atomic bomb when it is detonated is an expressed state. Before the detonation, the energy in an atomic bomb is a hidden state, only becoming apparent when interacting with external substances (detonated). Qi, however, is distinguishable from energy because regardless of interactions, QI functions remain the same.

Hùn Yuán Qì can be defined as a as the special existing state of a substance which contains the full, unique characteristics of mass, energy and information. For example, TV signals consist of radio waves, information and energy. Before the signal is sent out, the radio wave does not have any specific information (it has its own information such as wave length, but not added-on information). Only after the program information and energy are added and merged (the merging point is called Hùn Yuán Point) will the radio wave become a signal with particular characteristics (wave, information and energy) that can be called Hùn Yuán Qì.

Hùn Yuán Qì exists in two ways. One is in a formless, imageless and non-solid form. It is called Qì in traditional Qìgōng and Hùn Yuán Qì in Hùn Yuán Theory. Hùn Yuán Qì is a substance in a special existing state in which Xíng, Qì and Zhí are transmuted as one, evenly distributed (uniform) and indivisible. Ordinarily, Hùn Yuán Qì's physical form/mass is in a hidden state, neither seen nor touched, yet it still exists . A radio wave cannot be seen or be touched, but it still exists (its mass is in a hidden state). Hùn Yuán Qì exists in the same way; the formless, imageless and non-solid form is the most common form of existence. The other form of existence is in physical form. All physical things are a form of Hùn Yuán Qì. As the formless Hùn Yuán Qì condenses and its concentration reaches a certain point, it becomes a physical thing (has form and image/appearance). It is a special existing form of Hùn Yuán Qì, but it is still Hùn Yuán Qì. In order to distinguish the two, the formless form is called Hùn Yuán Qì, the physical form is called the solid object.

Inside all solid objects, there is uncondensed Hùn Yuán Qì circulating within its empty spaces. All solid things are not really solid since they consist of atoms, within which are protons, neutrons and electrons. Thus, the majority of the solid is empty space with Hùn Yuán Qì circulating inside. The Hùn Yuán Qì is not only within the solid object, it is also in its surrounding area. The Hùn Yuán Qì surrounding an object is called Hùn Yuán Qì Field. The solid object is the condensed Hùn Yuán Qì; the Hùn Yuán Qì Field is the diffused Hùn Yuán Qì. Together, a solid object and its Hùn Yuán Qì Field form an entity. This entity is called Hùn Yuán Entity.

There is a direct relationship between the solid object and its Hùn Yuán Qì Field. Generally, the higher the density and the bigger the object is, the bigger (spread further) and stronger the Hùn Yuán Qì Field will be. If the object's structure and/or function changes, it will affect the Hùn Yuán Qì Field and cause the Qì Field to change; and the reverse also is true. But changes do not affect each other instantly; the process takes time. If the structure of the solid thing is completely changed or disappears, its original Qì Field will remain a certain period of time before it changes or disappears. When changes occur in the Hùn Yuán Qì Field but not in the physical subject, the Hùn Yuán Qì Field (the diffused Hùn Yuán Qì) can condense to become part of the solid object and to a certain degree, the Hùn Yuán Qì Field can change the solid object to become something else.

When the solid object changes, usually it changes from within first; the surrounding Qì Field will remain and stay unchanged. Only when the "New" (changed) solid object's diffused Hùn Yuán Qì expands outward, will it gradually replace the old Hùn Yuán Qì Field. If the Hùn Yuán Qì Field changes first, the solid object will remain unchanged for a period of time. This will create an unbalanced phenomenon. When the Hùn Yuán Qì Field (diffused Qì) condenses and becomes part of the solid object, it will create a new equilibrium. If the changes in the Hùn Yuán Qì Field exceed a certain limit, it can change the original solid object and form a new solid object.

This is a very important concept in Qì healing. In Qì healing, if one focuses on the illness or has doubts, the illness may come back. Dissolving a tumor will be used as an example. The tumor is dissolved during the Qì healing (emitting Qì) session, which can be administered by a healer or by oneself, but its Qì Field may still be intact and the tumor's (Qì Field) information is still there. Or during the session, one focuses on the tumor only, mind intent will affect the tumor but not the surrounding Qì Field. If one has doubts and keeps thinking that the tumor may still exist, then one adds that information and energy into the Qi Field and the tumor may return. Normally, it will take some time for the Qì Field to change. Therefore, if one works on the Hùn Yuán Entity (tumor and surrounding Qì Field), the tumor normally would not return.

After a solid object is formed, the Hùn Yuán Entity (solid object and surrounding Qì Field) is not fixed permanently, changes still may occur. An advanced and complex Hùn Yuán Entity can dissolve into a simple Hùn Yuán Entity. By the same token, several simple Hùn Yuán Entities can transmute to become a complex Hùn Yuán Entity. Also, a Hùn Yuán Entity can interact with other Hùn Yuán Entities to form either a more or a less complicated Hùn Yuán Entity. For example, a thermal cup's special characteristic is to be able to the hold water temperature. If it is broken, its wholistic characteristic (holding water temperature) no longer exists, but it is still a physical substance with its own characteristics. The cup (complex Hùn Yuán Entity) no longer exists, it dissolves into pieces (simple Hùn Yuán Entities).

Hùn Yuán Qì is constantly merging from formless to solid and from solid to formless. In Traditional Qìgōng, concentrating Hùn Yuán Qì to become a solid object is called "from nothing give birth to something." From a solid object dissipating to become Hùn Yuán Qì is called "Have to become have not." These interactions between Hùn Yuán Qì and solid objects occur continuously in Nature.

2. Stages of Hùn Yuán Qì

Hùn Yuán Qì is the overall/unique manifestation of an object (mass, energy and information). Each object in the Universe has its own characteristics and particularity. In other words, each object has its own Hùn Yuán Qì. Although there are innumerable objects in the Universe, from simple to complex, Zhìnéng Qìgōng's Hùn Yuán Qì Theory catalogs them into five levels/stages of existing. The first two levels are the same as Traditional Theories, the last three levels are unique to Zhìnéng Qìgōng.

a) Hùn Yuán Element Stage 混元子層次

Hùn Yuán Element (混元子) is the most basic material in the universe. It is unimaginably small; it can be described only using a dot. Unlike the dots in mathematics, which occupy only space but not time, Hùn Yuán Element occupies both space and time. All things in the universe occupy space and move. When a substance moves from point A to point B, it creates a line in space called *Space Line* (a line in space). Time behaves the same way, as time moves from point A to point B, it also creates a line in time called *Time Line* (a line in time). When the *Space Line* and the *Time Line* intersect each other, the intersecting point occupies both space and time. But it is neither space nor time, it is a dot that contains both space and time. Hùn Yuán Element is a dot in the *Space Line* and a dot in the *Time Line*. In science, a dot occupies space but does not have length, width or height. Although Hùn Yuán Element is unimaginably small, it still has length, width and height. No matter how short the existence is, as long as it is within the *Time Line*, it occupies time. When the *Space Line* and *Time Line* intersect each other, changes will occur. Since both space and time are a dot, space will contain time, and time will contain space. This merged state is called Hùn Yuán Element. Fig. 2-1. Hùn Yuán Element.

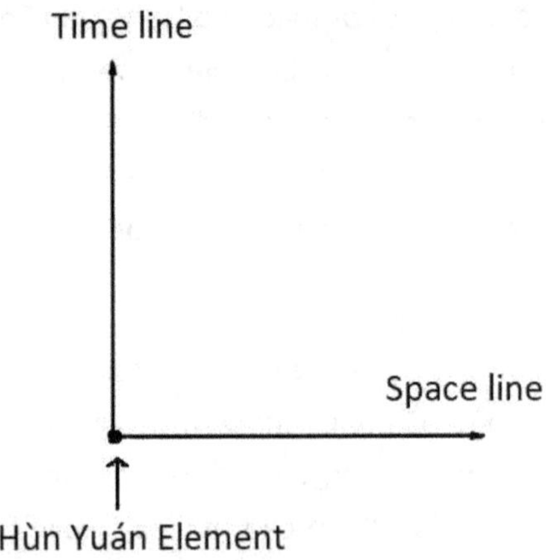

Fig. 2-1 Hùn Yuán Element

Hùn Yuán Element is so small, it cannot be divided any further. It is in an absolutely even and indivisible state, and is called "Hùnjí (混極)" in traditional Qìgōng. Hùn

Yuán Element is the result of the transmutation of space and time. In it, space, time, mass, energy and information are all transmuted as an indistinguishable one. Therefore, one (Hùn Yuán) Element is call Hùn Yuán Element, millions of (Hùn Yuán) Element are also called Hùn Yuán Element. One is many, many are one, and they are indistinguishable. Hùn Yuán Element is a very unique substance, it only exists in a very brief moment of time; it exists, and then it is gone. Hùn Yuán Element's space and time are absolute space and time. In traditional Qìgōng, this level is called Dào (道), Wújí (無極) or Hùnjí (混極).

Dào Dé Jīng (道德經) describes Dào as:

> *有物混成,先天地生,寂兮寥兮,独立而不改,周行而不殆,可以為天下母,吾不知其名,字之曰道.強為之名曰大.大曰逝,逝曰遠,遠曰返.*
>
> *In chaos, a thing is formed before Heaven and Earth;*
> *It is silent and formless; unique and unchanging;*
> *Revolving and inexhaustible, it can be the mother of all things;*
> *I do not know its name; I just call it Dào; reluctantly, I describe it as "Big."*
> *"Big" means it is (goes) everywhere; everywhere means it is infinite; infinite means it is returning.*
>
> Translated by Luke Chan. *8 Secrets of Tao Te Ching, p. 285.*

Dào Dé Jīng also says:

> *視之不見, 名曰夷; 聽之不聞, 名曰希; 搏之不得, 名曰微. 此三者不可致詰, 故混而為一. 其上不皦, 其下不昧. 繩繩兮不可名, 复歸於無物. 是謂無狀之狀, 無物之象, 是謂惚恍. 迎之不見其首, 隨之不見其後.*
>
> *Looked at, but cannot be seen; it is called Yí.*
> *Listened to, but cannot be heard; it is called Xī.*
> *Grasped at, but cannot be touched; it is called Wēi.*
> *These three things cannot be used to reach the end of inquiry. Therefore, they are blended as Oneness.*
> *Above is not bright; below is not dark.*
> *A continuous whole beyond description,*
> *It returns again to the nothingness of Dào.*
> *This is called the form of formless. The image of nothingness. This is also called being vague and elusive.*
> *Facing it, one cannot see its head; following it, one cannot see its rear.*
>
> Translated by Luke Chan. *8 Secrets of Tao Te Ching, p. 241*

Since Dào is before Heaven and Earth, it is easier to explain it backward. In the galaxies, once a black hole is formed, it continues to grow by absorbing additional matter such as stars and other black holes. As the density increases, it will create gravitational collapse; space and time form a singularity. The moment the singularity is formed, all gravitational forces will disappear, and this singularity is called Hùn Yuán Element.

b) Primal Hùn Yuán Qì Level/Stage 初始混元氣層次

Primal Hùn Yuán Qì evolves from the Hùn Yuán Element; its structure is extremely even, and it occupies the whole universe. In this level, space and time are separated and Qì begins to emerge. Traditional Qìgōng called this Qì "Yuán Qì (元氣)" or Tàijí (太極). All things are evolved from this Qì.

Primal Hùn Yuán Qì is the most basic level of existence and the root of the formation of the universe. It can transmute into formless substance (Hùn Yuán Qì) and into millions of things with physical forms in different stages of existence. When it transmutes/condenses into solid objects, it remains inside the object. Primal Hùn Yuán Qì permeates all things in the universe. The difference between Hùn Yuán Element and Primal Hùn Yuán Qì is that Hùn Yuán Element cannot transmute into solid objects nor remain inside the object. Hùn Yuán Element's space and time are transmuted as one; it can only give birth to Primal Hùn Yuán Qì. Primal Hùn Yuán Qì can change and give birth to millions of things.

How is the Primal Hùn Yuán Qì formed? As mentioned earlier, Hùn Yuán Element is a space and time singularity with no gravitational forces. When the gravitational forces disappear, space and time will "escape" and "break out" from the singularity. It becomes something that occupies both space and time and is called Primal Hùn Yuán Qì. In other words, Primal Hùn Yuán Qì is a merged but not transmuted state of space and time; the energy and mass are in a hidden state. This merged state is called "Space and Time Merged Element (時空複合子)." Depending on how the space and time merge, it will create different merged states that represent different space and time information. When space and time escape from the singularity, they acquire energy. As a result, Primal Hùn Yuán Qì gives birth to ten-thousand things.

Although it may not be well defined, all physical substances (Hùn Yuán Qì) in the universe have boundaries, and there are spaces between the boundaries of substances. How do the substances connect to each other beyond their boundaries? Science considers that the connections are created by gravitational forces. In Qìgōng, gravitational force is one of Hùn Yuán Qì's physical characteristics. Once the Primal Hùn Yuán Qì is formed, gravitational force will exist. Therefore, in Qìgōng, it is the Primal Hùn Yuán Qì that connects all substances.

c) Wànwù 萬物 (Ten-Thousand Things) Level

As the Primal Hùn Yuán Qì evolves, it becomes Yīn and Yáng. When Yīn and Yáng interact with each other, they create substances that are different from Yīn and Yáng. These substances have the characteristics of matter but not physical forms; they are called Wànwù Hùn Yuán Qì. This Hùn Yuán Qì is formless and invisible; as it concentrates and condenses, it forms simple physical elements called simple element Hùn Yuán Qì. When simple element Hùn Yuán Qì interacts with each other, complicated Hùn Yuán Qì is formed, and all existences are created. The Hùn Yuán Qì in this level is called Wànwù Level Hùn Yuán Qì. Wànwù are the things that one can see in the universe.

All entities are the transmutation and concentration of their own Hùn Yuán Qì. Every object in the universe has its own structural, physical and chemical characteristics; it is the manifestation of the object's own Hùn Yuán Qì (mass, energy and information). Therefore, Wànwù Level Hùn Yuán Qì refers to the completed/wholistic characteristics (space and time) of an object, which are mass, energy and information. In this level, Hùn Yuán Qì can be either the formless, invisible Qì or an object with mass, energy and information.

Every object has invisible Qì circulating inside and a layer of thinly dispersed Qì surrounding it. Ordinary sensory perception can only sense/be aware of partial characteristics of an object, such as mass, energy or information, but not all of them at the same time. In extraordinary wholistic perception, partial characteristics do not exist, there is only wholistic entity (characteristics), a very special state in which space, time, mass, energy and information are merged as one.

Normally, an adult's ordinary sensory organs are only able to see the physical object, not the surrounding Qì nor the invisible Qì circulating inside. Babies can see and sense the surrounding Qì. A baby does not have the concept of space. When a baby sees a ball, they would reach out to grab it. To the baby, there is no distance/space between them and the ball; all they see is the ball and the surrounding Qì. At the beginning, they are not able to reach the ball, then they move and finally they are able to touch it. With repeated experience, sensory organs will establish the position of the ball and the distance will be established. Once this becomes a habit, the position of the ball remains, and the surrounding Qì will gradually disappear from the sensory organs. Human beings are capable of seeing much more than is assumed to be possible. For example, a human being should be able to see a wider range of the light spectrum. But due to the fact that they do not hold on to that ability as they get older or during their daily life, they gradually lose that ability.

In Wànwù Level, materials can be divided into organic and inorganic. To maintain their original characteristics, inorganic materials must maintain their own internal Qì and cannot interact with other Hùn Yuán Qì. For example, sodium cannot interact with chlorine, if it does, it will become sodium chloride. Sodium chloride has its own wholistic characteristics. It is neither sodium nor chlorine and the original characteristics of sodium and chlorine no longer exist.

When sodium chloride is looked at from the formation point of view, one can see it is not directly from Primal Hùn Yuán Qì. It begins with simple element Hùn Yuán Qì evolving into complicated Hùn Yuán Qì with full characteristics of space and time. Both sodium and chloride are simple materials with their individual characteristics. When they transmute together, they form a new entity—sodium chloride, which has its own characteristics. Within sodium chloride, the original characteristics of sodium and chlorine no longer exist. To maintain its characteristics, sodium chloride cannot interact with other Hùn Yuán Qì (materials).

An organism (organic materials) is different; after it is formed, it must continuously interact with external Qì (metabolism) to maintain its equilibrium. Its Hùn Yuán Qì is the result of transmutation between original Hùn Yuán Qì (the Qì that forms the organism) and External Qì. In traditional Qìgōng, the original Hùn Yuán Qì is called Pre-Primal (prenatal) Qì, the External Qì is called Post-Primal (postnatal) Qì.

In the advanced form of organic materials such as plants and animals, their Hùn Yuán Qì is not the same. Plants normally grow in the same spots during their entire life cycle; therefore, their Post-Primal Qì is from two sources—earth (water and nutrition) and heaven (air and sun light). Water, nutrition and air are the concentration of formless and invisible Hùn Yuán Qì and are less complicated than plants' Hùn Yuán Qì. Plants can absorb the less complicated Qì into the body and transmute it with the Internal Qì to become part of the plant. The way plants change their physical shape and maintain their equilibrium is by using Internal Qì to interact with External Qì.

Animals have nervous systems that enable them to have subjective and active movements. With independence and movement, the distribution of an animal's Internal Qì is no longer restricted by the physical body. Internal Qì can change the way it is distributed when it follows the subjective movements. For example, the distribution of Internal Qì in an animal is different when it is running away from danger and when it is relaxing. With the exception of human beings, animals cannot consciously move Qì. In animals, the entity is called Xíng Qì Zhí (形氣質

body, energy and information); in human beings, it is called Xíng Qì Shén (形氣神 body, energy and mind activities).

Xíng Qì Zhí/Shén is the wholistic expression of the merged state of an object's structural and functional characteristics. Structural characteristics occupy and express in space, functional characteristics (the continuous changes of an object) occupy and express in time. The expression of structural characteristics is a process that must express in time. Space and time cannot be separated within an object. When one sees a thing, what one sees is the space expression (structural characteristics) and the time expression (functional characteristics) at that particular moment in time. For example, the Hùn Yuán Qì of a plant is the seed, the young tree, the adult tree, flowering, fruiting and death. When one sees a tree, what one sees is its structural and functional characteristics at a particular moment in time, not its whole Hùn Yuán Qì (complete information). Not being able to see does not mean it does not exist. The cross section of the tree shows the information of space (structures) and time (past). Since the tree needs to interact with External Qì to maintain its equilibrium and growth, the future information such as flowering, fruiting and death is in a hidden state.

An extension rod is a way to explain Hùn Yuán Qi. The Hùn Yuán Qi of an extension rod can extend from one length to another and also retract back to its original state. In the following diagram (Fig. 2-2), A is the original state; B is a point between the original state and the final state; C is the final state and D is Hùn Yuán Qì. From A to B to C, the rod changes from short to long to the longest, the structures and time change, but the Hùn Yuán Qì (whole information (D)) remains the same. Fig. 2-2 Extension Rod.

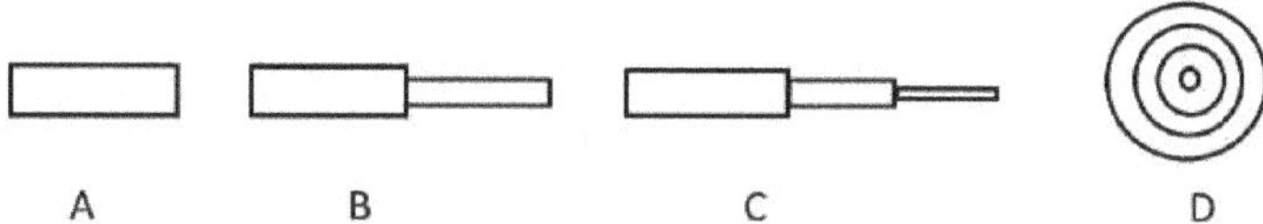

Fig. 2-2 Extension Rod

d) Human Hùn Yuán Qì

Although a human being's Hùn Yuán Qì belongs to Wànwù Level, a human being has mind/mental activities (consciousness) and overall life activities that are under the influence of consciousness. Compared with other animals, Human Hùn Yuán Qì evolves/belongs to an advanced level. Human Hùn Yuán Qì will be explained in detail in Chapter Four.

e) Yì Yuán Tǐ 意元體

When Hùn Yuán Qì in the brain has evolved to the point that it contains consciousness and logical thinking, it is called Yì Yuán Tǐ. It is the finest, most agile and important part of the Human Hùn Yuán Qì. Besides the ability to direct the body (Human) Hùn Yuán Qì, it can also direct/command all levels of Hùn Yuán Qì in the universe. It is very similar to the Hùn Yuán Element and Primal Hùn Yuán Qì, except it has initiative. It is the highest level of Hùn Yuán Qì and will be explained in detail in Chapter Five.

Note: Yì Yuán Tǐ is a unique term used only in Zhìnéng Qìgōng. All other forms of Qìgōng use the word Shén.

3. The Characteristics of Hùn Yuán Qì

The following are the common characteristics of the Hùn Yuán Qì.

a) Concentrating and Dispersing Characteristics

Hùn Yuán Qì exists in two ways: one is the formless, invisible, evenly distributed and non-solid form; the other is the concentrated visible substance form. The formless Qì concentrates and condenses into visible substances; the visible substances disperse into invisible Qì. The inter-change (the concentrating and dispersing) between the two is the most fundamental characteristic of Hùn Yuán Qì.

Hùn Yuán Qì's concentrating and dispersing is a natural process. In the universe, this process is caused by interactions between substances and it occurs by "accident." When Qì is affected by external forces such as pressure, movement and/or gravitational force, it will congregate. If the congregation reaches a tipping point at which it is no longer able to maintain balance, a physical substance will be formed. When the physical substance is affected by external force, it may disintegrate into Qì. A desk will be used to illustrate the point. A desk is the concentration point of wood, nails and paint. It is an entity with complex structural characteristics, which include adhering and supporting forces. If it is hit by external force or does not have sufficient adhering and supporting forces, it will disintegrate into pieces.

Organic materials are constantly maintaining this natural process of concentrating and dispersing of the Hùn Yuán Qì. In human beings, in addition to maintaining this concentrating and dispersing process, the mind intent can also activate the body Hùn Yuán Qì's concentrating and dispersing process. When the mind intent merges with the Qì and concentrates in an area, Qì will begin to concentrate and condense in that area. When the Qì concentrates reach a point at which it is no longer able to maintain balance, visible substance will form. Conversely, when the mind intent permeates inside an object and has dispersing intent, the object can be dissipated into formless and invisible Qì.

b) Wholistic Characteristics

A physical object is its Hùn Yuán Qì in a concentrated form. An object may have many parts with different functions, but all of them are still a concentrated form of its Hùn Yuán Qì. Because the object's Hùn Yuán Qì contains the complete information of the object, every part of the object contains the wholistic information. When the object or some parts of the object interact with an external object, both the object and the external object will have the full information of each other. For example, when John Doe writes something on a paper, the paper would have his Hùn Yuán Qì, which includes space (his physical conditions) and time (present and past); a person with extraordinary ability can detect it.

c) Distribution Characteristics

The formless Primal Hùn Yuán Qì is evenly distributed and permeates the universe; the universe is made up of evenly distributed Primal Hùn Yuán Qì. As the Primal Hùn Yuán Qì evolves to Wànwù Hùn Yuán Qì, it will become source material for the ten-thousand things. The distribution of Wànwù Hùn Yuán Qì will change with the formation of substances. The distribution of Hùn Yuán Qì in the physical substances is not even, it is closely related to the physical structure of the substance. In animals, body movements also affect the distribution of Qì. Normally, the center and surface/membrane have more Qì than the rest of the substance. A physical substance is concentrated Qì, besides the substance itself, there is a layer of Qì surrounding it. The distribution of this layer of Qì is also not even; it is closer to the substance having the higher density.

Why is knowing the distribution important? To change a substance, its Qì Field must change. Knowing the distribution gives us a better idea of how to proceed. For example, in Qì healing, to change the condition of a person, if the surrounding Qì Field is strong, one may process the Qì Field first. One can change the Qì Field to affect the membrane or from the membrane to change the Qì Field to achieve healing. If one's mind intent can penetrate deep inside the body, then one can directly penetrate into the center (of the body) and change from the inside out. No matter how one conducts Qì healings—starting from inside out or outside in, one should know that there are three areas to work on: the Qì Field, the membrane and the center (of the body).

d) Retaining information Characteristics

All levels of Hùn Yuán Qì, whether formless or with form, can retain information. Because a substance constantly interacts with the Hùn Yuán Qì surrounding it, it will also absorb and retain the information from the universe. Therefore, on a physical level, the information is from both within and without. As a substance evolves, the information inside the substance before the process is retained in physical form will combine with the new information to form a new wholistic entity. For example, a person's DNA contains/retains all the information about that person. DNA is the formless Hùn Yuán Qì which contains the person's wholistic information condensed into physical form. When DNA interacts with the surrounding Qì Field (environment), it will also absorb and retain the information from the universe and will form a new entity. The difference between the new and old DNA may be extremely small, but there are changes.

Information does not occupy space and time. Whether the information is strong or weak, once it exists, it will remain; it is just a matter of how to extract it. To extract information, the information (volume) either has to be strong or one will have to add energy to it. A house will be used as an example. When a person dies there, it will retain the information. If the person died in a trauma, that information is very strong and easy to extract, and the house may become a haunted house. If the person died in peace, normally the information is very weak, so it is more difficult to extract. Only after one consciously focuses (adds energy) on the house then one may be able to extract the information.

Human beings can deliver/send out the wholistic information and store it in any place. For example, paper itself is Hùn Yuán Qì, when some information is input into it, it will retain the information. However, for the paper to be able to retain information about an individual, the mind intent must be added to strengthen the information. To add mind intent means the way information is input into the paper; therefore, the individual must be consciously aware of what they are doing. The strength of the information about the individual is proportional to mindfulness.

e) Compatible Characteristics

Compatible means that Hùn Yuán Qì can co-exist/cohabit and retain information. Cohabiting and retaining information are directly related, there will be no retaining without cohabiting. Because information does not occupy space and time, cohabiting also refers to different levels of Hùn Yuán Qì (Hùn Yuán Qì occupies space). A lower level Hùn Yuán Qì can circulate freely in a higher level Hùn Yuán Qì (including solid substance). With the exception of human Shén (mind intent), which can permeate from higher level to lower level, Hùn Yuán Qì can only permeate from a lower level to a higher level. Therefore, the most basic form of Hùn Yuán Qì, the Primal Hùn Yuán Qì, can circulate freely through all levels of substances in the universe and becomes the basic materials for all levels of Hùn Yuán Qì. An organism can strengthen its vitality by absorbing this Qì directly.

The reason that the lower level Hùn Yuán Qì can circulate freely in the higher levels is because Qì in a higher level is much more complex and creates space for simpler Qì to enter. For example, the bigger the element in a substance is, the greater is the empty space in the element. A small element can easily enter and circulate the empty space inside the bigger element; however, a bigger element cannot enter a smaller one.

II. Hùn Huà (Transmutation) Theory

Hùn Huà (Transmutation) Theory describes the formation process of Hùn Yuán Entity, which involves at least two or more substances. It also explains the governing patterns and changes within the Hùn Yuán substance itself. Hùn Huà Theory has two components: Substance Hùn Huà (Transmutation) Theory and Space and Time Hùn Huà (Transmutation) Theory.

A. Substance Hùn Huà Theory

To form a Hùn Yuán Entity, there must be at least two ingredients (materials) present. Before these ingredients can transmute together, they must go through two processes: to evolve internally and to transmute. These processes include the internal movement of the substance and the interaction of two or more substances.

Because the characteristics of a substance cannot be changed until the internal changes reach a certain point, the process of transmutation begins with the substance's internal changes. The process of internal changing/movement does not involve another substance, therefore, it is not a transmutation. Transmutation involves at least two or more substances and depends on internal changes. Without internal changes, there will be no transmutation among substances. After a substance is formed, it will continue to interact with external substances. When the interaction reaches a certain point, transmutation will occur. In other words, if the substance's movements stay within a certain boundary, which would not affect or change the characteristics of the substance, it is called Internal Movement. If the movements exceed the limit and no longer maintain its original characteristics, it is called Transmutation.

1. The movement of Hùn Yuán Entity

The internal movements of Hùn Yuán Entity can be divided into four categories: Open-Close, Concentrate-Disperse, In-Out, and Huà. They are the most basic movements of all substances and they exist in every substance.

a) Open-Close

This is the most basic form of movement and refers to the movement or changes in the Hùn Yuán Entity's surface. Open means the surface area opens and expands outward. When the surface area opens and expands outward, it becomes bigger. Close means the surface area closes and retracts inward; the surface area becomes smaller. For example, in human beings, Open-Close occurs in the skin area, including respiratory and digestive tracts, that contract externally. Each cell has a membrane which is the contact surface with the external world. Therefore, the Open-Close movement occurs in every cell of the body.

Every substance has boundary and range (area within the boundary), and its open-close movements occur on the surface of the boundary and range. In human beings, the range and boundary/surface of the Qì layer surrounding the skin cannot be defined. Therefore, in Qìgōng practice, one focuses on the skin; the Open-Close occurs on the surface of the skin.

b) Concentrate-Disperse

This refers to the movement of elements/components within the Hùn Yuán Entity. Inside a physical substance, there are many elements. When the elements condense and concentrate, the Hùn Yuán Entity will become smaller and its density will increase; this is called "Concentrate." When the elements disperse outward, the Hùn Yuán Entity will become bigger and its density will decrease, this is called "Disperse."

When the element's concentrate or disperse reaches a tipping point at which it is no longer able to maintain balance, the physical appearance of the Hùn Yuán Entity will change. Matter can exist in three states, gaseous state, liquid state and solid state. In gaseous state or formless Hùn Yuán Qì, the density is very low and the gravitational force between the elements is very weak. As it begins to concentrate, the density and the gravitational force will increase; when it reaches a certain point, it will become liquid. If the process continues, it will become solid. In Qìgōng theory, it is called "concentration would form a substance" or "formless give birth to form." And in reverse, when a physical substance gradually dissipates, it will become formless/non-physical Hùn Yuán Qì; and it is called "solid dissipates to become wind" or "form disintegrates to formless." The Concentrate-Disperse movement occurs naturally in nature. In human beings, mind intent can activate this Concentrate-Disperse movement and consciously change the Hùn Yuán Entity.

c) In-Out

"In" refers to internal Qì (of the substance) or External Hùn Yuán Qì goes inside the surface/boundary; normally it occurs in combination with Close and Concentrate. "Out" refers to the substance's Qì leaving the surface/boundary and moving outward; normally it occurs in combination with Open and Disperse. When the internal Qì going out and the external Qì coming into a substance reach a point in which balance is no longer able to be maintained, then the exchanging of Qi causes characteristic change within the substance. The characteristic change is called transmutation. Normal In-Out movement may not necessarily result in transmutation, but it will lead to some changes. The degree of changes is in proportion to the amount of In-Out movements; the bigger the amount of movement, the bigger the changes will be.

Open-Close, Concentrate-Disperse and In-Out have their own special functions. Open-Close is the surface/boundary of the Hùn Yuán Entity open-up and close-in movement; Concentrate-Disperse is the element inside the Hùn Yuán Entity movement; In-Out is the in and out of the surface movement of the Hùn Yuán Entity's Qì.

d) Huà (化)

Huà means change or transmutation. Its function depends on the movements of Open-Close, Concentrate-Disperse and In-Out. In order to beget a new thing, there must be transmutation. It is called Shēng Huà (生化 beget and transmute) in Chinese culture. The Yellow Emperor's Classic of Internal Medicine (黃帝内經) says "a substance is begotten is Huà (物生謂之化)." When the movements (Open-Close, In-Out and Concentrate-Disperse) reach a certain point, the substance's structures and information will change and need to be rearranged to maintain balance. With rearrangement, a new substance will emerge; this process is called Huà or Beget (生).

These four movements are not isolated from one another. They interact, influence and interconnect with one another, and there is a "from simple to complex process" between them. "Not isolated from one another" has two meanings.

- The movement can start with one and becomes more complicated as it progresses (with more than one movement). Or it can start with the most complicated (with all four movements) and progress to simple.
- In advanced (complex) physical substances, all four movements exist at the same time, they would not be in isolated existence.

These four movements can have different combinations. Some have all four, some have three, and some have two or just one. Among them, Open-Close is the simplest and is the foundation for all others. It exists in all levels of Hùn Yuán Qì and is the most common form of movement. All levels of Hùn Yuán Qì have Open-Close movement.

Generally speaking, in the physical world, all four movements exist at the same time and interact with one another. In a physical substance, when there is In-Out movement, usually it is accompanied with Concentrate-Disperse and the surface's Open-Close movements. It is Open-Disperse-Out, and Close-Concentrate-In. Although Open usually associates with Disperse and Out; Close associates with Concentrate and In, they are not absolute and can have different combinations.

For example, when there is a force inside a physical substance, no matter whether it is a retracting force from within or a suppressing force from without, it belongs to Concentrate, and the surface area would close/contract inward. If the contraction extends over a certain point, the surface collapses and disintegrates/opens up. Once the surface is Open, inside pressure/density will decrease, and external Qì will continue to concentrate inward. This is a Concentrate-Open-In combination. When we inhale, our lung expands, it will create negative pressure and the air will come in; this is an In-Open-In combination.

The relationships between the four movements are different in each level of Qì. Hùn Yuán Element level is a singularity. It is so small, it does not have Concentrate-Disperse, In-Out movements; its Huà is Open-Close. When the Hùn Yuán Element opens, it is no longer Hùn Yuán Element; it is changed/Huà to Primal Hùn Yuán Qì. The Close occurs when space and time return to singularity — Hùn Yuán Element. The process of Open-Close of Hùn Yuán Element is the process of Birth and Death of the Universe.

In the Primal Hùn Yuán Qì level, the Open-Close movement is very small. Space-Time separation is Open, Space-Time merging is Close. Primal Hùn Yuán Qì can be described as one thing (entity) or as a collected whole in the chaos (the formless matter before the creation of the universe). The Open-Close movement in this level refers to the Open-Close movement among the "Space and Time Merged Elements (the merged state of space-time-aka Primal Hùn Yuán Qì)."

Although there is no difference between the "Space and Time Merged Elements," they all have open outward and close inward movements. Space and Time Merged Elements follow the Open-Close movement to concentrate (congregate) and disperse. Consequently, Elements will congregate together in various sequences and produce various amounts of energy. With energy, the Hùn Yuán Qì inside the

Element will have Concentrate-Disperse movements. The Concentrate-Disperse movement will form Wànwù Hùn Yuán Qì.

There is no In-Out movement in the Primal Hùn Yuán Qì level, only when the Hùn Yuán Qì evolves to become physical substances then the In-Out movement exists. With the Open-Close, Concentrate-Disperse and In-Out movements, the substance will change/transmute. Physical substances belong to Wànwù Level. Therefore, only Wànwù Level has all four movements. Generally, the movements in an inorganic substance are much smaller than in an organic substance, and the degree of movement is proportional to the complexity of the substance; the simpler the substance, the smaller the movements.

2. Wànwù Level's Transmutation

All changes/transmutations in the physical substance are the results of the transmutation of its Hùn Yuán Qì. There are two types of transmutation in this level. One is the transmutation of simple substances into complex substances; the other is the dissolution of complex substances into simple substances. To form a Hùn Yuán Entity, a non-physical entity must be formed first, then from the non-physical it forms a physical entity. These processes are called "Yǒu (有 Have) and Wú (無 Have Not) beget each other (有無相生)."

Yǒu (Have) and Wú (Have Not) refer to the wholistic characteristics of the substance. For example, water is a whole entity by itself; the Yǒu (Have) is the whole characteristic (function, color, shape) of the water expressed in physical form, and the Wú (Have Not) is that the water no longer exists in physical form or no longer possesses the characteristics of water. The relationship between Yǒu (Have) and Wú (Have Not) in water is: water (Yǒu physical form) → (becomes) Hùn Yuán Qì (Wú non-physical water) → hydrogen + oxygen, and hydrogen + oxygen → Hùn Yuán Qì → water. Water cannot become hydrogen and oxygen or hydrogen and oxygen cannot become water directly; they must go through the process of transmutation.

Transmutation is the process of transforming the original characteristics of the participating elements into something else; it is also the process of forming a new wholistic entity. To form water, hydrogen and oxygen must transmute together. During the process, both hydrogen and oxygen will lose their original characteristics, but a new entity (water), which has its unique characteristics, is formed. In the transmutation process, some substances may disappear, and some new substances may be created. This is not a simple chemical reaction; it is a very complex transmutation process. It is easier to explain the process using the metabolism of organic substances as an example.

After an independent substance is absorbed into the body, metabolism is the process of breaking down the independent characteristics of the substance, and transforming it into part of the host body. The process has the following sequence:

a) An independent substance (Yǒu, Have) → Huà (change/transmute) → the substance's Hùn Yuán Qì (Wú, Have Not).
b) The substance's Hùn Yuán Qì → Hùn Huà (混化 transmute) → New Hùn Yuán Qì without substance's independent characteristics.
c) New Hùn Yuán Qì → concentrates and Huà (anabolism) → becomes part of the new entity (Yǒu, Have) (independent substance no longer exists).

Catabolism works the same way. Part of the substance separates from the main body, and changes to Hùn Yuán Qì with the characteristic of the substance. Hùn Yuán Qì with the characteristic of the substance transforms/transmutes to Hùn Yuán Qì without the characteristic of the substance. The new Hùn Yuán Qì concentrates to become an independent substance with its own characteristic. The process has the following sequence:

a) Part of the substance (Yǒu (Have)) → Huà (change/transmute) → the substance's Hùn Yuán Qì (Wú, Have Not) with the characteristic of the substance.
b) The substance's Hùn Yuán Qì → Hùn Huà (混化 transmute) → New Hùn Yuán Qì without substance's original characteristics.
c) New Hùn Yuán Qì without substance's original characteristics → Concentrate and Huà (anabolism) → become the new entity/independent substance (Yǒu, Have).

In conclusion, the process of from "simple to complex" means to break down the original entities and their Qì Field, and then merge and transmute to form a new entity and Qì Field. The process of from "complex to simple" means to break down the original entity and its Qì Field to become many elements, and then each element transmutes to form a new entity and Qì Field. The breaking down process is called Hùn Huà (混化 transmute apart), the forming of the new entity is called Hùn Hé (混合 transmute together). Hùn Hé depends on Hùn Huà, Hùn Hé cannot occur without Hùn Huà.

3. The mechanism of transmutation in Wànwù (Ten-Thousand Things)

Although the transmutations in Wànwù can be divided into two categories, simple substances forming complex substances and complex substances dissolving into simple substances, the mechanism for both are the same; it is the transmutation of space-time in the wholistic structures of the substances.

Usually, the Hùn Yuán Qì in substances is intertwining and permeating each other. When the interaction between their space-time structures (information) reaches a certain point, the original space-time structure will disintegrate. A new space-time structure will be formed to gather energy and to form mass. When a complex substance's space-time structure is disintegrated due to the effect of External Hùn Yuán Qì, the internal elements (components) will become relatively independent. These elements will transmute with each other to form new space-time structures that can concentrate energy and evolve into new Hùn Yuán Entities. This is the process and mechanism of forming Hùn Yuán Entity through transmutation.

Transmutation involves changing the substance's space-time structure. Small changes within a substance are internal changes, not transmutation. Only when internal change reaches the critical point that the characteristics of the substance change has true transmutation occurred. Transmutation can be divided into three categories.

a) Space-time structure change/transmutation powered by energy

The characteristic of this category is to use energy to change a substance's energy equilibrium, so that the substance (space-time structure) will lose it balance (equilibrium) state with the original energy and lead to new transmutation.

Changes in Nature and all things human beings do depend on energy. Things cannot change without energy. Without energy as a power source, one cannot make changes in the space-time structure of a substance. In a physical substance, although mass (space-time structure) is in a dominant position and energy and information are in a hidden state, they are bonded together and are inseparable. In order to break the substance's equilibrium and change its space-time structure, more energy is needed. For example, to change the space-time structure of water, one needs energy (electrolysis). With only air, water and nutrition, plants cannot grow; they need energy (sunlight) to perform photosynthesis, to create change.

b) Space-time structure change/transmutation induced by Space-time structure

Advanced living organisms mainly use this method to induce transmutation. In human beings and animals, metabolism occurs constantly. In order to save energy, it usually occurs under normal temperature and conditions. After we consume something, the substance will change and go through the process of transmutation. As a result, energy will be produced. Aided/induced by enzymes (space-time structure), the process of digesting (transmutation) is faster, more efficient and uses less energy. Complicated life activities depend on the inducing method to power the transmutation. It can further divide into two types.

(1) Complementary induced transmutation among space-time structures

This refers to a space-time structure that acts as a catalyst for the transmutation of another structure. In metabolism, the enzyme is the catalyst. A lot of energy will be needed to break down a substance if only mechanical force is used. When a space-time structure is present that can transmute and dissolve the substance, it is called complementary transmutation among space-time structures. The presence of an enzyme is the reason human beings can quickly break down and reconstruct the nutrients.

(2) Replication of space-time structure induced transmutation

This refers to the new structure's space and time structure that is a replica of the original structure. For example, in molecular biology, DNA replication is the biological process of producing two identical replicas of DNA from one original DNA molecule. This process occurs in all living organisms and is the basis for biological inheritance. DNA is made up of a double helix of two complementary strands. During replication, these strands are separated. Each strand of the original DNA molecule then serves as a template for the production of its counterpart, a process referred to as replication-induced transmutation in Qìgōng.

All these transmutations (powered by energy and induced by Space-time structure) naturally occur in all things in Nature.

c) Space-time structure change/transmutation induced by Consciousness

One of the most basic features that separate human beings from other species is that human beings have consciousness (mind activities). Consciousness is a special form of movement that can affect things in nature and cause them to transmute. It is different from using consciousness to assemble energy or information. For example, to build a table, gathering wood, nails and constructing the table is assembling, it is not Hùn Hua (transmutation). Hùn Hua is the consciousness that directly causes wholistic changes in a substance, such as using the mind intent to kill bacteria. Basically, all human consciousness activities are a form of transmutation. Because transmutation induced by consciousness is a very complicated process, the focus will be only on using consciousness as the power source to induce transmutation in a substance's space-time structure.

In experiments using external Qì to kill bacteria or cancerous cells, many participants are not successful because they are not aware that the External Qì's nature of action is determined by consciousness. The External Qì one uses in the experiments is mainly human Qì. Human Qì has vitality and growth information. When it is applied to an outside substance, it will strengthen the substance's vitalities. In order to kill the bacteria, most participants use more Qì and intensify the effort, but this would still not have the intended results. The key to killing the bacteria is not to use more Qì, it is to use the mind intent (consciousness).

Consciousness is a very complicated state of space-time structure. It does not have energy or mass, but it can concentrate Hùn Yuán Qì, assemble energy and can condense them into mass. Consciousness as a power source means that one uses these special functions of consciousness to induce transmutation in a substance. Although consciousness is the power source, this "power" is not involved in transmutation directly. Unlike the transmutation induced by a space-time structure method, which uses a physical substance directly to induce transmutation, consciousness does not transmute directly with a substance. Consciousness concentrates Hùn Yuán Qì and assembles energy to create a template, which has both complementary and replication functions, then the template transmutes with the substance to form a new space-time structure. When emitting external Qì, if one has a more detailed template, it will be easier to affect the substance. Consciousness transmutation is one of the most important tools in consciousness (mind intent) healing and remote healing. When one says that consciousness is the power source, what is the power for? There are two main purposes, one is to provide the energy to create a template; the another is to provide the energy during the transmutation between the template and the substance. This energy is called Consciousness Force in Qìgōng.

The effects of the template are very difficult to be aware of. Consciousness (the brain) has all the information of the person. It can receive and store the information of a person's vitality, Nature's vitality and all kinds of life information that with which one has contact . One interacts with objects in the external world constantly; these objects contain all kinds of vitalities, which include their whole (space-time structure) information. All this information about the object is received and stored in the brain, but it is very weak and does not have enough energy to stimulate one's attention; therefore, one is not able to extract the information. Qìgōng practice is to increase the brain's sensibility and ability so one can extract the information.

Birth will be used as an example. In our life, we encounter lots of things related to birth; our brain has the "birth" information. When the thought of "birth" arises, information on birth will be activated. The brain will automatically extract and arrange the information and forms a birth structure to interact with the substance. In consciousness transmutation, the important part is that consciousness directly activates the information in the brain and rearranges all the related information. If one has more detailed and concrete information about a subject such as birth, one can strengthen the process during the arrangement. For example, in emitting

Qì to help a seed to sprout, without the template, the result would be minimal. But if one has a template (image) of what the growth would look like, this information would behave like a catalyst and the result would be obvious.

To create a template, one needs information. This information must exist in the objective world. If the information does not exist, it would not exist in one's brain; therefore, consciousness cannot create a template. Consciousness transmutation is based on existing information. A hundred years ago, no one could make a template of people talking to one another face to face hundreds of miles away. That information was not available.

In conclusion, transmutation can be divided into three categories.

- Transmutation powered by energy.
  A simple inorganic substance's chemical and physical reactions belongs to this category.
- Transmutation induced by space-time structure.
  An organism does not totally rely on energy; its transmutation evolves to use space-time structure. Metabolism in an organism belongs to this category.
- Transmutation induced by Consciousness.
  This only exists in human beings; it means to use subjective consciousness to induce changes in substances. It can apply to the chemical and the physical world or to an organism.

4. Transmutation is the integration of heredity and mutation

As mentioned previously, an organism must constantly interact with external Qì to maintain its equilibrium. Interactions lead to transmutation and change of the space and time structure of an organism. In other words, an organism is constantly mutating. In an organism, heredity and mutation cannot be separated; it is impossible to have heredity without mutation or to have mutation without heredity. The characteristic of heredity is that organisms interact/transmute with the external world and change to become new space-time structures (new genetic makeup) that are inherited by the next generation. The process is heredity — mutation — heredity. A newborn is defined by its heredity (genetic makeup); as it grows, it is defined by environments. With mutation, it becomes heredity. The process of heredity and mutation is integrated by transmutation.

For example, a seed's DNA has the space-time (sprouting, growth, flowering, fruiting and death) information of the plant; but the seed alone would not be able to produce a plant, it must transmute with the right space-time structure in the right environment to make that possible. In a seed, the internal information (DNA) transmutes with external information (environment) to form a new entity (plant) with new characteristics. If the external space-time structure (environment) is comparable, the changes in the seed's characteristics will be minimal; the seed will sprout and genetic makeup will be the dominant force. If the environment is not comparable but close, the changes in the characteristics will be small and the seed will adapt and become a mutation. If the changes in the characteristics are too much or the environment is not comparable, the seed will die. An organism's hereditary characteristics are expressed via the environment. For a seed to become a plant, it must have a suitable environment. When the seed and environment interact and form a new entity, this new entity has it wholistic Hùn Yuán Qì that can condense into a physical substance and becomes genetic material.

An organism's existence and mutation depend upon its inherent structural characteristic of space-time (life information). This information is the blueprint and foundation for the metabolic and life functions of organisms. But by itself, an organism cannot sustain its life functions and its metabolism cannot take place. Only through the movements of Open-Close, In-Out, Concentrate-Disperse and transmutation to interact/transmute with External Hùn Yuán Qì, can the organism become an independent Hùn Yuán Entity. In the Yellow Emperor's Classic of Internal Medicine, the internal foundation (life information) for transmutation is called Shén Jī (神機), the external foundation (environment) for transmutation is called Qì Lì (氣立) 根於外者命曰氣立，根於中者曰神機. It states that life's existence depends on the external root which is Qì Lì and the internal root which is Shén Jī. Qì Lì and Shén Jī each contain half of life's functions. Qì Lì's function is to exchange Qì with the external environment via In-Out movements, and Shén Jī's function is internal movements. Only after they are transmuted together, they can become a wholistic Hùn Yuán Entity.

Note: For the life function to exist, it must have a certain independence and stability. There are two forces, internal and external, that maintain the life function's independence and stability. The internal force is called Shén Jī and the external force is called Qì Lì.

Shén Jī combines the materials (internal organs, meridians, Jing and Qì) that power the life functions into an organic entity, and follows the Yīn-Yáng characteristics of the components to separate the entity into three Yīns and three Yángs. Because the Yīn-Yáng characteristics among the three Yīns and three Yángs are not the same, they create imbalance. To maintain stability, a Yīn-Yáng balancing movement occurs. The internal expression of the balancing movement is Up-Down movement, the external expression is mind activities.

Shén Jī cannot maintain life functions by itself, humans must exchange substances and information with Nature. Only when the function of exchanging Qì between humans and Nature is normal can the life functions be sustained. Exchanging Qì is to bring in energy and information to a person and carry out the waste to the external world. The In-Out of the body Qì function is Qì Lì. In TCM, the In-Out of the body Qì is called Yīn Qì and Yáng Qì. Qì Lì can be the foods humans eat and air humans breathe or the influence of the environment (Wǔ Yùn 五運: Wood, Fire, Soil, Metal and Water, or Wind, Heat, Humidity, Dryness and Cold).

B. Space-Time Hùn Huà (Transmutation) Theory

In this text, space and time are mentioned quite often, but space and time are very elusive. No one can touch space or catch time. Most people consider space to be empty and that time is a one-directional concept. However, space is not truly "empty," but one cannot say it is not empty either; time is a one-directional concept because it refers to the changes in the universe. When space changes/expands, time moves forward. Can time go backward? In theory, it is possible (some people with extraordinary abilities may be able to be aware of it), but to ordinary people, it is not probable. To reverse time involves space. The changes in space have too many variables.

For example, we assemble chairs in a hall to watch a movie. After the movie is finished, we put the chairs back to their original places. To reverse time, we have to reverse every step of every person at every exact moment of time; any discrepancy in the process will lead to a different outcome. Also, every change is related to its environment; it is impossible for the substance and environment to return/repeat the past. One variation will have a different result. It is possible to play the movie backward, but not the actual event. The movie goes backward, but the surroundings do not. Therefore, time would not be going backward. This is the reason time is considered one directional. It is not that time cannot go backward, just that the probability is impossibly small.

Qìgōng theory considers space and time as a wholistic entity. In this context, space and time refers to the space and time of the physical substances in the universe. According to Hùn Yuán Theory, space and time are the substance's space structure and time structure, they are the expression of the physical substance. In the Hùn Yuán Element, space and time are transmuted as one which is similar to Newton's concept of absolute space and time. Primal Hùn Yuán Qì's space and time are the Primal Hùn Yuán Qì's space structure and time structure, so they are close to absolute space and time. After the Big Bang, space and time changed and the space and time of Wànwù are the same as Einstein's relativity of space and time.

According to Qìgōng theory, there is another space and time structure called Consciousness space and time. Consciousness space and time are similar to Primal Hùn Yuán Qì's space and time.

In Qìgōng, the process of changing or the continuing expressions of a substance's Hùn Yuán Qì functions is called time; the process of structural change/extension of a substance's position is call space. Space and time are inseparable. Time (the changing process) is only able to be revealed through space (position's continuing changing/ expanding). For example, a plant's life cycle, as far as time is concerned, is a continuous process, i.e., sprout, seedling, young plant, flowering, fruiting and death. The process is completed via time, and the time structure for the process is a whole unit (wholistic entity). But the process of growth—from small to full grown, is revealed via space. Therefore, time must express via space and functions must reveal via the changes of space. By the same token, the change of the space structure of a substance is not instantaneous; it is a process and must integrate with time. Space and time are two sides of the same coin, each presents part of the characteristics of the substance. Together, they form the wholistic entity.

1. Transmutation of time

Basically, time is one directional movement; it never ceases moving. All things one contacts with or know of in nature follow time's movement; none of the things in nature can stop moving forward. When one sees a substance, it is its space expression at that particular moment. Within the substance, there is time information which includes the past, present and future. In other words, in any instance, time is a transmuted state of past, present and future. The following diagram will be used to explain the transmutation of time. Fig. 2-3 The Transmutation of Time.

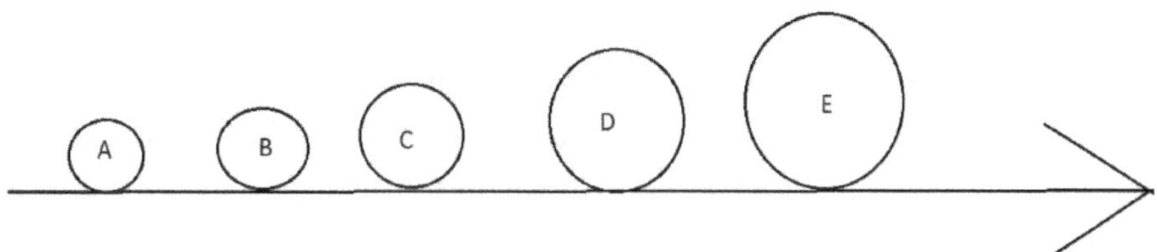

Fig. 2-3 The Transmutation of Time

The circles represent a plant in different stage of growth. A is two years ago, B is a year ago, C is the present, D is next year, and E is two years in the future. It is easy to see the five stages in a spatial structured view, but not as easy to see these stages in the physical plant. C is the physical plant at this moment in time, A, B, D and E do not occupy space (A and B no longer exist, and D and E are in the future). What happened to A and B? They are stored in C. Within the physical plant C, there is transmuted past time (A and B). How about D and E? They are the genetic blueprint inside C. In any particular moment, C is composed of space structure and time structure. Space structure is A, B and C, and time structure is from A to E. In C, time is transmuted as the present and is called the transmutation of time.

The present information is easy to understand, but how does one know there is information about the past and the future? The human being will be used as an example. When a person meditates in a room, after they leave, an aura camera (a DSLR camera calibrated to take aura photographs) still can pick up the information about the person in the room. For a person, the past information will stay with them and becomes part of the genetic inheritance. An ultrasound image of the fetus can show the future information of the person. But whether the fetus will develop to be a person or not is not set, it depends on the environment. For the fetus to develop, it must interact with environment. The plant will be used as an example again. Before C can become D, C's formless outer layer Hùn Yuán Qì will interact with External Hùn Yuán Qì, and the Internal (C's outer layer) and External Hùn Yuán Qì will transmute. The transmuted Qì will interact and transmute with solid C, which contains the transmuted A and B time and space information, to form D. Both D and E depend on the genetic makeup of the plant, but how D and E develop depend on the environment. The past (A and B) is set/fixed, but the future is not. The future can go multiple directions because the environment has numerous variables. The future is like a weather forecast, the closer to the present, the clearer is the picture. Therefore, time is both set/fixed and unsettled/unfixed. If time is not set, there will be no heredity; if time is set without changes, the plant will die.

2. Transmutation of space

All physical things occupy space. Because the universe has evolved from and is occupied by Primal Hùn Yuán Qì; when space is mentioned, it refers to Primal Hùn Yuán Qì. Primal Hùn Yuán Qì exists as space. This space (Primal Hùn Yuán Qì) does not have physical substance, but a physical substance's Hùn Yuán Qì, which is in a transmuted state and contains all the information of the substance, can exist within this space. When Primal Hùn Yuán Qì evolves, it begets substances which have different time and space information. In turn, substances interact with Primal Hùn Yuán Qì and ten-thousand things are born. Information does not occupy space and all substances' information can congregate within the space (Primal Hùn Yuán Qì).

Physical substance occupies a certain amount of space which contains the substance's information. Because this particular space is inside Primal Hùn Yuán Qì, it also contains the information within Primal Hùn Yuán Qì. It is physical substance space within Primal Hùn Yuán Qì space and this particular space contains both spaces' information. This space within space is called space transmutation. For example, when John Doe mentions his mother's health, an accomplished Qìgōng healer can do a remote diagnosis and receive the health information about his mother from John Doe's body. John Doe's body contains his mother's health information. The closer the relationship between John Doe and his mother, the stronger the information. Remote diagnosis and healing rely on space transmutation.

Summary

Hùn Yuán Theory explains the characteristics of a wholistic entity and describes the wholistic concept of substances/contents. There are three theories/concepts that Hùn Yuán Theory uses to explain the wholistic entity.

1. The concept of Hùn Yuán Substance

Unlike Traditional Qìgōng which considers all substances have their own Yuán (Primal) Qì that is singular (a singularity), Hùn Yuán Theory implies that nothing in the universe is singular. All existences, including the universe, are the result of the transmutation between two or more physical substances and/or formless Qì. The process of two or more things transmuting together to form an entity is called Hùn Hé; Zhìnéng Qìgōng calls this new entity "Hùn Yuán Qì (Entity)." Hùn Yuán Theory catalogs Hùn Yuán Qì into five levels/stages of existing. They are Hùn Yuán Element, Primal Hùn Yuán Qì, Wànwù (Ten-Thousand Things), Human Hùn Yuán Qì and Yì Yuán Tǐ. Within the universe, substances exist in all different levels of Hùn Yuán Qì. Hùn Yuán Qì evolves from simple Hùn Yuán Element to complicated Wànwù Hùn Yuán Qì and to the advanced Yì Yuán Tǐ. No matter whether Hùn Yuán Qì has form or is formless and in what level of existence, it is a substance formed by Hùn Hé (transmutation). This characteristic/concept of substances is called the concept of Hùn Yuán Substance in Zhìnéng Qìgōng, which uses this concept to explain the common characteristics of the Hùn Yuán Qì in the chapter.

2. The concept of Hùn Yuán Movement

By definition, Hùn Hé is a movement. Once an entity is formed, it has internal movements and interactions with external substances/environment. With movements and interactions, there will be changes. The changes are called Hùn Yuán Movement. There is no absolute stillness substance, the universe is evolving. The internal movements can be divided into four categories: Open-Close, Concentrate-Disperse, In-Out, and Huà (transmute). In the physical world, all four movements exist at the same time and interact with one another. All changes/transmutations in the physical substance are the results of the transmutation of its Hùn Yuán Qì. There are two types of transmutation, one is the transmutation of simple substances into complex substances; the other is the dissolution of complex substances into simple substances.

3. The concept of Space and Time Transmutation

Space and time are the substance's space structure and time structure, they are the expression of the physical substance. In Qìgōng, the process of changing or the continuing expressions of a substance's Hùn Yuán Qì functions is called time; the process of structural change/extension of a substance's position is called space. Space and time are inseparable. Time is only able to be revealed through space. Wholistic space is a point in space that contains the information/contents of the whole universe. Wholistic time is a point in time that contains the past, the present and the future.

In conclusion, Hùn Yuán Theory describes the formation process of wholistic entity and explains the characteristics of Hùn Yuán Entity, which involve at least two or more substances; Hùn Yuán Theory also describes the governing patterns and changes within the Hùn Yuán substance itself. Hùn Yuán Theory states that the characteristics of a substance cannot be changed until the internal changes reach a tipping point at which the substance is no longer able to maintain balance. The process of transmutation begins with the substance's internal movements/changes.

第三章：整體論

Chapter Three: Wholistic Entity Theory

Wholistic Entity Theory and Transmutation (Hùn Yuán) Theory are the two aspects of a process; they are inseparable. Transmutation Theory describes the characteristics of a transmuted entity in a theoretical point of view. Wholistic Entity Theory describes the wholistic characteristics of an entity; it focuses on the relationship between parts/components of the entity. The transmutation process is called the Hùn Huà and the new entity is called Hùn Yuán (Transmuted One or One). Transmuted One or One is a wholistic entity. The transmutation (process) belongs to the Transmutation Theory, and the Transmuted One belongs to the Wholistic Entity Theory. An entity is not the sum of all its parts, it is an entity formed by the interactions between the parts, and all parts obey/subordinate to the entity.

I. The Concept of Wholistic Entity

By definition, a wholistic entity is a completely/wholly integrated entity. As mentioned in the last chapter, all entities are the result of the transmutation of two or more substances. Each entity has its unique prescriptive characteristics; therefore, they are different from one another. To be maintained as an entity, these unique prescriptive characteristics cannot be destroyed. Although an entity is transmuted together from two or more substances, these component substances cannot be separated, otherwise, it is no longer the same entity. To a limited degree, the integrated entity may have some small changes. If these small changes do not affect the prescriptive characteristics, the entity will remain as a wholistic entity. If an entity is changed to a point that it is not able to maintain its unique prescriptive characteristics, it is no longer a wholistic entity. In other words, a wholistic entity is an integrated entity that maintains its unique prescriptive characteristics.

A. How a wholistic entity is formed

A wholistic entity exists in two forms, one is as Formless Qì (Hùn Yuán Qì) and the other is as a physical substance. A physical substance, which has a layer of diluted (slightly condensed) Qì surrounding it, is a condensed form of its Hùn Yuán Qì. The formless Hùn Yuán Qì is a very evenly distributed entity, but the physical substance is not. A physical substance has many components, which are different from one another and have different distributions of Qì, and the components are connected by the formless Hùn Yuán Qì inside the substance to form an entity. For example, in a human being, the physical body has many different components, such as hands, legs and organs. Each component is different from one another, and each has its own functions, shape and distribution of Qì. But within a person's body, uncondensed Hùn Yuán Qì is evenly distributed and permeates every cell. When the physical body parts are connected by the formless Hùn Yuán Qì, they form a wholistic entity.

A wholistic entity is not the sum of all its parts. It is an entity with special properties/characteristics resulting from the interaction between the parts. When individual parts interact with each other or with an external substance, they will form a special property that has different characteristics from the individual parts. In Qìgōng, an entity with special property is a wholistic entity. Therefore, a wholistic entity is not only the entity's structure but also its functions. For example, when we say a table is an integrated entity, what we refer to is the structure and shape. But a table is more than its structure, its functions are part of the table. As a wholistic entity, a table is a special merged form including its structure and functions.

A wholistic entity is an entity in which space structure and time structure are merged; a wholistic entity can be defined as its Hùn Yuán Qì (space and time structure). This space-time structure determines the characteristic features of the entity. For example, electromagnetic waves have different frequencies and wavelengths; these frequencies and wavelengths determine the functions of the wave. If a different wave is added to the original wave, the merged wave will have a different structure and will carry different information. It is the structure of the wave that determines the outcome. Structure and characteristic features (functions) are directly related; a certain structure will have certain characteristics. In all levels of existence, whenever there is structure, there are characteristic features. When we mention an entity that has a unique independent characteristic, we refer to the substance's formless Hùn Yuán Qì. To be more specific, it is its Hùn Yuán Qì's space-time structure.

When the formless Hùn Yuán Qì of substances interact with one another, it will beget entities which have their unique prescriptive structure and characteristic features. Each entity's Hùn Yuán Qì (space-time structure) functions as a template for its components to follow.

For example, if there is a triangular structure with many components inside, normally it would be described as a triangular structure with many components. In Wholistic Theory, a triangular structure includes its structure and functions. Once the structure is formed, it becomes a template for the components to establish their positions inside and to become part of the structure. The position and size of the components may be different, however, the structural information (the template) is the same. This information is also in every layer/level of the structure. Every component is part of the wholistic entity, and they follow and conform to the template. Inside the components, every structure has the space-time structure information of the entity. To maintain the space-time structural information of the entity, the component cannot separate from the entity and be independent.

An integrated entity is the most fundamental form of expression for Wànwù (Ten-Thousand Things) level substances. Different substances have different formation processes and the probability for different formations is limitless. The formation process can be categorized into either a natural process or a manmade process. In a natural process, when Wǔ Yùn 五運 and Wǔ Xíng 五行 interact with one another, Heaven and Earth are created, weather appears, and ten-thousand things evolve. With the exception of raw materials, most products in the world are manmade. No matter whether it is a natural process or a manmade process, the formation process depends on time-space structure information. The time-space structure concentrates energy and condenses it into a physical substance. Therefore, the formation of a substance is the formation of its time-space structure. The characteristics of a wholistic entity is its time-space information. Once the substance is created, the wholistic entity is formed. For example, a seed follows its space-time (wholistic) information to transmute water, fertilizer and energy (sun light) together to form a tree. From "Nothing" to "Something," it is a natural process. To assemble a table, one needs a table's space-time information. The blueprint is the space information, and the assembly sequence (including collecting materials) is the time information. Following the space-time information, one adds energy (labor) and a table (wholistic entity) is formed. It is a manmade process.

Note: Wǔ Yùn 五運 refers to wood, fire, soil, metal and water and Wǔ Xíng 五行 refers to five shapes: Water is round (•), Wood is straight (l), Fire is point (Λ), Soil is square (L), and Metal is thin surface (口).

B. Levels/layers of wholistic entity

In Chinese culture, a wholistic entity is described as a Tiāndì (天地 Heaven & Earth or Universe) or Taiji. Everything is/has an independent body; inside the independent body, there is a Tiāndì. For example, the universe is a large Tiāndì, earth is a small Tiāndì, the human being is a smaller Tiāndì. Therefore, there are many layers/levels of wholistic entities. Each entity is connected with its surroundings through space and time. A smaller entity is a part of the bigger entity, which is part of the universe. Within an entity, there are many levels. No matter what level the entities belong to, they all have their unique and independent characteristics, which obey/follow the laws of the bigger entity. For example, the human heart is a level, but it is a sublevel of the human being;

therefore, it must obey/follow the laws of humans. The human being is a level, but it is a sublevel of animal (biologically, humans are classified as animals, and are a type of animal known as a mammal), it must obey/follow the laws of animals. Animal is a sublevel of organic materials and must obey/follow the laws of organic materials. Dào Dé Jīng explains it this way:

> *Human obeys/follows the laws of Earth; Earth obeys/follows the laws of Heaven; Heaven obeys/follows the laws of Dào; Dào obeys/follows the laws of its owe nature.*
>
> 人法地, 地法天，天法道, 道法自然 —《道德经》

No matter whether it is a large or a small Tiāndì, substances inside the Tiāndì are independent from one another but they are not isolated, they are connected to one another. Because they are independent and yet connected to others, they form layers (levels). Each level has its specific functions (laws, behavior patterns) and locations. For example, in Wànwù level, there are organic and inorganic substances, and the laws of physics and chemistry. Although inorganic substances such as a piece of iron and organic substances such as a tumor have different functions and obey different laws, they are made of Hùn Yuán Qì. In the wholistic point of view, they are two small Tiāndìs with different behavior patterns within a larger Tiāndì. To understand a Tiāndì's behavior patterns, one must start out with a smaller Tiāndì. For example, instead of focusing on the large Tiāndì that contains both inorganic and organic substances, one should focus on either the inorganic or the organic substance. For most people, the behavior patterns of the body are more familiar than the patterns of a piece of iron; therefore, it is easier to use the mind intent to dissolve a tumor than to dissolve a piece of iron.

The levels within a Tiāndì can change. A lower level can change into a higher level, and a higher level can change into a lower level. For example, simple substances can transmute into complex substances; evolution is the perfect example of a lower level changing to a higher level. When an animal dies, organic materials dissolve into inorganic materials, into elements and finally into energy. This is an example of a higher level changing to a lower level. After human beings eat something, Qì will change from a lower level to a higher level. When nutrients are absorbed into the body, they become Body Qi (higher level), and the changes continue from Body Qi to Organ Qi (higher level), and from Organ Qi to Brain Qi (highest level). But if a person has a mental condition such as depression or sadness, then the person may become overweight. This change may be because Brain Qi does not function normally, and it moves downward to become Body Qi.

Although all entities contain wholistic information, the way an organism expresses the information is related to the stage of its development. The organism's space-time information is gradually completed with its development. For example, the wholistic information of a plant contains a seed, a seedling, a young to mature tree, and the processes of flowering, seeding, and dying. From seed to death, it is a process of space and time transmutation. Every stage of the plant's life (development) displays only partial information—the information of that stage. The wholistic information of the plant is in its latent stage and is expressed as whole information only after the plant is mature. A mature plant contains the space and time information of the growing process. It is a transmutation of Internal Qì (seed) and External Qì (water, nutrients and sunlight), and has roots, leaves and stems. When the plant becomes mature, the expression of wholistic information is complete; then the Hùn Yuán Qì can condense into a physical substance—a seed. The seed will contain all the space and time (wholistic) information; this information will be in its latent state. The wholistic information in the seed and the mature plant is not the same. The mature plant's information is realized information; the seed's information is potential and latent information. The seed's information may or may not become realized as a plant.

C. Space and Time

Space in this book refers to the space that contains physical substances. Space is where physical substances exist and expand. All substances occupy a certain amount of space. Because Dào is the mother of all things, all substances (spaces) are within Dào. In Dào, space and time are absolute and all spaces (including individual space) inside Dào permeate each other. The space occupied by a cup is not only a space in the universe. it is also space occupied within Dào. A cup is a condensed form of Hùn Yuán Qì, therefore the cup occupies a specific space. At the same time, the cup has uncondensed Qì surrounding it. From a wholistic point of view, the cup's space includes the condensed Qì and surrounding Qì. The boundary of the surrounding Qì is unknown; it is proportional to its mass. The surrounding Qì connects the cup and the external substances and/or their surrounding Qì to form a space entity. This space is a universe space and also a Dào space; they are overlapping and permeating one other.

Within Dào, the Hùn Yuán Qì in all substances interacts with and permeates each other. During the concentration (Hùn Huà) process, the information contained in the Hùn Yuán Qì of the substances will merge as one. Therefore, the cup's space has all kinds of information, which includes the information from the surrounding substances, and the information from the past. When a physical substance is seen, it is an entity made with condensed Qì; the process that makes it a reality is Hùn

Huà. The characteristic of wholistic space entities is that they permeate each other and are inside each other.

In Qìgōng, a substance's continuously changing process or movement is called time. Every independent substance has a birth-death process. The birth-death process is the substance's wholistic time (entity). A time-entity must be expressed through space. The substance we see is its momentary space expression—the space it occupies and its space structure at that particular moment. This space structure contains the wholistic time of the substance. For example, a tree's wholistic time is from its birth to its death. The cross section of the tree contains the information of age, health record and the weather conditions since its birth. The tree's timeline of the past is clearly established and is expressed through its physical space. Since time must be expressed through space, the future cannot be shown; it is there but unrealized. The past is easy to understand. Since the future is not here at this moment, it is more difficult to comprehend. Fig. 3-1 will be used to explain the wholistic timeline of a tree.

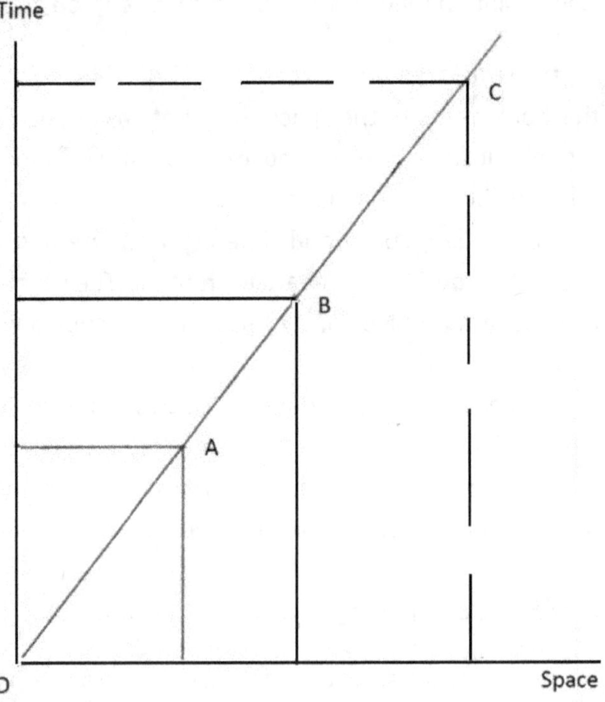

Fig. 3-1. Wholistic Timeline of a Tree

Assume that the wholistic time of a tree is twenty years and that it is ten years old now. Point A is 5 years old, Point B is present (10 years old) and Point C is the future (20 years old). From Point 0 to Point B, the space is realized so that the timeline shows how the tree has grown from Point 0 to Point B. From Point B to Point C, the space is unrealized so the timeline cannot be seen. When the tree is 5 years old at Point A, the physical tree from Point A to Point B is not yet realized so time is in a hidden state. As the tree continues growing, time becomes apparent. From Point A, the space from Point A to Point B is the future, and from Point B, it is the past. This pattern also works in this manner from Point B to Point C.

The tree (substance) has the wholistic time information within, but the future is outside of the physical structure of the tree and is contained in the surrounding Qì. The unrealized information spreads out from the physical body to the surrounding Qì and to the boundary of the Qì Field. At the same time, the surrounding Qì concentrates inward to become a physical substance (realized space). When the Qì changes up to a specific point, changes in the physical substance will occur. For example, when a towel is new, it may be white, and after time passes , the color changes to yellow. It is very difficult to say what day the color changed. This change may have occurred before the towel changed color. The external (surrounding) Qì transmuted with the external substance's Qì and changed first, and then gradually internalized into the towel. The towel changes color slowly. The Qì changes first and then the physical substance changes. Therefore, any split second of time contains the future, but the future is not fixed. The changes in physical substances are the transmutation of Qì which involves unlimited probabilities; it is not something that can be fully controlled.

Space and time are a wholistic entity; they cannot be separated. A substance's space is the result of time movements, and the expression of time relies on the space. In Qìgōng, the "realized" space and time is called Shí (實), the "unrealized" space and time is called Xū (虛). Shí and Xū are the two faces of the same entity that is a very important concept in developing extraordinary abilities. Moving something with the mind intent relies on this concept.

II. The Concept of the Universe as a Wholistic Entity

In Chinese writing, the Universe consists of 宇(Yǔ) and 宙(Zhòu). 宇(Yǔ) means space, 宙(Zhòu) means time. Chinese culture considers the Universe (an entity) to be the result of merging space and time. Space and time are evolved from and stay within Dào. Dào is the most basic or absolute state of space and time.

Dào Dé Jīng explains Dào this way:

> *I do not know its name; I just call it Dào; reluctantly, I describe it as "Big." "Big" means it is (goes) everywhere; everywhere means it is infinite; infinite means it is returning.*
> *吾不知其名, 字之曰道. 强为之名曰大. 大曰逝, 逝曰远, 远曰返.*
>
> *A continuous whole beyond description; it returns again to the nothingness of Dào. 繩繩兮不可名，复歸於無物.*
>
> *Revolving and inexhaustible, it can be the mother of all things.*
> *周行而不殆, 可以为天下母.*
>
> *Facing it, one cannot see its head; Following it, one cannot see its rear.*
> *迎之不見其首，隨之不見其後.*

The quoted passage means that time has no beginning nor ending, and space has no boundaries. The Universe is Dào. Dào evolves to become Primal Hùn Yuán Qì, Primal Hùn Yuán Qì evolves to become Wànwù (Ten-thousand Things) and the reverse also is true. The Universe is an entity that consists of formless Hùn Yuán Qì and physical substances. The Universe (primarily refers to Wànwù level) is an end result of constant interactions and transformations between the physical substance and the formless Hùn Yuán Qì. The universe has time and space wholistic structures. Every moment of time contains the past and the future. Every part of the space is connected with the wholistic entity and contains the wholistic information. Time is the changing process, and space is a transverse section of timeline. We will use the structural characteristics of time, space and ten-thousand things to explain the wholistic feature of the Universe.

A. Wholistic characteristics of the Universe's time structure

The time structure of the Universe is its evolutionary process. In physical cosmology, the Universe began with the Big Bang. For 13.8 billion (± 130 million) years, the Universe's space and time has been continuously expanding. It evolved from a singularity to the first subatomic particles, simple atoms, stars, galaxies, and into today's known universe. According to Hubble's law, the Universe is expanding, and the galaxies are moving rapidly apart. If we reverse the expansion scenario, then the galaxies must have been clumped together and denser in the past. As we keep going back in time, the whole universe will converge to a point of infinite density. Originally, the universe itself was an infinitely dense point, a singularity, which expanded to its present size. With telescopes, one can literally look back in time. In 2016, the Hubble telescope saw the oldest galaxy ever spotted—it's located 13.4 billion light years away. In context, that means that the galaxy existed just 400 million years after the Big Bang. Like tree rings, galaxies are an evolutionary process that demonstrate a timeline. From the Big Bang to the present, the timeline contains all the information; it is the Universe's wholistic time structure.

B. Wholistic characteristics of the Universe's space structure

According to the Big Bang Theory, the Universe evolved only once. How do we know it is a wholistic entity? As mentioned earlier, every space and time intersection of a wholistic entity contains the information of the entity and obeys its laws. The physical laws which govern the Universe are: Gravitation, Electromagnetic Force, Strong Force and Weak Force. The contents of matter are made of six quarks and six leptons, along with their antiparticles. From physical cosmology, it is known that the physical laws which govern the dynamics of the Universe are still the same. All the content of matter surrounding us is still made up of six quarks and six leptons, along with their antiparticles. They are all bound together by the four fundamental forces of nature mentioned above. When going back in time, space structures still obeyed the same laws which indicate that the Universe space structure is a wholistic structure.

III. The Concept of Human and Heaven (Nature) as a Wholistic Entity

Although human beings belong to Wànwù level, and all things are from the same source (萬物同源), the Chinese consider the human being to be above all others. The ancients believed that the basic elements that constituted the phenomenon of life and the meaning of life were Heaven, Earth and Man. They considered Heaven, Earth and Man (human beings) to be the Three Pillars (三才) of the universe. In Chinese culture, Man refers to the human being, and Heaven (normally means Heaven and Earth) refers to the natural and social environment. The concept of Human and Heaven as a Wholistic Entity is not only important in Qìgōng, it is one of the cornerstones of Chinese culture and an essential part of daily life. This concept means that the human being is part of Nature and society; if a human being violates the laws of Nature or society, they will perish. This concept can be divided into two parts: Human and Nature; and Human and Society.

A. Human beings and Nature are a Wholistic Entity

1. Human beings evolved from Nature

Human beings evolved from Nature and belong to Wànwù Level of Hùn Yuán Qì. Nature provides the necessary environment such as food, energy and shelter for human evolution. To maintain life functions, human beings must exchange Qì (materials) with Nature. In other words, the life process of a human being is to exchange, to merge, and to transmute external Qì for their own use. This process occurs in three areas.

- Physical substance exchange.
  The human being obtains materials from outside, such as food, and assimilates them to become part of the body. At the same time, the human being excretes unwanted materials as waste.
- Energy exchange.
  The human being directly or indirectly absorbs and exchanges energy with the external world. For example, the human being absorbs and consumes energy from the sun and releases energy from the body.
- Information exchange.
  Information refers to a substance's special space-time characteristic. Information is associated with language, but language is a kind of information that does not contain energy. The reason that language may affect human beings is because of the information that it contains. Information is a space-time structure which is composed of three elements--the information matrix, the quantity and the form/shape. Every substance has its unique information. A human being constantly exchanges information with Nature. Compared with physical substance and energy exchanges, information exchange is more subtle and is not easily noticeable, but it has an impact on the body. For example, in a particular house, no matter how it is decorated, one might feel uncomfortable as soon as one steps inside the house. On the other hand, one may feel very comfortable in another house with the same decorations. It is the information that the house presents which makes the difference.

  How a building is situated and its relationship with its surroundings determine the space-time information of the building. When a person is inside a building, this space-time information will interact with the person constantly. A well-situated house gives comfortable information. An ill-situated house gives uncomfortable information; and it may even cause illness to the person who stays there all the time. Fēngshuǐ 風水 is an art that interprets this space-time information and is widely used to situate buildings.

  Note: Fēngshuǐ is one of the Five Arts of Chinese Metaphysics which is a philosophical system of harmonizing everyone with their surrounding environment.

These three exchanges are equally important. Physical substance and energy exchanges are very obvious and noticeable in human evolution, but information exchange is not. According to genetic engineering, all human beings evolve from the same source; therefore, all human beings should be the same, but they are not. The reason is that the human metabolism is not just material (physical materials and energy) metabolism but also information (the surrounding environment) metabolism. Human evolution cannot be separated from the surrounding environment. Human beings can be "complete" only when they have evolved along with the information of the surrounding environment.

Mental activities (consciousness) are the responses/reflections of the objective world. Nature not only provides human beings with the materials and environment in which to thrive, but Nature is also the human being's objective world. When one interacts with Nature, mental activities will occur, and these activities will cause structural changes within the body. One of the purposes of consciousness is to cognize Nature; therefore, all mental activities such as science, arts and cultures directly or indirectly reflect Nature. Mental activities and Nature are tightly intertwined. The deeper the reflection and understanding of Nature, the better the brain functions will be. This in turn will cause the body functions to become mature/developed. These changes are the result of the transmutation of Qì between Nature and the human being; thus, we call it "Nature created Human."

2. The Human Being is changing Nature

The human being is created by Nature and at the same time, the human being is not only impacting and changing Nature, the human being is also "creating" Nature. Creating Nature means changing Nature's materials to create different structures. By itself, the world is evolving according to the laws of Nature. The human being is independent and has mental activities. When interacting with Nature, human beings consider themselves as the center of the universe, but also change Nature according to mental activities that suit their needs.

The human being has conscious activities. Once conscious activities are combined with physical activities, they will create new things and ideas that become realities. For example, to build a bridge is an idea (conscious activity) and building the bridge is the physical activity. When energy (building—physical activities) merges with subjective information (idea—conscious activity), new things (bridge) will be created in the objective world (Nature); this is called "Human creates Nature."

Human activities, whether they are impacting the environment or gathering materials for internal consumption, are the actors carrying out conscious activities. Nature provides human beings with materials for survival. In turn, human beings change Nature according to conscious activities. Human beings evolved from and are part of Nature and obey/conform to the laws of Nature; therefore, human beings are called Nature's Human (dominated by Nature). Human activities change how Nature behaves so that Nature moves from its original state to one that reflects human interaction and becomes Human's Nature (dominated by humans).

3. The Human Being is part of Nature and reflects Nature's wholistic characteristics

Although human beings belong to the most advanced level of Hùn Yuán Qì in Nature (earth), they are still a part of Nature. Human beings evolved on the earth, therefore, they contain and can reflect the wholistic characteristics of the earth. For example, the levels of material structure the human body contain are very similar to the earth. The earth contains levels of inorganic, organic materials and organisms and the human being contains similar materials. On a basic level, the human being contains inorganic elements such as Carbon, Sodium, Iron, Potassium and Calcium, and organic elements such as amino acids. On the compound level, the human being is composed of water, carbon dioxide, calcium phosphate, calcium fluoride, calcium hydroxide, sugar, fat and protein, and also all the twenty basic amino acids of the earth. All these material structures are in proportion to those on the earth. This is the result of evolution; it is called "Heaven and Man are the same 天人相類" in Chinese writings.

The earth (Nature) has physical, chemical, and biological movements; the human being has all these movements plus conscious movement. In a sense, the human being is a condensed form of Nature with material structures and functional (physical, chemical and biological) movements. Many classical writings called the human being a small Tiāndì (Universe). Specifically, they considered human consciousness a Tiāndì. To find out or to understand the secrets of the Universe, Chinese Buddhism and some Chinese philosophies (such as Ming Dynasty Yáng Míng philosophy 明朝陽明哲學) focus on consciousness. They believe if consciousness is understood, the universe is understood. Confucianism considers the human being to be the most precious thing in the universe because only the human being has the Five-Element Qì (Metal, Wood, Water, Fire and Soil/Earth) well balanced.

Because human beings have conscious movement (subjective thinking), they separate themselves from Nature. This type of concept creates two worlds—the subjective world (human) and the objective world (Nature) in the human being's mind. But in reality, there is only one Nature; the human being is part of Nature. The subjective and objective worlds only exist in our consciousness.

B. The Human Being and Society are a Wholistic Entity

When people group together to share common goals such as survival and prosperity, a society is formed. No matter what size the society is, all human beings are part of a society; there is no such a thing as a completely isolated human being. Even when someone lives in an extremely isolated environment, they are still connected with society because the tools they use for survival are the products of society. Human beings and society are one entity and cannot be separated.

According to Karl Marx, the conception of human nature is formed by the totality of social relations. All newborns, including human babies, follow the laws of Nature, their metabolism is innate. The differences between human beings and animals occur because human beings have conscious activities and languages, which are the products of society. The main ingredients of a society are communication and interactions. With communication and interactions between the members of the society, there will be rules and regulations. Once a society is formed, it becomes the environment in which the group will live. All human activities are carried out based on society's environment. The conditions of the society, such as productions, knowledge, culture, language, moral and ethical standards, not only will dictate the individual and the group's behavior, but will also dictate society's evolutionary development.

Although most Classical Qìgōng writings do not mention the relationship between the human being and society, this omission does not mean it does not exist or is not important. In ancient times, societies were small, population was homogeneous, technologies were primitive, and life was relatively simple; therefore, the impact between the human being and society was not that obvious. Today, there are many races, all kinds of societies, technologies have advanced by leaps and bounds, and life is complicated; the impact between human beings and society is very profound. With human activities, many things in Nature become part of the society.

All communications between individuals and groups rely on Nature. Whether using a phone or a computer, one needs external things (wave, electricity) to finish the task. Therefore, things from Nature will enter society and become part of the society. By continually absorbing external things from Nature, society will be "naturalized" by Nature. As stated previously, the human being is part of Nature; more importantly, the human being is part of society. To change Nature, we need a group effort, no single person can do it. Society is the intermediary between human beings and Nature.

IV. The Concept of the Human Being as a Wholistic Entity

Each human being is a wholistic entity, but a "human wholistic entity" has many definitions. Many people consider the human being to be an entity that consists of a physical body and mental activities. Traditional Chinese Medicine describes the human being as an entity that is based on the inner organs, guided/commanded by the mind and connected with Qì, blood and Meridians. Qìgōng considers the human being to be an entity that consists of Jìng, Qì and Shén. In Qìgōng, the physical body which includes inner organs, limbs and blood belong to Jìng. Mental (conscious) activities belong to Shén, and the formless, colorless and moving/circulating substance inside the body belongs to Qì. In explaining the concept of the human being as a wholistic entity, focus will be on the relationship between Jìng, Qì and Shén, and describing the human entity in two contexts:

A. The human being is a Wholistic Entity consisting of Jìng, Qì and Shén.
B. The relationship between parts of the body and the whole body.

A. The Human Being is a Wholistic Entity consisting of Jìng, Qì and Shén

Jìng 精 means "essence." Traditional Chinese Medicine considers the physical substance that contains "essence" materials and/or reproductive information as Jìng. In Qìgōng, the physical body is called "Xíng 形" and Jìng is considered as part of Xíng; Jìng and Xíng are the same substance. In Qìgōng, the human body is composed of cells, and each cell has a nucleus which has reproductive capacity. The nucleus and reproductive Jìng (sperm and egg) are essence materials, therefore, they belong to Jìng. The human's life functions/activities occur in the physical body. A human being relies on the physical body to carry out the life functions; therefore, the Xíng (physical body) is also considered as Jìng. Jìng is the root that maintains the entity's life functions, and it is also the foundation for reproduction. Xíng and Jìng are the same substance.

The physical body is Qì in a concentrated state. Qì is formless and dynamic, and it is constantly moving in and out of physical form. Therefore, the physical body is not in a fixed state, it is mobile and dynamic. Every part of the physical body has uncondensed Qì engulfing it. For example, there is Qì within and without each cell, and there is Qì between each cell. Before the (Body) Qì condenses into physical form, the uncondensed Qì circulates in the body freely and unimpeded. All parts of the body are connected by this Qì. Traditional Chinese Medicine uses Meridian theory to describe how Qì connects all parts of the body. When Meridians are mentioned, people have an impression that the Meridians are tubes or vessels. In reality, there is no tube/vessel, the Meridians are the cells' engulfing Qì aggregating together to form tube-like structures.

The human brain is very dense and consists of billions of cells. The Qì that is in and out of the cells and that engulf the cells form a very unique Qì field. The activity of this Qì field is called Shén. Because the nervous system of the brain and Body Qì connect with every part of the body, Shén can direct the life activities. Shén is the commander of all life activities.

Jìng, Qì and Shén are different expressions of Qì. When it is non-active, Qì is in a natural formless state called Qì; when it condenses, it is in a physical state called Xíng. When it has special activities, it is called Shén. Traditionally, Body Qì is divided into three grades, the coarser one is called Xíng, the regular one is called Qì and the finer one is called Shén. Fig. 3-2.

Dàoist Qìgōng emphasizes cultivating Jìng into Qì, and Qì into Shén. Jìng, Qì and Shén are interconnected and interchangeable. They can concentrate in any one of the three grades, and the concentrated area will become more prominent. The following figure (Fig. 3-3) demonstrates the relationship between the three grades.

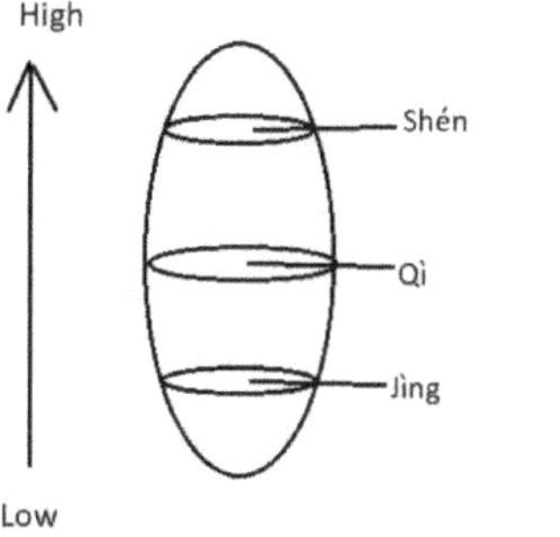

Fig. 3-2. Three Grades of Qì

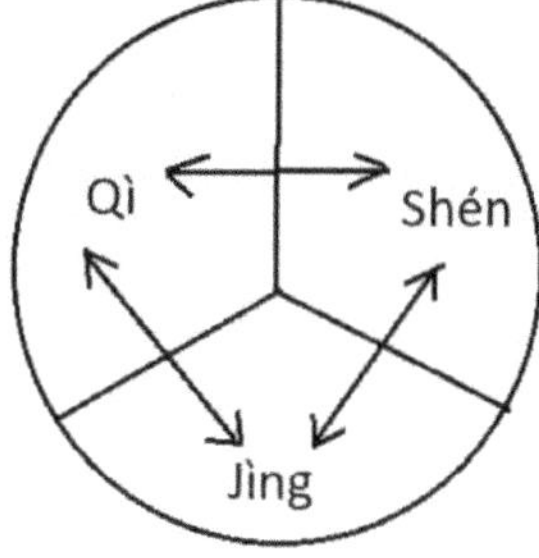

Fig. 3-3. Jìng, Qì and Shén

A human being is an entity consisting of three parts: Jìng, Qì and Shén. If the Qì is strong, Xíng (Jìng) and Shén will concentrate/pull toward Qì; if Xíng is strong, Qì and Shén will concentrate/pull toward Xíng; and if Shén is strong, Xíng and Qì will concentrate/pull toward Shén. Different concentration points and different degrees of concentration will create different prominent functions/areas. As a result of different degrees of concentration, the entity will express different prominent functions resulting in unique human characteristics. The attracting/pulling force among the three is based on the quality and activities of life functions and the mental conditions of the person. Therefore, the human entity can be changed from within and can place emphasis on a certain area (Jìng,

Qì and Shén). What does it mean to place emphasis on a certain area? This can be explained from three contexts: Unintentional, Intentional and Advance Level.

1. **Unintentional Level—normal daily activities**

   a) Shén and Qì integrate/unite within Xíng

   This integration refers to life activities that are most prominent at Xíng (Jìng). Shén and Qì concentrate toward Xíng, with both serving Xíng. Because most life activities are carried out by the physical body, all normal life activities belong to "Shén and Qì integrates within Xíng." Therefore, Xíng (Jìng) is the most prominent among Jìng, Qì and Shén. The simple movement of picking up a glass will be used to explain this concept. The normal procedure of picking up a glass is the following: have an idea of picking up a glass, look at/for the glass, and pick up the glass. Once the idea of picking up the glass arises, Shén (mind intent) will give the command to the eyes. As the eyes search for the glass, the muscles in the eyes will move and Qì will follow. Once the glass is located, Shén will command the hand to reach out for the glass and Qì will follow the hand movement. The whole process of Shén and Qì concentrating toward Xíng (hand) is not a conscious effort, it is carried out automatically.

   When Shén and Xíng are well integrated, Qì will concentrate in Xíng, and Xíng's functions will be strengthened. For example, the right-hander's Shén, Xíng and Qì are concentrated on the right hand side of the body; consequently, the functions in the right hand are much stronger than the left hand; and the reverse is true for a left-handed person. When saying that a certain person is very agile, it means that their Xíng is agile. Shén directs Xíng, and when Shén and Xíng merge, Qì permeates Xíng. If Shén, Qì and Xíng are well integrated, Shén can direct Xíng at will, and then the person becomes agile.

   b) Shén and Xíng integrate/unite within Qì

   This integration refers to the sudden and dramatic change in Qì that causes Shén and Xíng to involuntarily unite within Qì. Normally, it is very difficult for a regular person to achieve this kind of integration under normal conditions. However, under certain circumstances, this integration may occur and it is usually related to emotions. When a person's mental state is stimulated, they may have an emotional reaction. If the emotional reaction is strong and concentrated, it will create changes in Qì, which will become dominant. Shén and Xíng will integrate into one within the dominate Qì. Anger is one example. When one is provoked and becomes angry, one will have an emotional reaction and will feel the Qi rushing upward through the body; the face becomes red, the eyebrows raise, and the eyes become wide open. This emotional response activates Qì, Xíng and Shén to concentrate toward Qì and become integrated within Qì. Traditional Chinese Medicine says "when Qì and blood move upward, it can cause a person to become angry easily; when Qì concentrates in the lungs, one will become sad, anger causes Qì to rise, happiness causes Qì to run smoothly, being startled causes Qì to dissipate, and sadness causes Qì to disperse." All these emotional responses describe when Shén and Xíng are integrated within Qì.

If the integration of Shén and Xíng within Qì is too deep or too long, it can cause illness/imbalance. For example, anger damages the liver and sadness damages the lungs. The imbalance only occurs after Shén and Xíng are integrated within Qì, and Qì has time to work on Xíng. This response becomes an illness when it exceeds the limits of normal emotional boundaries. Basically, "Shén and Xíng integrate/unite within Qì" is to use Qì to change a person's emotional condition.

c) Xíng and Qì integrate/unite within Shén

This integration refers to when Xíng and Qì united within Shén. This only happens under highly concentrated and extraordinary circumstances, not in normal conditions. For example, when a person is chased by a dog, they may be able to jump over a wide ditch which is impossible under normal circumstances. When a child is pinned underneath a car, a mother is able to lift the car to free the child. The person can jump over the ditch because they intensely concentrate on running away from the dog, not the ditch; the mother can lift the car because she is focused on freeing the child. Under these types of extraordinary and extremely urgent circumstances, Xíng and Qì are integrated within Shén.

2. Intentional Level—conscious activities

To increase the ability of certain life functions, one has to change the distribution among Jìng, Qì and Shén. This change can occur with conscious activities. It can also be divided into three categories.

a) Shén and Qì integrate/unite within Xíng

This integration refers to one consciously integrating Shén and Qì within Xíng by focusing on particular body movements to improve that particular body function. For example, in body building, every movement is focused on strengthening a particular part of the body. Once the body moves, Shén will focus on that particular part of the body, and Qì will follow. Shén and Qì will integrate within Xíng, as a result, a muscular body is formed. Martial Arts training is another example of how the Xíng functions of the practitioner can surpass regular people so that the marital artist is able to move faster and punch harder. In Hard Style Qìgōng (硬氣功), the practitioner can perform many extraordinary tasks that are impossible for regular people to do. For example, when Shén and Qì are highly integrated within Xíng, such as in the throat, a spear cannot pierce through it.

b) Shén and Xíng integrate/unite within Qì

This integration occurs during Qìgōng practice or any mindfulness exercise when Qì functions are activated; therefore, Shén and Xíng follow Qì's movement which causes the body to move automatically. Although the body movements can be either the purpose or the byproduct of the practice, the principles behind the movement are the same. In some Qìgōng practice, once the Qì functions are activated during the practice, a Qì current will form inside the body which will flow toward the intended body parts. As soon as the mind focuses on the intended body parts, Shén and Qì will merge, and as a result, the body parts will move. These kinds of body movements are mainly caused by Qì movement; it is Shén and Xíng following the movement of Qì. In other words, Shén and Xíng integrate/unite within Qì means when Shén moves, it activates Qì inside the body which causes the body to move, then Shén follows the body movement to move.

Certain types of Qìgōng, such as Spontaneous Movement Qìgōng (自發功), are designed to activate Qì functions. Other types, such as Five Animal Form (五禽戲), would unintentionally cause the body to move spontaneously. Although Qì practice is a higher level of practice (Xíng—Qì—Shén, low to high), Shén is very important in this level of practice. The most important aspect of this practice is when the body has spontaneous movement, Shén must stay in a "non-engaging, observation-only" state. Shén must be able to maintain its commanding functions and be able to follow the actions of Qì. The practitioner must stay in an alert and clear state of mind to observe and to experience the Qì action and body movements. The practitioner cannot assist or restrain the Qì action and body movements. For example, when Qì moves, Shén just observes its movement and lets it run its course. If Shén and Qì are separated, one may lose control of the Qì. If the uncontrolled Qì is very strong, the body may have uncontrollable movements. With strong Qì movement, some practitioners may have illusions. If one has illusions and follows them, or tries to direct the Qì flow, these types of actions may lead to mental disorders.

c) Xíng and Qì integrate/unite within Shén

This integration refers to Xíng and Qì completely following Shén's command. When Shén moves, Xíng and Qì move, and when Shén is static, both Xíng and Qì are static. This is a very high level of practice that very few people can achieve. In Traditional Dàoist Qìgōng, after the Dà Dān (大丹) is formed, Xíng and Qì's functions completely follow Shén's command. When Shén is highly tranquil and concentrated, both breathing and heartbeat can stop. In this stage, some people can levitate.

3. Advanced/Extraordinary Level

At this level, Xíng is dissipated into Qì and Qì is dissipated into Shén, and Jìng, Qì and Shén are almost integrated as one (Hùn Yuán) and become nearly indistinguishable. Shén is the key for all the integration. At this level, Shén can transmute/condense into Qì or Xíng at one's will (any time). The condensed Qì is formless, existing yet non-existing substance. The condensed Xíng is a physical body that consists of Jìng, Qì and Shén. Chinese Buddhism calls Jìng, Qì and Shén at this level "Miào yǒu" (妙有 existing yet non-existing). When it is Shén, it is "non-existing;" when it is Jìng, it is existing.

Different integration combinations will have different outcomes. When Shén and Qì integrate/unite within Xíng, Xíng will be immortal. When Shén and Xíng integrate/unite within Qì, Xíng will be invisible. When Xíng and Qì integrate/ unite within Shén, Xíng can be visible or invisible at one's command. The Xíng in this level is different from the Unintentional and Intentional Level. This Xíng is a Qì body, it can go through other materials such as walls. Under the sun, this Xíng does not have a shadow. If someone puts a hat on their head, the shadow of the hat would show but not the Xíng. In Qìgōng, this level of practice is called Fǎn bǔ guīzhēn (返補歸真 return to origin, back to the essence.)

B. The relationship between the whole body and its parts

From the perspective of anatomy, the human body is an entity that consists of cells, tissues, organs and systems. Traditional Chinese Medicine considers the human body to be an entity that consists of five solid and six hollow organs inside and limbs and bones outside, and they are united as an entity with Meridians. In Qìgōng, the body consists of Jìng, Qì and Shén. Points of view are different, but the common theme among them is that the entity (body) is dominated/dictated by Shén (consciousness).

Note: The five solid organs are the heart, spleen, liver, lungs and kidneys. The six hollow organs are the stomach, large intestine, small intestine, bladder and Sānjiāo 三焦.

According to Hùn Yuán Wholistic Theory, all physical parts of the body are condensed Hùn Yuán Qì, and there is formless Hùn Yuán Qì inside and engulfing the body. Therefore, every part of body contains the wholistic information of the body and can mirror the whole body; all parts obey the body. The most basic element of the body is the cell, and all cells, except specific cells such as sperm and egg, contain the same DNA with the same information. The heart and lungs have different gene expression, but from a wholistic viewpoint, they both have the same DNA and the same life information.

Each cell can represent the whole body, and each part of the body is a miniature of the whole body. This concept is widely used in Traditional Chinese Medicine and Qìgōng Healing. In healing, instead of working on the organ or system directly, very often the healer would insert a needle into the corresponding part of the ear, or would do Tuīná (推拿 Chinese Massage) on the feet, and/or would emit Qì to the hands. The nose, ears, feet and hands will be used to illustrate this relationship.

1. Nose

The nose and its immediately surrounding area have corresponding points that represent various body parts or organs. When these points are connected vertically, they form five lines (center and two on each side of the nose). The central line starts from the middle of the forehead, passes through the tip (center) of the nose and ends on Rén zhōng xué (人中穴 DU-26 under the nose, above the upper lip on the midline). This line is called Zàng (脏 Zàng normally refers to solid organs in TCM). The inner lines (closer to the nose on each side) are Line One and the outer lines are Line Two. Line One starts from close to the bridge and ends underneath the nostrils, and is called Fǔ (腑 hollow organs). Line Two, which runs along the outside of Line One, begins from the inner side of the eyebrow and ends beneath the nostrils. According to Traditional Chinese Medicine, the nose relates to Kidneys which belongs to Prenatal Qì, Fig. 3-4. Nose and Corresponding Body Parts.

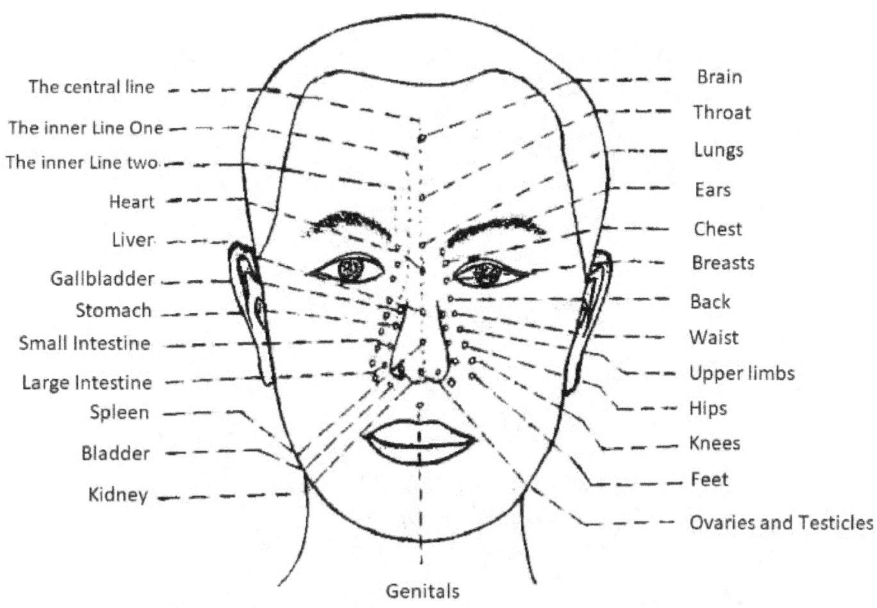

Fig. 3-4. Nose and Corresponding Body Parts

2. Ears

When the face reflects the body, the corresponding points are reflecting a standing person. The way the ear corresponds to the body is slightly different, it reflects an upside down sitting fetus. The center of the ear corresponds to the inner organs, the helix (the outer rim of the ear) is the limbs, the head is pointing to the ground. The ear resembles an upside-down fetus inside the mother's womb. The ear relates to the Spleen which belongs to Postnatal Qì, Fig. 3-5. Ear and Corresponding Body Parts.

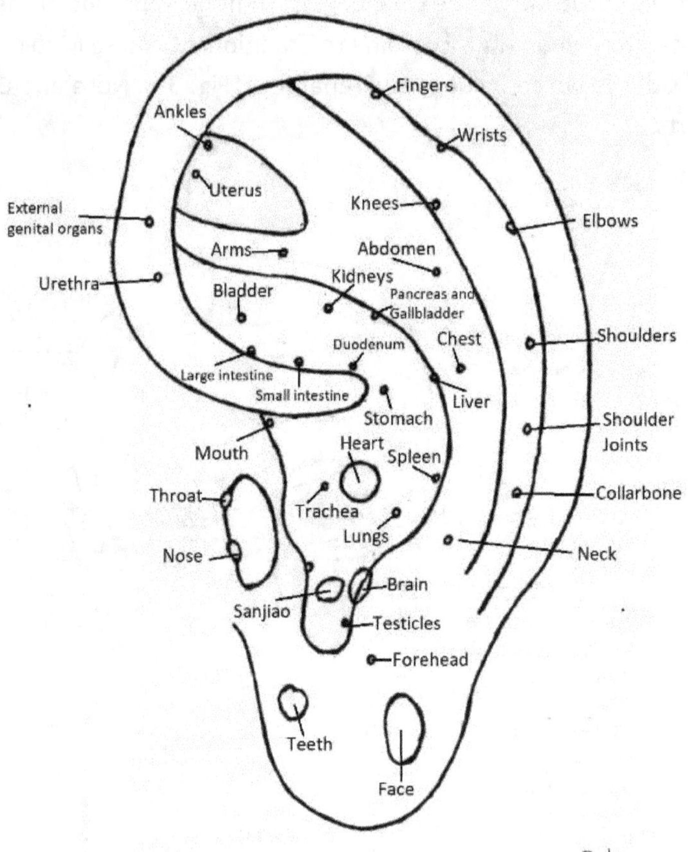

Fig. 3-5. Ear and Corresponding Body Parts

3. Feet

The soles of the feet are miniature representations of the body. The toes correspond to the head, followed by the upper cavity (the organs), and the lower cavity (organs) and the limbs. Each foot corresponds to half the body, Fig. 3-6. Feet and Corresponding Body Parts.

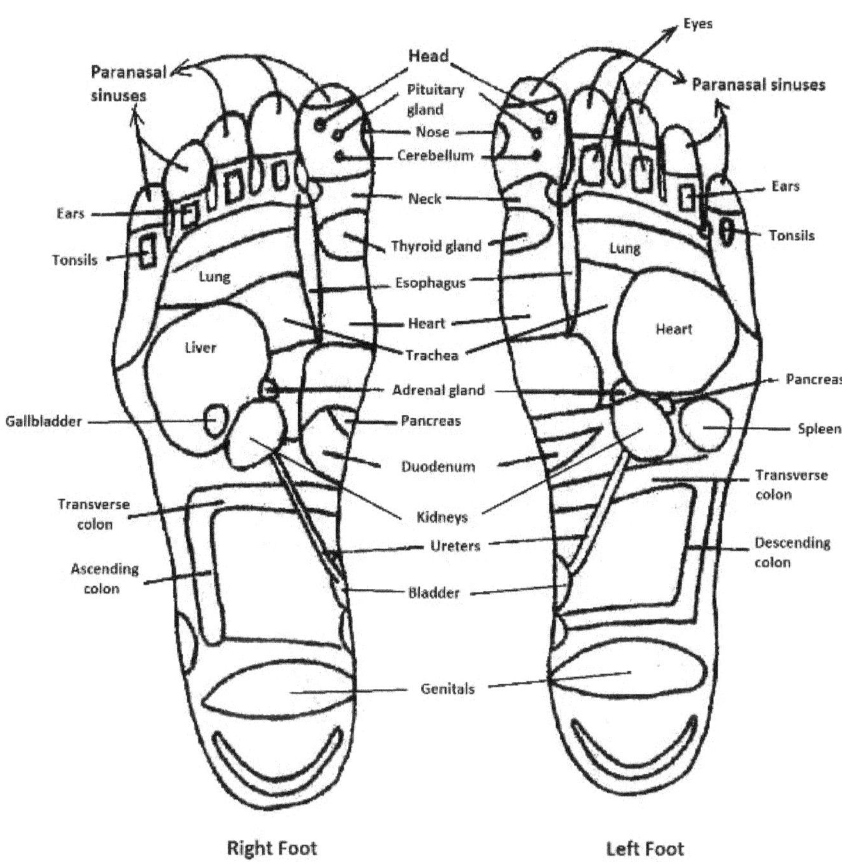

Fig. 3-6. Feet and Corresponding Body Parts

4. Hands

The inner side of each palm of the hand corresponds to the inner organs. The outer (back) side of the fingers mirrors the limbs and back; the fingernail represents Sānjiāo 三焦 (the tip of the fingernail mirrors Upper Jiāo 上焦, the center mirrors Middle Jiāo 中焦 and the base mirrors Lower Jiāo 下焦). Both sides of the finger joints mirror different part of the limbs; on the side that is pointing to the thumb direction, the bottom joints mirror the shoulders, the middle joints mirror the elbows and the top joints mirror the wrists. On the side that is pointing in the direction of the little finger, the bottom joints mirror the hipbones, the middle joints mirror the knees and the top joints mirror the ankles. The upper part of the back of the palm corresponds to the back of the body, and the lower part corresponds to the waist, Fig. 3-7. Hands and Corresponding Body Parts.

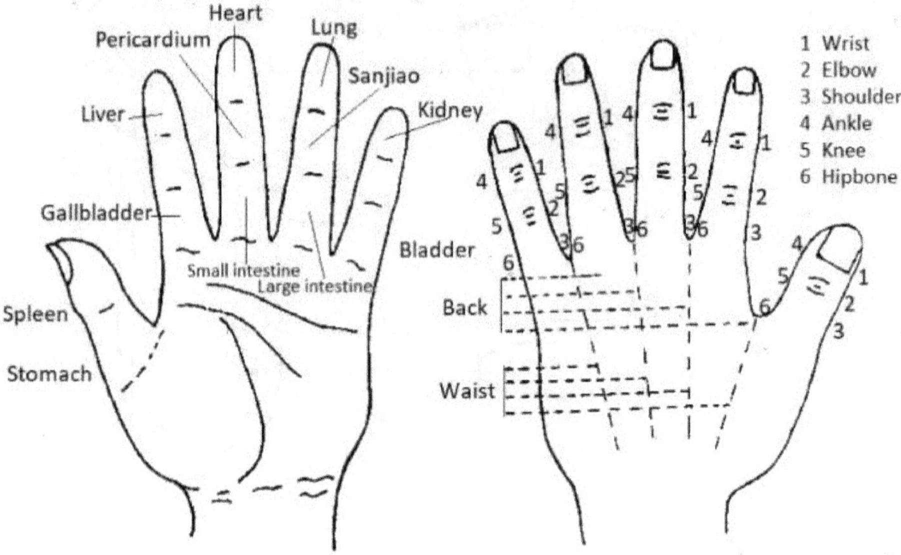

Fig. 3-7 Hands and Corresponding Body Parts

Summary

Wholistic Theory describes the characteristics of a wholistic entity. In science, an entity mainly refers to an object that occupies space. In Qìgōng, a wholistic entity is an entity in which time structure and space structure are transmuted as one, and within the wholistic entity, all individual parts obey and conform to the entity. The Wholistic Theory is divided into three subcategories/concepts: the concept of the universe as a wholistic entity, the concept of Human and Heaven (Nature) as a wholistic entity, and the concept of the human being as a wholistic entity.

The concept of the universe as a wholistic entity explains the space structure and time structure of the universe. The universe is a wholistic entity that consists of materials with form (condensed Hùn Yuán Qì) and without form (Hùn Yuán Qì). These materials are constantly transmuting with each another and are expressed as space and time. Time is the process of changing or continuing expressions of a substance's (wholistic entity) Hùn Yuán Qì functions, and space is the process of structural change/extension of a substance's position. Qìgōng is an exercise with mindfulness, therefore, one of the most important requirements in Qìgōng practice is to regulate mental activities. Buddhist Qìgōng emphasizes emptying the consciousness. Empty is not devoid of all things; it is consciousness that means not to be aware of or fixed on any particular thing. It is extremely difficult to do. Dàoist Qìgōng emphasizes returning back to Nature. But no one can give an exact definition of what it means. The concept of the universe as a wholistic entity gives a practitioner a clearer way to obtain emptiness. The universe is a transmuted state of space and time. From the earth, the sphere of the universe is more than 92 billion light-years in diameter. It is so big that it cannot be comprehended in a normal sense. When one visualizes the universe, one would not be thinking about concrete things and all existences will become vague. The bigger the universe one visualizes, the blurrier the existences will be, and finally, all existences become empty (existing and non-existing). Because human beings are part of the universe entity, while practicing Qìgōng, if the practitioner can be aware of the space (universe), they would be able to let go of themselves and immerse themselves in the vastness of space (emptiness). The mind will be able to relax and open up, and becomes "empty," and in turn, the consciousness will merge with Primal Hùn Yuán Qì.

The concept of Human and Heaven as a Wholistic Entity is not only important in Qìgōng, it is one of the cornerstones of Chinese culture and is an essential part of daily life. This concept means that human beings are part of Nature and society. The human beings rely on the External Hùn Yuán Qì (environment) to survive. If a human being violates the laws of Nature or society, they will perish. Because human beings and Nature are one entity, all Qìgōng emphasizes following the rhythm of Nature to harmonize with the environment. The characteristics of Nature Qì change with the seasons and the time of day. Many Qìgōng methods utilize this unique phenomenon to cultivate Qì to strengthen the body functions.

Each human being is a wholistic entity. Qìgōng considers the human being to be an entity that consists of Jìng, Qì and Shén. Jìng, Qì and Shén are different expressions of Qì. When it is non-active, Qì is in a natural formless state called Qì; when it condenses, it is in a physical state called Xíng (Jìng). When it has special activities, it is called Shén. In Qìgōng, the physical body which includes inner organs, limbs and blood belong to Jìng. Mental (conscious) activities belong to Shén, and the formless, colorless and moving/circulating substance inside the body belongs to Qì. Since the human being is a wholistic entity, Qìgōng has many different ways to use Jìng, Qì and Shén to cultivate Qì. Methods such as Jìng practice, Qì practice and Shén practice are widely used in all types of Qìgōng to cultivate Qì.

第四章：人的混元氣

Chapter Four: Human Hùn Yuán Qì

The fundamental difference between human beings and animals is that human beings have high levels of mental activities and social consciousness. In Zhìnéng Qìgōng, Hùn Yuán Wholistic Theory considers Human Hùn Yuán Qì to be the fourth level of Qì. In previous chapters, the wholistic features of human beings have been briefly discussed. In this chapter, focus will be on the Human Hùn Yuán Entity, and the evolution, movement and formation of Human Hùn Yuán Qì.

I. Human's Hùn Yuán Entity

According to Hùn Yuán Theory, Hùn Yuán Qì can condense into a physical substance which is engulfed by the uncondensed Qì. The merged physical substance and the surrounding Qì is called Hùn Yuán Entity. Therefore, the Human Hùn Yuán Entity is the physical body and its Qì. To understand the Human Hùn Yuán Entity, one needs to know its wholistic features and its transmutation movements. The wholistic features are the characteristics of Human Hùn Yuán Qì and its distribution.

A. Human Hùn Yuán Qì

Human Hùn Yuán Qì is the result of the transmutation of the Prenatal and Postnatal Qì. It consists of invisible Qì and concentrated Qì (physical substances). The concentrated Qì is called Xíng (形 entity) or Jīng (精 essence). The invisible Qì consists of formless Qì (氣) and formless Shén (神). Xíng, Qì and Shén are the expression of Human Hùn Yuán Qì.

Xíng has form/shape and is Hùn Yuán Qì's expression of physical substances. Qì is formless and is Hùn Yuán Qì's expression of a formless characteristic which is inside every part of the body and the space surrounding the body. Shén is the finest grade of formless Qì and is mainly inside the brain. Xíng, Qì and Shén are not isolated, but are interconnected and interdependent to form an entity. Within Xíng, there are Qì and Shén; inside Qì, there is Shén. Traditionally, Human Hùn Yuán Qì is divided into three grades, the coarse one is called Xíng, the regular one is called Qì, and the refined one is called Shén. When Qì condenses, it becomes Xíng; when it is refined, it becomes Shén. In order to understand their relationship, we will describe each in the following sections.

1. Qì

As in all other kinds of Hùn Yuán Qì, Human Hùn Yuán Qì is invisible and formless. It is not solid, liquid or air (gaseous state), but is a special existing condition. It occupies space, but not physically. It can co-exist with everything and is in every part of the body and its surroundings. It is very evenly distributed and colorless but is not transparent and can be seen in certain circumstances. In addition to the common characteristics of the Hùn Yuán Qì, Human Hùn Yuán Qì has the following unique features.

a) Characteristics

(1) Contains all information

Every element and organ of the body has its unique characteristics and is interconnected with each other through the Qì that surrounds them. This surrounding Qì is transmuted together to form a wholistic entity (Human Hùn Yuán Qì) which contains all the information of the person. Because this Qì contains all of the information, it can merge with the genetic material in the cells of different organs to form physical substances (cells); it also can merge with brain cells to nourish Shén.

(2) Mobility

Hùn Yuán Qì in the body can move. There are two forces that move the Hùn Yuán Qì. One force is the physiological changes in the human body. During activity or movement, the body or the organs will consume and attract Qì; in turn, these will move Qì. Also, the metabolism will consume and move Qì. The other force is mind intent; mind intent can direct Qì's movement.

(3) Attachment

Hùn Yuán Qì has the characteristic of even distribution, but once it becomes part of an organ/element, Hùn Yuán Qì with the same characteristic as the organ will attach to the space surrounding the organ. For example, the human body is the expression of Hùn Yuán Qì in physical form, and there is a layer of Human Hùn Yuán Qì that surrounds the body. The closer to the body, the stronger and denser is the Qì. Also, the amount of attached Qì is proportional to the density of the substance.

(4) Concentration and Dispersing

Hùn Yuán Qì can concentrate or disperse according to the body's structural needs and the directions of the individual's mind intent.

(5) Energy

Hùn Yuán Qì has energy in different kinds of forms. Under certain conditions, it can change from one form to another.

b) Distribution and function

Hùn Yuán Qì and the physical body exist in a merged state; without the physical body, Qì has nothing to which it can attach. The functions of Hùn Yuán Qì are dependent upon where it is located inside the body, and the locations can be the body or Shén. Depending on its locations and functions, the Human Hùn Yuán Qì can be divided into Body Hùn Yuán Qì, Organ Hùn Yuán Qì and Yi Yuán Ti.

Note: Traditionally, Body Hùn Yuán Qì is called Dāntián Qì, Organ Hùn Yuán Qì is called Middle Dāntián Qì, Yì Yuán Tǐ is called Upper Dāntián Qì.

(1) Body Hùn Yuán Qì

The Qì that supports cell metabolism and physical functions is called Body Hùn Yuán Qì. For example, in a hand movement, Qì involves muscles and bones. It will need the Hùn Yuán Qì for two purposes—one is to maintain and replenish the consumed energy and the other is to maintain the metabolism of the cells involved. Although Body Hùn Yuán Qì is distributed in every part of the body, it is concentrated in the area between the navel and Mìngmén. Traditionally, this area is called the Lower Dāntián. Body Hùn Yuán Qì can follow the mind intent to circulate to any part of the body. Most Qìgōng methods focus on strengthening the functions of Body Hùn Yuán Qì during the early stages of cultivation.

(2) Organ Hùn Yuán Qì

The Qì that powers the function of hormone/internal secretion of the organs is called Organ Hùn Yuán Qì. In addition to being part of the physical body, each inner organ can produce or secrete substances which are not only for its own use but also for that of the whole body. Therefore, there are two kinds of Qì, Body and Organ Qì, involved in each organ. For example, in the digestive system, the Qì that maintains the life cycle and metabolism of the cells belongs to Body Hùn Yuán Qì. The production and function of digestive enzymes belong to Organ Hùn Yuán Qì. The digestive enzyme does not exist until it is needed. The digestive enzyme is formed when Organ Hùn Yuán Qì is condensed from formless state into physical substances. The process of moving from non-existing to existing is called Wú 無 (none/nothing) to Yǒu 有 (have/something) in Qìgōng. Organ Hùn Yuán Qì nourishes the secretion function and does not relate to the organ's functions. It does not follow the mind intent and is concentrated in the Epigastric region, or Middle Dāntián.

(3) Yì Yuán Tǐ

When Hùn Yuán Qì in the brain cells concentrates and becomes extremely even and fine, it will have special characteristics such as the ability to search, memorize and analyze. This Qì is called Yì Yuán Tǐ. Mind activities are the functions and processes of Yì Yuán Tǐ. Yì Yuán Tǐ can permeate every part of the body and has a commanding role in the body's life functions. The movement (activity) of the Yì Yuán Tǐ is called Shén. Yì Yuán Tǐ is the most refined type of Hùn Yuán Qì.

Note: In all Qìgōng (except Zhìnéng Qìgōng) writings, Shén can be either Upper Dāntián Qì or mind activity.

2. Xíng (Jīng)

Xíng (physical body) is Human Hùn Yuán Qì in a physical form. It is formed by concentrating/condensing Human Hùn Yuán Qì into a fixed physical form. Once the formless Hùn Yuán Qì is concentrated into a physical body, the Qì movement inside the body and in its surrounding area (Qì Field) will be restricted and its movement is significantly different from the previous unrestricted form of movement. The Qì Field's density and range are confined by the physical body—the more massive that the physical body is, the denser and larger the range of the Qì Field will be.

Note: In most Qìgōng, Jing is exclusively for human beings, Xíng is for all others.

All forms of Human Hùn Yuán Qì contain all of the information (space, time, and functions) of the person, but the information is very weak in the formless state. Compared with formless Qì, the physical object contains a tremendous amount of information and energy. For example, when one cubic meter of formless Qì is condensed into a one cubic centimeter object, according to the laws of physics, the condensed object (1 cm^3) will contain the same amount of data and energy. Therefore, a one cubic meter object will contain numerous amounts of data and energy; and the amount of energy the object contains is proportional to its mass, $E= mc^2$.

All living things need to exchange Qì with Nature. One of the purposes of Qìgōng practice is to collect and cultivate Nature Hùn Yuán Qì. Because a physical substance contains so much information and energy, is it necessary to spend so much time collecting Nature Hùn Yuán Qì? Why not just focus on collecting and cultivating Qì from the concentrated/physical object? The reason that the focus is not on consuming a physical substance (food) is that each individual object (food) has its own characteristics which are not comparable to those of the individual who consumes it. In order to absorb an object into the body, one must change the object into Qì (its original characteristics are still intact in this step), neutralize its characteristics, and then merge and transmute it with one's own Qì. These changes consume a great amount of energy. If one cannot completely neutralize the object, and if the object retains its own characteristics, it may be harmful to the body.

The genetic information, which is compressed in the physical body and is expressed in physical form as DNA is called Jīng. Jīng is also referred to as sperm or egg. In that context—Jīng is a very special form of Qì. The sperm or the egg is a part of the physical body and contains the characteristics of the Body Hùn Yuán Qì. Sex hormones are produced when Jīng (sperm or egg) is formed, so it has the characteristics of Organ Hùn Yuán Qì. The discharge of sperm normally is accompanied by high excitement—this is Shén's characteristic. Therefore, Jīng's (sperm or egg) birth and maturity must involve Body Hùn Yuán Qì, Organ Hùn Yuán Qì and Yì Yuán Tǐ. Jīng (sperm or egg) contains the most genetic information within the physical body and is the essence of Human Hùn Yuán Qì.

Although the egg or the sperm contains all the genetic information, by themselves, the eggs or the sperms are not comparable and cannot be transmuted together. However, the egg and the sperm are complementary to each other since each one contains half of the information needed for the resulting transmuted entity (human being). The human being will be genetically male or female and the Hùn Yuán Qì in a male and female is not the same.

3. Shén

As noted previously, the finest grade of Human Hùn Yuán Qì is called Shén. But Shén is more than just Qì, it is also mental (conscious) activities. Shén as a substance (Qì) and Shén as a function (consciousness) cannot be separated. Shén is "body and functions/use as one." To distinguish between the two aspects of Shén, Zhìnéng Qìgōng calls the concentrated, but not solid, brain cell Hùn Yuán Qì "Yì Yuán Tǐ" and the activity of Yì Yuán Tǐ "Shén." Shén represents the activities (functions and processes) of the brain cell Hùn Yuán Qì. Shén is the highest form of human activity that can direct and dictate life activities. In addition to the characteristics of In-Out, Open-Close, Concentrate-Disperse and Huà, Yì Yuán Tǐ (brain cell Hùn Yuán Qì) has special functions such as the capacity to select, memorize, and to take initiative. If Yì Yuán Tǐ is considered as an object, Shén will be that object's functions, uses and applications.

> *Note: Shén is mentioned in all of Qìgōng, only Zhìnéng Qìgōng separates the two concepts.*

4. The relationship between Jīng (Xíng), Qì and Shén

The relationship between Xíng and Qì is that they are interchangeable. Under certain conditions, the formless Qì condenses into a solid substance and the solid substance disperses into formless Qì. This interchange is called "Yǒu (有 have) and Wú (無 have not) beget each other" in Qìgōng, and it occurs in the body constantly. Once the formless Qì is condensed into a solid object, the information it contains will be fixed/confined within the solid object. This process is very similar to regular Hùn Yuán Qì, except that human beings can use the mind intent (Shén) to regulate information in this process.

To regulate/influence the process is to use Shén to merge with Qì, but the density of formless Qì is very low and the mind's influence is relatively minor; moreover, a solid thing's density is very high and is difficult to permeate. When we observe something, our consciousness will have it “fixed” in a certain way and it will be difficult to influence that fixed perception. Because the interchange of Xíng and Qì into form and formlessness occurs constantly within the body, the mind exerts the most influence when the Qì is in between the two states. During Qìgōng practice, one should not just focus on the physical body or the formless Qì. One should imagine that the physical body is not solid but that it is composed of concentrated Qì and pay attention to the interchanging process between the concentrated Qì (physical body) and formless Qì. If one adds information/mind intent under this circumstance, one can change the outcome of the process. Adding information/ mind intent during the process is especially important in treating illness. An intention of wellness will speed up recovery from an illness.

Shén’s existence depends on the physical brain cells and it also needs Qì’s nourishment. The brain cells are different from all other cells in the body; in addition to normal metabolism, they store and disperse information and communicate with the rest of the body. The endocrine system is a major communication system for the body. Unlike the nervous system, which uses neurotransmitters as its chemical signals, the endocrine system uses hormones. The organs such as pancreas, kidneys and heart are all sources of hormones. Therefore, to nourish Shén, one needs Organ Hùn Yuán Qì. Among the organs, kidneys are the most important; they store the Prenatal Qì and contain reproduction Jīng (essences). The kidney’s reproduction Jīng is the concentration of Jīng from all inner organs; therefore, kidney Jīng contains the most information and energy. To be more effective in nourishing Shén, one must use the kidneys’ Jīng. In Traditional Dàoist Qìgōng, after cultivating Xíng into Jīng, the next step is to change Jīng into Qì to nourish Shén.

In Conclusion, Xíng, Qì and Shén all are part of Human Hùn Yuán Qì. Shén controls Xíng and Qì, and Xíng and Qì can nourish Shén. The formless Qì transmutes into the physical body, and the physical body gives birth to formless Shén. To maintain normal life functions, Xíng, Qì and Shén depend on, interchange with, and permeate each other. The human physical body contains both characteristics of formless Qì and Yì Yuán Tǐ. For example, brain cells are the condensed physical form of Hùn Yuán Qì, and they have Qì and Shén. The cells in the nervous system have Qì and Shén. Yì Yuán Tǐ is the finest form of Hùn Yuán Qì, and can permeate directly or through the nerve cells into every cell of the body.

B. The Distribution Characteristics of Human Body Hùn Yuán Qì

Human Body Hùn Yuán Qì is part of Human Hùn Yuán Qì which consists of Jīng (Xíng), Qì and Shén. Human Body Hùn Yuán Qì refers to the formless and changeable Qì inside Human Hùn Yuán Qì; therefore, the distribution characteristics of Human Body Hùn Yuán Qì will not include Jīng (Xíng) and Shén. The following are characteristics of the formless Human Body Hùn Yuán Qì.

1. Same structure as the physical body

Human Body Hùn Yuán Qì is distributed according to the physical structure of the body. The physical body is the Hùn Yuán Qì in concentrated form with very high density. In addition to the uncondensed Qì inside the body, there is a layer of diluted Qì in the area surrounding the physical body. This Qì, both inside and outside, can circulate in and out of the physical body. This Qì's distribution is fixed/confined by the structures of the body. Qì's distribution will be the same without regard to the structure of the physical body. The body structure is fixed when the fetus is formed and is determined by Prenatal Qì. For example, most people were born with five fingers and will have a five-finger Qì Field in the area surrounding the hand. If a person loses a finger in an accident, the Qì Field remains the same. Using a special camera, the image of a five-finger Qì Field remains visible. But if a person was born with only four fingers, the image will show a four-finger Qì Field.

2. Qì bodies inside and outside of the body

There are three layers of Qì outside the body. The first layer extends about 3 cm to 5 cm outside of the body; it is distributed along the body's axis. This layer of Qì directly mirrors the body's structure and covers the whole body. It reflects the physical condition of the body—the healthier the body, the denser the Qì layer. The second is a thinner layer of Qì outside of the first layer surrounding the body. It is formed by the "escaped" first layer Qì, and is related to the amount of Internal Qì one processes. The third is a diluted Qì layer, and radiates outward. The mind activities can influence these three layers of Qì, and practicing Qìgōng can strengthen the Qì Body.

There is a Qì body inside the physical body. The distribution of Qì is not even inside the physical body because of the circulation of Qì and blood, and the Qì concentrating underneath the skin/membrane. Also, deep tissues and bones have a large amount of Qì. Because the distribution of Qì is the same as the body's structure, it is as if there is a Qì Body within the physical body. Because Human Hùn Yuán Qì follows the mind intent, the shape and size of the Qì Body will change automatically according to the mind's activities. The Qì Body (both inside and outside of the body) is called Fǎshēn (法身) in Traditional Qìgōng.

3. The uneven distribution of Hùn Yuán Qì

Because the body structure restricts (fixes) the Hùn Yuán Qì's movements, different parts of the body have different Hùn Yuán Qì concentration centers/points. The concentrations centers/points follow two major rules.

- The organ or system with strong and vigorous functions has more Qì.
- Qì circulates and concentrates more easily in an area with less densely packed structures/tissues, a denser area is more difficult for Qì to go through.

These two rules dictate the outcome of the concentration points and their locations. There are three major Hùn Yuán concentration points in the body: Body Hùn Yuán Qì which concentrates inside the navel area; Organ Hùn Yuán Qì which concentrates inside the Epigastric region; and the brain cells' Hùn Yuán Qì (Yì Yuán Tǐ) which concentrates in Shén Jī Qiào 神機竅 (located at the center of the brain).

a) Body Hùn Yuán Qì concentration point

The purpose of Body Hùn Yuán Qì is to support the metabolism and functions of the physical body at the cellular level. It concentrates deep inside the navel (umbilical area} for the following reasons:

(1) For humans, the main source of Postnatal Qì is from food. The small intestine's digestive enzymes break down the food to become Qì and absorb it into the body. Therefore, the small intestine area becomes the Qì center. From the perspective of the Prenatal Qì (before birth) point of view, a fetus receives the Hùn Yuán Qì (nourishment) from the mother through the umbilical cord; the navel area becomes the center for receiving and distributing the Hùn Yuán Qì.

(2) According to Traditional Chinese Medicine, the kidneys in a fetus include the adrenal glands, urinary system and reproductive system. The reproductive system is the area that produces the Prenatal Qì. In adults, the testicles and the ovaries are not next to the navel; as a fetus, both belong to the urogenital system. When the inner organs are formed, the testicles and the ovaries are between the kidneys and slightly above the navel; they will move downward as the fetus grows. As noted previously, the distribution of Qì is determined by the fetus's structure. Although the testicles and the ovaries move downward, their Qì Field remains deep inside the navel, and close to and between the kidneys. Traditionally, this area is called Mìngmén (not the acupuncture point Mìngmén Xué). The Prenatal Qì and Shén are formed in the Mìngmén area. The transmutation of Prenatal Qì to Postnatal Qì, which contains all the life information, is also originally from this area. Therefore, this area is the concentration point for both Prenatal and Postnatal Qì.

(3) The waist (lumbar vertebrae) is the most important structural part of the physical body. The waist connects the upper and lower limbs and maintains the body's balance. It is a key area that supports and regulates all physical movements. This area needs a significant amount of Qì to maintain its functions. This is one of the reasons that Body Hùn Yuán Qì concentrates in the navel area.

All physical activities need the support of the spine. In Martial Art Qìgōng, it is said that the "force is issued by the spine." This phrase means that one needs the spine to maintain body posture. With strong posture, Qì will follow the mind intent to move outward as force. The spine has a Qì central point; if the body is divided into upper and lower sections, the central point is located in the middle or Mìngmén area. This point is where the force and Qì concentrate.

One of the reasons that most Medical and Martial Art Qìgōng focuses on the Lower Dāntián is because of the need to cultivate the Body Hùn Yuán Qì and to strengthen the physical body. Without a healthy body, how can one practice a martial art? Zhìnéng Qìgōng uses the Three Centers Merge Standing Method to accumulate Body Hùn Yuán Qì.

b) Organ Hùn Yuán Qì concentrates in the Hùn Yuán Qìào (混元竅)

"Organ" mainly refers to the heart, liver, lungs and spleen which includes the pancreas and digestive system, and the kidneys which include the reproductive system. Although organs have their own special functions, they have two common characteristics.

Note: Qìào 竅 is not a physical point and does not exist until one accumulates enough Qì. The Hùn Yuán Qìào is located slightly below the center of the diaphragm.

(1) They all receive and distribute substances from and to the rest of the body. For example, the heart circulates blood and lymphatic fluid. The lung receives carbon dioxide and distributes oxygen. These receiving and distributing functions congregate the Organ Hùn Yuán Qì in the organs.

(2) Each organ produces hormones to nourish the body and regulate emotions. Because the organs are either located in the Thoracic cavity or in the Abdominal cavity, how can their Hùn Yuán Qì concentrate at the Hùn Yuán Qìào? The Hùn Yuán Qìào is located in the Epigastric region (slightly below the diaphragm) and at approximately the center among these organs. The outer layer of each organ's Hùn Yuán Qì overlaps each other in this area and it becomes a concentration point. More importantly, the movements of the diaphragm bring all the organ's Hùn Yuán Qì together. As one inhales, the diaphragm moves downward and brings the lung and heart Qì downward to congregate with the liver Qì, spleen Qì and kidney Qì in the Hùn Yuán Qìào area. With repeated up and down movements, the diaphragm's movement will bring all of the Organ Qì together and they will merge as one. In this area, Prenatal and Postnatal Qì are transmuted as one and this Hùn Yuán Qì is better equipped for the "Wú (無 nothing) to the Yǒu (有 something)" process. Because Organ Qì can change to become Body Qì to nourish and strengthen the physical body, many Qìgōng practices use Abdominal Breathing to increase diaphragm movements to achieve enhanced vitality.

c) Yì Yuán Tǐ (brain cell Hùn Yuán Qì) concentrates in Shén Jī Qìào 神機竅 (located at the center of the brain)

Brain cell Hùn Yuán Qì is not only distributed throughout the body but also outside the body. It behaves very similarly to the Primal Hùn Yuán Qì; but it has a central point which is located at the center of the head. This central point is the hub and commencement point for all Shén's activities.

The Body Hùn Yuán Qì follows the mind intent. Therefore, Shén (mind activities) can change the distribution of Body Hùn Yuán Qì. When the mind concentrates on a certain part of the body, Qì will congregate in that area. The part of the body that lacks the mind's attention has less Qì. For example, our hands have a significant amount of Qì because of the attention that is paid to them. Each time we move the hands, Qì congregates there. Also, the human sensory organs (eyes, nose, ears, etc.) are the congregation points of Body Hùn Yuán Qì. Generally speaking, the degree of congregation is directly related to the activities/uses of the organ. The more one uses a particular organ, the more Qì will congregate in that organ, and its functions will be enhanced further. This may lead to extraordinary abilities. For example, when a child is born with a certain disability such as blindness, they will develop much better listening ability than people who have normal vision.

If one concentrates frequently on an area, Qì will congregate in that area and form a fixed Qì Field. Over a period of time, the fixed Qì Field will evolve, and its functional structure will change. When the functional structure changes, it will create structural changes. The fixed Qì Field may/will transmute into a solid form. Because the mind intent can change the distribution of Qì, in Qìgōng, Shén dictates how one should practice, what to practice, how to work on a certain part of the body while working on the whole body, what to practice first, and how to progress.

d) The Skin and Mó Luò (膜絡 membranes) have more Body Hùn Yuán Qì

Mó (膜) means membranes and refers to all the membranes of the skin, organs, tissues, and cells in the human body. Traditional Chinese Medicine considers tiny blood vessels in the membrane to be closely related to or part of the small lateral meridians. These tiny blood vessels and small lateral meridians are called Luò (絡 lateral meridian). Together, the membranes and the small lateral meridians (including tiny blood vessels) are called Mó Luò (膜絡). The Qì inside the Mó Luò is called Mó Luò Qì and belongs to Body Hùn Yuán Qì.

In general, compared to other parts of the body, the Skin and Mó Luò have more Qì. For example, muscle membrane has more Qì than muscle fiber. Why does Mó Luò have more Qì than other parts of the body? There are three reasons.

(1) Compared to the rest of the tissues, the density of the membrane structure is relatively low. This low density will allow Qì to go through easily, and also creates space to store the Qì.

(2) The exchange of Qì between the internal and external elements occurs at the membrane level. For example, the exchange of Qì with Nature is carried out primarily by the skin or mucosa; as a consequence, these areas will have more Qì. Similarly, the mucosa carries out the exchange of Qi between the different tissues and organs inside the body. The membranes are the elements' contact surfaces with external elements. When there is contact, there will be exchanges. With exchange, Qì volume will increase.

(3) Normal mind activities for humans are outward focusing. In other words, one tends to focus on outside of the body rather than on the inside of the body. This focus would cause the Qì to disperse outward and congregate in the membranes of the body. The main reason that the Lift Qì Up/Pour Qì Down Method in Zhìnéng Qìgōng focuses on External Hùn Yuán Qì is to increase the Mó Luò Qì.

In conclusion, the distribution of Body Hùn Yuán Qì is determined by the structure, functions and mental activities of the body. Qìgōng practice uses the mind intent to influence the function of Qì in order to improve body functions and enhance health.

II. The Evolution of Human Hùn Yuán Qì

The formation of Human Hùn Yuán Qì begins with a sperm and an egg. When a sperm fertilizes an egg, it creates Human Hùn Yuán Qì. From a single fertilized egg to an adult, the Human Hùn Yuán Qì goes through five stages of complex Hùn Huà process.

Note: Although the formation of Human Hùn Yuán Qì is divided into five stages, in most writings, when human Qì is mentioned, it refers to Adult Hùn Yuán Qì.

A. Fertilized Egg Hùn Yuán Qì

In macroscopic observation which medical science uses, a complete cell (zygote) is formed when a sperm and an egg fuse together. One of the reasons a sperm can fertilize an egg is because each gamete contains only 23 chromosomes, which is half of the normal cells. In a natural context, sperms or egg cannot simply fuse among themselves to form a zygote; by themselves, the sperms' (or the egg's) characteristics are not comparable to each other.

Qìgōng uses microscopic observation. According to Hùn Yuán Wholistic Theory, when a sperm fertilizes an egg, a new entity is created. In fertilization, the new entity is a fertilized egg. This new entity's Hùn Yuán Qì exists as a physical substance and as a Qì Field. The physical substance (fertilized egg) is this new entity's Hùn Yuán Qì in condensed form, and the Qì Field, the uncondensed Qì inside the egg and in its surrounding area, is its formless form. The fertilization is a Hùn Huà (transmutation) process.

As an individual entity, and before the Hùn Huà process, each gamete's (sperm/egg) Hùn Yuán Qì has its own characteristics. During the fertilization, the gamete's individual characteristics will disappear, and once fertilization is completed, the zygote has a completely different set of characteristics. Therefore, fertilization is not a simple fusion between a sperm and an egg, it is a Hùn Huà (transmutation) process. The process is the following: existing to non-existing to existing (Yǒu 有 – Wú 無 – Yǒu 有). The following diagram is used to explain this process. Fig. 4-1 Process of Existing to Non-existing to Existing.

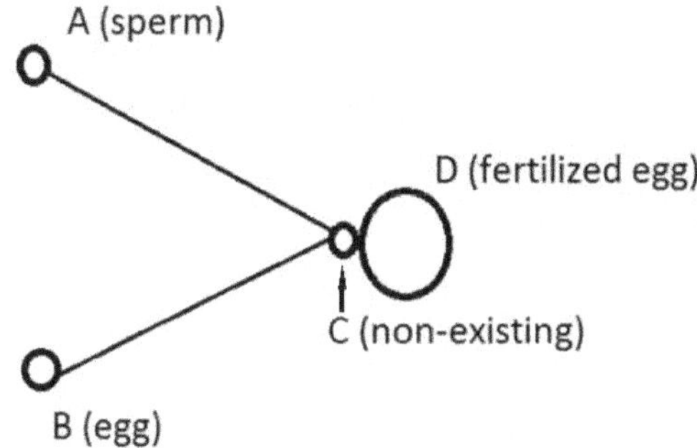

Fig. 4-1 Process of Existing to Non-existing to Existing

When the Hùn Yuán Qì at point A and point B meet at point C, the characteristics of A and B are neutralized and no longer exist and D is not yet formed. C is a very evenly distributed Qì state, similar to Primal Hùn Yuán Qì, and its existence is extremely brief. C forms D's Hùn Yuán Qì, and in turn, D's Hùn Yuán Qì will form a physical substance (fertilized egg) and its Qì Field. This is a two-step process.

- Step one: the transmutation (Hùn Huà) between the gamete's (sperm/egg) chromosomes to form a complete cell (zygote).
- Step two: the transmutation between the nucleus of the zygote and the ovum's cytoplasm.

The process is continuous but is divided into two steps for easy explanation. Before the sperm fuses with the egg, the formless Hùn Yuán Qì of the gametes will first begin to transmute the physical substances of the gametes into the formless Hùn Yuán Qì of the fertilized egg; at the same time, the formless Hùn Yuán Qì of the fertilized egg will condense to form the fertilized egg and its Qì Field.

Traditionally, the Qì one is born with is called Prenatal Qì. Before the baby is born, they receive most of their Qì from the mother; therefore, there are two types of Prenatal Qì. The zygote's (fertilized egg) Hùn Yuán Qì is called Pre-Prenatal Qì, and the Qì from the mother is called Post-Prenatal Qì. Dàoist Qìgōng considers Qì in point C as the true Prenatal Qì.

A fertilized egg contains the wholistic (space and time) information of the parents, and this information which is in a hidden state will guide its future development. As the fertilized egg grows and develops, it will gradually display the whole characteristics of space and time information that it has inherited. Therefore, the conditions of the sperm and egg are extremely important. The human being constantly interacts with the environment, thus, the information that one possesses changes from moment to moment. The age, health condition, experience and mental conditions of the person influence the gamete's Hùn Yuán Qì. A very young person may have a lot of vitality, but their body may not be mature enough and the brain may not be fully developed. An older person may have a well-developed brain that contains a significant amount of information, but their body may lack vitality. Under these circumstances, the information that a gamete contains may not be optimal.

B. Embryo Hùn Yuán Qì

From a one-celled zygote to full-term fetus, the fertilized egg goes through three periods of development: the zygote period, embryonic period and fetal period. The zygote period is the first week after fertilization, and during this period, there is no growth in the overall size of the embryo, as it is confined within a glycoprotein shell. The zygote relies on its cytoplasm as an energy source for division, and each division produces successively smaller cells. Therefore, the Hùn Yuán Qì in the zygote period belongs to Fertilized Egg Hùn Yuán Qì.

The Hùn Yuán Qì in the embryonic period, which is from week two to week eight, is very special; it contains mainly Pre-Prenatal Qì and a huge amount of information. As the cells divide, the Embryo Hùn Yuán Qì will expand and disperse outward. Once the neural tube is closed and skin is formed, Qì begins to absorb inward; energy, Qì and information will stay inside to nourish the embryo. In Qìgōng, the movement of dispersing outward and absorbing inward is called "One Open, One Close." Open-Close movements connect the Embryo Hùn Yuán Qì with the external Qì—Qì from the mother and the environment, and it allows the embryo to create a Prenatal center to collect external information for future development. The amount of external Qì and information that the embryo receives is proportional to its strength; the stronger the Embryo Hùn Yuán Qì, the farther it will disperse and it will absorb more information and Qì. The root and main source of the external Qì for the embryo is the mother; therefore, the environment and health condition of the mother during pregnancy are extremely important and they are a vital part of fetal development.

C. Fetus Hùn Yuán Qì

Unlike medical science which states that the fetal period begins in week eight after fertilization, Qìgōng theory considers that Fetus Hùn Yuán Qì begins to form when the neural tube is closed, which is about four weeks after fertilization. "Fetus" in Fetus Hùn Yuán Qì is not just the fetus, it refers to the whole system, which includes the fetus, umbilical cord, placenta and other functions that support the

life of the fetus. The Fetus Hùn Yuán Qì is the space-time structure of the fetal system.
Every stage that an organism moves through during evolution involves Hùn Huà (transmutation) process between the organism's Hùn Yuán Qì and the external (environment) Hùn Yuán Qì. These Hùn Huà processes change the space-time structure of the organism and make it more complex and able to contain more information. The additional information will become part of the space-time information stored in the "new" organism. This stored information will become the basis for the next Hùn Huà process. In a human being, a fertilized egg contains the wholistic (space and time) information of the parents, and this information, which depends on the right environment for expression, is the blueprint for the development of the fetus. There are two types of Hùn Huà process in the development of the fetus, one is Internal Hùn Huà and the other is External Hùn Huà, and both occur simultaneously.

- Internal Hùn Huà. Internal Hùn Huà refers to the development and growth of the fertilized egg; in the fetus, it is the transmutation (interaction) between different structures/organs.
- External Hùn Huà. External Hùn Huà refers to the Hùn Huà process with the mother—the exchange of Qì (nutrition, energy and information) via umbilical cord and placenta.

As the fetus develops, a physical body with human characteristics will be formed. Human Hùn Yuán Qì consists of Jīng, Qì and Shén, but the fetus's Jīng, Qì and Shén have not been separated. In other words, the functions of the fetus's Jīng, Qì and Shén are not independent, they are united to perform one single task—physical development. The fetus connects with the external environment through the umbilical cord, and the organs with important endocrine functions such as the kidneys, the adrenal gland and the sex glands that are all located near the navel area; therefore, the navel area becomes the Fetus Hùn Yuán Qì center. Classical Qìgōng theories consider the navel area (the area between Navel and Mìngmén) to be the area that stores/generates Prenatal Qì. As the fetus becomes mature, the mother's Hùn Yuán Qì is no longer able to provide the optimal conditions for the process of External Hùn Huà; therefore, the birth of the baby will occur.

D. Infant/Child Hùn Yuán Qì

The Infant/Child period refers to the time between birth (newborn) and eight to ten years of age. Once a baby is born, they become an independent entity. The infant/child Hùn Yuán Qì is not set due to the internal environment of the baby's organs not having been fully developed, as well as ongoing changes in the baby's external environment. The infant/child will therefore undergo the Hùn Huà process constantly. The most important change during this period of time is the transformation of the baby's functions/Qì from Prenatal to Postnatal Qì. Prenatal Qì is from the parents and Postnatal Qì is from self-cultivation.

As noted previously , Open-Close is the foundation of Qì functions. Before a baby is born, they have experienced three Open-Close processes.

- The first Open-Close process is the meiotic division that produce sperm and egg which is Open, and the fertilized egg which is the Close part of the process.
- The second Open-Close process is the development/expansion of Fetus Hùn Yuán Qì which is Open, and the closure of the neural tube which is the Close part of the process.
- The third Open-Close process is the formation of the organs/system which is Open, and the united Jīng, Qì and Shén which is the Close part of the process.

After the baby is born, they no longer have the comfort and protection of the prenatal environment (mother's womb). As the baby's organs/systems start to carry out their relevant functions, they create the separation of the Infant/Child Hùn Yuán Qì into Jīng, Qì and Shén. The separation and unification of Jīng, Qì and Shén occurs in two stages.

1. Stage One

The first stage of the separation and unification of Jīng, Qì and Shén is from Birth to about age three. The first to separate and function independently is Qì. The Infant/Child Hùn Yuán Qì is different from the Fetus Hùn Yuán Qì. The fetus receives Qì, which is already processed and contains the human information from the mother. Basically, the fetus can receive and use the mother's Qì directly without any further refinement. Everything changes once the baby is born. The baby must obtain Qì from external substances and from Nature through the refinement process. They must break down the less complex and simpler, lower level substances into Qì, and add human information to make it comparable to their own Qì. Then Qì is transmuted with their own Qì to make it available for use by the body. Following Qì's Open-Close, Concentrate-disperse, In-Out and Huà movements, one forms a unique distribution system to supply the transmuted (postnatal) Qì to the body. This Postnatal Qì is more complex than the Prenatal Qì and is independent from Jīng and Shén.

Xíng is the next to separate and be independent. Xíng refers to the broader aspect of Jīng—the physical body which consists of cells, organs and systems. Although the fetus has a complete body, the organ functions are not operational. The sole purpose of the Fetus Hùn Yuán Qì is for physical development (the rapid multiplication of cells). Once the baby is born, they need to obtain and refine the external Qì to maintain life functions, and these actions are required to activate the functions of the organs/systems. Because each organ performs different functions that require a significant amount of Qì, once they become operational, the baby must provide the Hùn Yuán Qì to power these functions. In other words, the baby uses Hùn Yuán Qì in two ways, one is for physical development and growth and the other is for organ/system functions such as liver functions, heart functions and kidney functions. Since the baby's Hùn Yuán Qì is no longer just for physical development, Qì and Jīng will separate from the merged state of Jīng, Qì and Shén.

Shén is the last one to separate and be independent. It is established on the foundation of Xíng's separation, and as soon as the nerve cell functions are activated, Shén is separated. Xíng separation refers to the expression of individual organ/system functions; therefore, Shén's separation (the expression of nerve cell functions) should belong to Xíng separation. However, brain (nerve) cells are fundamentally different from other kinds of cells—they do not divide and multiply. The metabolism in normal cells provide energy to carry out their functions and self-multiplication; therefore, the Hùn Yuán Qì of normal cells has two purposes, one is for physical multiplication (material metabolism) and the other is for maintaining their functions (energy metabolism). Although brain cells have metabolism, it is not for self-multiplication. With one less function to perform, the sole purpose for the Hùn Yuán Qì of the brain cells is to carry out its functions which, at this stage, is to receive, to send and to transmute information. Since brain cells do not self-multiply, their efforts are united to carry out their functions. The function or activity of the brain cells is called Shén. Shén is based on the activity of brain cells that is independent from that of regular cells.

As soon as a baby is born, Jīng, Qì and Shén will begin their separation and unification. Separation and unification do not follow one another, they happen simultaneously. Separation means Jīng, Qì and Shén have their independent functions; unification means Jīng, Qì and Shén are united in action which is guided by Shén, carried out by Qì and expressed in Xíng. A baby's first independent movement will be used to explain the point.

All metabolism produces by-products and a newborn baby has no means to discharge them once the umbilical cord is cut. The first by-product that a new born needs to discharge is carbon dioxide built up in the body fluids and bloodstream. As the carbon dioxide concentration increases, it will stimulate the vascular wall, nerves and respiratory centers. With stimulation, the body will follow the genetic blueprint to concentrate carbon dioxide in the lungs and expel it with the first cry (exhalation). This exhalation involves the coordination of brain (nerve) and physical activities. To cry, the chest muscles, throat muscles and facial muscles must move. In order to move the muscles in the correct way, the movement must be controlled/directed by the nerves. A simple exhalation involves intercostal, laryngeal, lingual, hypoglossal, glossopharyngeal, vagus and phrenic nerves. To cry, all these nerves need simultaneous stimulations and perfect coordination. The first cry is the first separation of Jīng, Qì and Shén, and also this is the first unification of Jīng, Qì and Shén's functions to perform a common task.

As the baby develops, sensory organs/systems will separate and be independent; these developments enable the baby to see, hear and feel the external substances. External substances are wholistic with characteristics such as color, taste and shape when interacting with a human being. Because each human organ/system receives only partial information, the separation of Jīng, Qì and Shén is initially limited to basic life activities with innate abilities gradually uniting with individual functions to perform more complex functions. For example, when a baby hears a sound, they would be stimulated initially. Gradually, when a baby hears a sound, they would look for it, and the visual and auditory functions will be united. When they touch and feel the object, the visual, auditory and tactile sensory functions are united.

When a baby hears a sound, the body would not turn toward the sound or reach out to touch something unless instructed to do so by Shén (the brain) as the instructions are delivered by Qì and carried out by Xíng. Although there are sequences in the movement, they are carried out simultaneously. In the beginning, the separations within Jīng or Qì or Shén are macro separations. When a baby wants to touch something, they would move both legs and arms—the movements are whole body movements. As the baby grows, they will develop micro separations when all movements are more limited. For example, to look at something, the baby uses only the eyes, and to touch something, uses only the hands.

2. Stage Two

This stage refers to the period between age three and age six. The first stage is the separation of Jīng, Qì and Shén. Stage two is the refinement of the separated Jīng, Qì and Shén. In addition to growth and development, Jīng does not have too many changes between Stage One to Stage Two, but Qì and Shén have major developments.

In Stage One, Qì is evenly distributed. Following the changes in life activities, Qì functions begin to separate. From age three and beyond, Qì with similar functions begins to congregate in certain areas. Qì distribution becomes uneven, and some areas have more Qì than others. Consequently, according to its functions, three types of Qì emerge and form three congregation centers. The three types of Qì are Body Hùn Yuán Qì, Organ Hùn Yuán Qì and Yi Yuán Ti (Brain Hùn Yuán Qì). In Qìgōng, a congregating center is called Dāntián; the three centers are Lower Dāntián, Middle Dāntián and Upper Dāntián. A newborn does not have a Dāntián because the Qì of an infant is evenly distributed. Because an infant's Qi is evenly distributed, a baby can continue crying without becoming hoarse; however, an adult's Qi is divided and will become hoarse with sustained crying because the throat does not have enough Qi. This divided/uneven Qi also allows an adult to perform a particular task more efficiently.

In this stage, Shén begins to have its independent activities. A child's mental activities (Shén) gradually advance from sensorimotor thinking to logical thinking. Logical thinking is a unique human mental activity; therefore, it does not only separate Shén from life activities, it enables Shén to direct/control life activities. Basically, by the age of six, although a child's nerve cell is not fully matured, its structure is about the same as that of an adult; therefore, Shén can take the initiative to change life activities from reactive to active. The ability for Shén to direct life activities is not innate but is based on training.

> *Note: A child from 5 to 9 is not primarily a logical thinker. Mental activities/skills are developing but a lot of mental learning is rote. The chief characteristic at this stage is the development of emotional and imaginative capabilities. This stage is the final separation of Jīng, Qì and Shén. Shén separation is the beginning of mind activity. Logical thinking (Shén) is a learned behavior, not innate.*

A baby does not have the concept of space; therefore, when they see an object, no matter how far it is, they would reach out to touch it because there is no space between them. For example, when the baby sees a red pen, all that is seen is the color red and they assume that the color red is the pen. When the baby reaches out to touch the pen, there is nothing there. After many attempts, the baby would only recognize a particular red, not the red color in front of them which is actually the pen; therefore, the concept (shape) of the pen and space will be established. An object has weight, and one needs strength to pick it up. Touching an object with intent to pick it up would transform Qì into force, and this transformation will establish the connections between the baby and physical substances. All these "concept and connection" processes are slowly established in daily life activities and become automatic. When a child wants to pick up an object, Shén (mind intent) activates first. Once Shén focuses on the hands, Qì would follow and will be concentrated in the hands, and the concentrated Qì will change to force to move the hands. This process is called "Mind induces Qì, Qì induces Xíng," and "Shén moves, Qì moves, Qì moves, Xíng moves."

In conclusion, the changes in Infant/Child Hùn Yuán Qì can be summarized as the following.

- **Qì.** The content of Qì changes from Prenatal Qì to transmuted Qì. The Infant/Child absorbs the external (Postnatal) Hùn Yuán Qì and it is transmuted with the body (Prenatal) Hùn Yuán Qì to become Infant/Child Hùn Yuán Qì.
- **Xíng.** The main change in Xíng is the formation of Xíng functions. Life activities need Xíng to carry out/realize; and changing from Xíng to Xíng function needs Qì. The transformation and interchanges among Xíng, Qì and Xíng's functions are carried out in this stage.
- **Shén.** Shén absorbs the external information and Hùn Huà (transmutes) with the internal information. In this stage, Shén functions mainly to absorb as much external information as possible and transmute it to become their own. To function as an independent individual, one's Hùn Yuán Qì must be transmuted Prenatal and Postnatal Qì. The main function of Infant/Child Shén is to transmute the internal (genetic) information and external (environment) information together. Therefore, Shén not only permeates Xíng and Qì, it directs the functions of the body and unites with Jīng and Qì to form a wholistic entity.

E. Adult Hùn Yuán Qì

The fundamental difference between Infant/Child Hùn Yuán Qì and Adult Hùn Yuán Qì is that the former does not have the reproductive function Hùn Yuán Qì. As noted previously, in different stages of life, a plant has different wholistic characteristics. A seed may contain the wholistic information of the plant, but this information will not be fully expressed in all stages. Only when the plant is mature can all of the wholistic information be expressed, and only after expression (flowering and fruiting) can the realized Hùn Yuán Qì (Qì with wholistic information) be condensed into the seeds.

This change is also true for human beings. A baby/child contains the wholistic information of the person, but some of the information would not be expressed unless the organ is mature. Reproductive organs, which begin to mature around age twelve, are among the last systems to express their functions. When a person's reproductive organs begin to mature and express their functions, their Hùn Yuán Qì will become relatively whole and complete. Then Hùn Yuán Qì can be condensed into a substance forming a new entity (sperm or egg) which contains the wholistic (including reproductive) information. Therefore, a fully matured reproductive system indicates the optimal state of a person's development.

Basically, human beings have three types of cells, which express different life functions. The first type is the reproductive cells which have the sole function of reproducing offspring. They are sperms and eggs and exist as single cells. The second type is the regular cells and its functions are to self-multiply, to power life functions and to produce hormones. They are multi-cells such as muscle cells and kidney cells. The third type is nerve cells which cannot multiply and its functions are to receive, to send and to transmute information (between internal and external environment). In a sense, these three types of cells represent the evolutionary process of the biological world: from single cells needing a host object having only reproductive function to multi-cells having reproductive and life functions, to nerve cells which can interact with external factors, and to brain cells having logical thinking capacity.

In human beings, the reproductive cells are the foundation for reproduction, the regular (body) cells are the foundation for life activities and the nerve cells are the foundation for Shén (mind activities). These three types of cells are inter-related, they serve, complement/nurture and restrain each other. They all consume Hùn Yuán Qì and are affected by the area where the mind concentrates. When one's attention/mind concentrates in a certain area of the body, Qì will go there, and the functions in that area will be strengthened. One of the subjects of Qìgōng practice is to deal with this phenomenon.

Once an area is strengthened, should one keep on strengthening it or let go of it? For example, if Jīng, Qì and Shén concentrate on Jīng (reproductive system), Jīng will be very strong. Dàoist Qìgōng has two ways to deal with this issue. One is to follow the life functions of sperms and egg, and it will lead to reproduction. The other is to absorb the sperms and egg back to the body, and it will lead to the formation of a Dān (丹) to promote longevity of life. If Jīng, Qì and Shén concentrate on Xíng, the physical body will be strong; but doing things unnaturally will waste energy and will be harmful to the body. Following the natural way of doing things will be healthy. If Jīng, Qì and Shén focus on Shén, then the mind will be alert, but a self-centered attitude will harm Qì and a generous nature will increase wisdom.

III. The Movement of Human Hùn Yuán Qì

As noted in Chapter Two, Hùn Yuán Qì has seven movements, they are Open, Close, In, Out, Concentrate, Disperse, and Huà. The pattern of these seven movements is as follows : Open-Close, In-Out, Concentrate-Disperse, and Huà. Human Hùn Yuán Qì is part of Hùn Yuán Qì and it will obey/follow the same pattern. The human being is a very complicated entity, and its Hùn Yuán Qì movements are more complicated than Nature Hùn Yuán Qì. Hùn Yuán Qì movements can divide into two parts. Part one is Open-Close, In-Out, and the Concentrate-Disperse movements; part two is the Hùn Huà (混化 transmutation) movement/process. They are parts of the whole and cannot be separated. Part one is the preparation process for part two, and part two is the destination/purpose of part one.

A. Part One: Qì movement

The Open-Close, In-Out, and Concentrate-Disperse movements occur in two areas. One is on the external surface that is the contact surface between the body and the outside world. The other is the internal surface of the human being, a multi-level entity, which is the contact surface between different levels of the cells/tissues/organs.

1. The Open-Close, In-Out, and Concentrate-Disperse movements are on and in an external surface

The external surface means all the surfaces in contact with the outside world. The human being is a "donut" with a long-enclosed tube, which consists of the respiratory tract and the digestive tract, in the middle of the body. The external surface includes all the skin and the mucosa membranes of the tube.

According to the Hùn Yuán Theory, Hùn Yuán Qì exists in physical form and in non-physical (formless) form; therefore, the Qì movements inside the body also include the physical substance movements and the formless Qì movements. The movement of the physical substances depends on the physical body and follows the skin's Open-Close and Concentrate-Disperse rhythm. For example, there are pores, sweat glands and adipose glands in the skin; when they open, they can produce secretions such as sweat and sebum. These secretions will follow the Open movement to disperse outward. The skin can also follow the Close movement to absorb physical substances into the body. For example, many medications are applied externally and are absorbed through the skin. Body functions such as the skin and the mucous membranes of the respiratory tract absorbing oxygen and releasing carbon dioxide are accomplished through the movement of Open-Close, In-Out, and Concentrate-Disperse on the external surface of the body. The movement of physical substances is easy to understand

and observe, but it is not that easy to understand with the formless Qì. The Hùn Yuán Qì Theory considers formless Qi movement to be the more important of the two. When mentioning Qì movements, normally, reference is to formless Qì.

As mentioned in Chapter Two, every physical substance has a Qì Field surrounding it; together, they form the Hùn Yuán Entity. This is also true for human beings. The physical body is the physical form of Hùn Yuán Qì, and there is a layer of formless Hùn Yuán Qì engulfing the body. This layer of formless Hùn Yuán Qì is formed by the physical body's Hùn Yuán Qì dispersing outward through the openings on the body surface (skin), such as pores and acupuncture points. This formless Qì is at the forefront of the interactions between human Hùn Yuán Qì and Nature Hùn Yuán Qì; also, it is the transition area between Nature Hùn Yuán Qì and the human Hùn Yuán Qì. The closer to the body, the denser is the human Hùn Yuán Qì. When Qì reaches the body's surface (skin), structural changes will occur and the formless Qì will become physical Hùn Yuán Qì. This change is directly related to the Qì movements on the external surface. The external surface or a physical substance's Open-Close movement can affect formless Qì's movements (Open-Close and Concentrate-Disperse, etc.). Different types of Hùn Yuán Qì have different ways to adjust and to balance the two (form and formless Qì) movements. Human beings use breathing, tissue metabolism, and mental activities to regulate the Qì movements.

a) Breathing

In general, the skin's In-Out movement affects the Qì outside of the body directly. When one inhales, the body surface closes inward. Qì will follow the inward movement to go inside the body. The volume and density of the surrounding Qì will decrease and the surrounding Qì Field will contract inward. When exhaling, the surface area will expand outward, pores will open wide, and Qì will dissipate outward. The volume and density of Qì surrounding the body will increase and the surrounding Qì Field will expand outward. These movements are very obvious and noticeable in the large acupuncture points such as Yìntáng, navel, Huìyīn, Yǒngquán, and Láogōng. Some people can feel the Qì movements in these acupuncture points. The outward moving Qì is Body Hùn Yuán Qì that has structures that are more complicated and contain more information than the inward coming Nature Hùn Yuán Qì. Body Hùn Yuán Qì is a "coarse" Qì and Nature Hùn Yuán Qì is a "finer" Qì. Most people will feel the outward moving Qì, not the inward coming Qì. However, the In-Out movements occur simultaneously.

b) Metabolism

When the metabolism is vigorous, the amount of Qì will increase inside the body and create a higher (Qì) pressure than on the outside of the body. This difference makes it easier for the Qì to disperse outward. Consequently, the surrounding Qì Field will be strengthened. With a strong Qì Field, it is easier for the external Qì to go inside the body. One of the reasons practitioner feels very comfortable in a frequently used practice room is because the Qì Field's pressure increases with time and makes it easier for Qì to enter the body. Most External Qì healing methods use the Qì pressure technique. When one gathers External Qì, the collected and compressed Qì will create a Qì Field with higher pressure than the surrounding area to press the Qì into the body. Once Qì is inside the body, the pressure will be higher inside than that outside, then the body Qì will disperse outward.

c) Mental activities

Mind intent and emotions can affect the distribution of Qì. The mind intent's influences are controlled by subjective activities. Emotions are natural and objective activities. When one's mind intent moves or focuses outward, Qì follows and when one focuses inward, Qì concentrates inward. Visiting a museum should be a very relaxing experience, but after walking around viewing art for extended periods of time, one may feel exhausted. The reason for this fatigue is that one is focusing outward all the time, resulting in the dissipation of too much Qì.

According to Traditional Chinese Medicine, emotions such as startle/fright (恐), anger and sadness would disperse Qì, and pensiveness and fear can cause Qì to congregate inside. One might ask, is it possible to use just emotions to activate Qì movement? The answer is yes, but it is extremely difficult to regulate how much emotion one should use to do so. Too much emotion can lead to stagnant Qì and may cause illness. Instead of using emotion, most Qìgōng practices use sentiment/attitude. For example, instead of being fearful, one might become cautious.

> *Note: The Five-Element Method of Zhìnéng Qìgōng uses emotions/ sentiments to regulate Qì.*

Qì movement is a natural process—breathing is natural, metabolism is natural, and emotions are natural. Once the rhythm of Qì movement is understood, including the effects of mental activities on the Qì movement, the practitioner can enhance the benefits and avoid the hinderances to the natural process of Qì movement. The Open-Close and In-Out movements have been mentioned in this chapter often but not the Concentrate-Disperse movements. In fact, all of these movements are interconnected; they are not isolated from one another. Normally, the Open (of Open-Close) process is accompanied by the Out (of In-Out) process which will disperse Qì. Likewise, the Close process is accompanied by the In process which will concentrate Qì. However, the relationship between the movements is not absolute. Open does not necessarily accompany Out, nor Close accompany In; they are determined by three factors—breathing, Qì pressure, and mental activities.

Under normal circumstances, inhale would accompany Close, and exhale would accompany Open. With vigorous metabolism, Qì pressure inside the body is stronger and higher than outside pressure. When exhaling, it is natural to open and to release the pressure; consequently, Internal Qì will have Open, Out and Disperse movements/processes. As soon as the pressure is released, Qì pressure outside of the body will be stronger than inside and the External Qì will have Close, In and Concentrate movements/processes into the body. If Qì pressure is strong inside the body, it is difficult to press ("Close" and "In") Qì into the body from outside. Pressure inside may create resistance and closure to prevent Qì from entering; under this circumstance, Qì will become lopsided/unbalanced and it will be difficult to maintain life functions. Therefore, mental guidance is crucial to lead Qì In-Out of the body. These three factors (Breathing, Qì pressure and Mental activities) are interconnected. Qìgōng practice uses mental activities to direct the movements.

2. The Open-Close, In-Out, Concentrate-Disperse movement on the internal surface

The human body is a very complicated system consisting of many sub-systems; and each sub-system consists of cells. Within each sub-system, each cell has a membrane that acts as a contact surface/boundary with the external world (outside of the independent cell). Fig. 4-2. Cell Membrane Relationship to Human Body and External World.

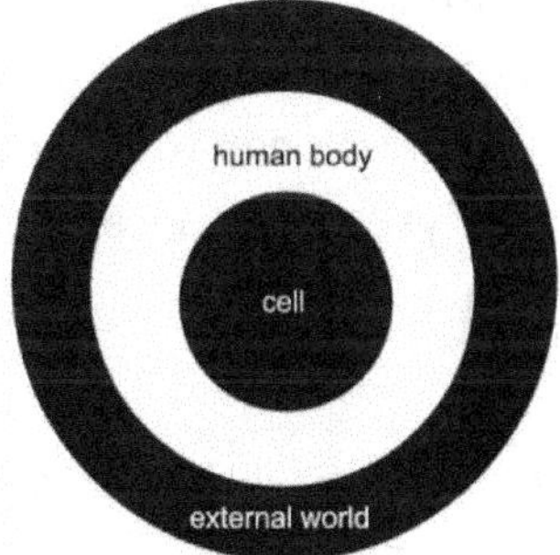

Fig. 4-2 Cell Membrane Relationship to Human Body and External World.

As indicated in Fig. 4-2, the human body is an independent entity that interacts with the external world. Qì movement occurs in the skin and the mucosa membranes of the respiratory tract and the digestive tract. The cell is an independent entity within the body. It uses the membrane to isolate itself from and to interact with the external environment. Qì movement occurs in the mucosa membranes.

While the body uses breathing, tissue metabolism, and mental activities to regulate the Qì movements, the cells use metabolism to create different Qi pressure among cells to lead to Qi movements since humans cannot consciously use their cells to breathe and their mental activities cannot reach the cellular level. With metabolism, Qì pressure inside the cell will be higher than on the outside of the cell, the membrane will expand outward and will open up the Qì pathways in the membrane. Qì inside the membrane will disperse outward to become part of Body Hùn Yuán Qì. Simultaneously, the Body Hùn Yuán Qì will be absorbed into the cell via the membrane.

B. Part Two: Hùn Huà (混化 transmutation) of Human Hùn Yuán Qì

The Hùn Huà process is based on Qì movements and occurs on both external surfaces and on internal structures. The Hùn Huà process can occur directly with the formless Qì which usually is the whole body Hùn Huà or indirectly with physical substances which usually are isolated (a certain part of the body) Hùn Huà. The transmutation of physical substances is very obvious—we digest (transmute) something we eat, and it becomes energy and nutrition. The transmutation of formless Qì is very difficult to comprehend, but it exists. The formless Qì transmutation can occur with very little physical substance such as food or be totally devoid of any physical substance to maintain life functions. In other words, human beings need nutrition from food to stay alive, but under certain circumstances, such as practicing a type of Qìgōng called "Bìgǔ (避谷)," some practitioners can live a normal life without any food for long periods of time. This is an innate ability in human beings except that some can do it better than others. All human beings are "programmed" to accept the fact that they must rely on nutrition absorbed from physical substances to maintain life functions; therefore, the formless Qì Hùn Huà "Bìgǔ (避谷)" function does not exist in our consciousness.

Note: Bìgǔ 避谷, Bì 避 means avoid, gǔ 谷 means food.

1. The external surface Hùn Huà (transmutation)

The external surface refers to the contact surface between the body and the outside world. The external surface Hùn Huà means the transmutation that occurs on the surrounding surface Hùn Yuán Qì Field. Because the transmutation between the skin and the outside physical substance is extremely limited, the external surface Hùn Huà mainly refers to the transmutation of food inside the stomach and intestine.

All physical substances have their basic elements/components. For example, cells are the basic elements of complex living organisms; amino acids and proteins are the basic elements of cells. A physical substance cannot be formed if the conditions for the basic elements' particular space and time do not exist. For the external substances to become part of the body, they must transmute with the human body to become basic elements for the human body. For the cells to form, physical substances must become amino acids first and this transmutation occurs on the surface of the digestive tract.

After the food is consumed, it must go through the Hùn Huà (digestion) process and becomes basic elements (nutrition and energy) before it can be absorbed into the body. For example, milk cannot be injected into the muscles; otherwise, it would cause fever. Without Hùn Huà, the milk Hùn Yuán Qì retains its own original characteristics which are not compatible with that of human beings. The Hùn Huà process breaks down large elements into small elements without their original characteristics so it can be absorbed into the body. For example, if one has a small house and wants to use its bricks to build a large house, one cannot just put the smaller one into the large house and make it part of the larger house. One must take apart the small house brick by brick to make these bricks part of the materials for the large house.

Breaking down food into basic elements is performed by enzymes. Enzymes are Organ Hùn Yuán Qì in physical form. Enzymes transmute the food into basic elements and transmute the incompatible food elements into compatible basic elements that can be absorbed into the body. After the external surface Hùn Huà (digestion), nutrition will be absorbed into the body and proceed to internal surface Hùn Huà to become part of the body.

2. The internal surface Hùn Huà

The internal surface refers to the surfaces of different layers of internal structures/systems/organs of the body. No matter whether it is the nutrients from the digestive system or the oxygen from the respiratory system, they must be conveyed to the cells by the blood before metabolism can occur. In Qìgōng, metabolism is a Hùn Huà process between the absorbed External Hùn Yuán Qì (nutrients) and the Human Hùn Yuán Qì, and it occurs inside the body. For the nutrients in the blood stream to become basic elements and to be absorbed into the body, they must go through further Hùn Huà (refinement). To become part of the Human Hùn Yuán Qì, the external substances must go through two processes. One is to break down the external substances into small elements, and the other one is to reconstruct the new small elements into larger elements. A physical substance is concentrated Hùn Yuán Qì with its own characteristics, and to break it down into small elements is to dissolve these characteristics. Reconstructing small elements into larger elements forms the basic elements that are compatible with Human Hùn Yuán Qì. For example, food is broken down into amino acids, amino acids are absorbed into the body, and amino acids Hùn Huà become proteins and become part of the body.

These concentrating and dispersing processes occur continuously inside the body. In the concentrating process (anabolism), the simple Hùn Yuán Qì is transformed into complex Hùn Yuán Qì (new entity). In the dispersing process (catabolism), large elements (complex Hùn Yuán Qì) break down into small elements (simple Hùn Yuán Qì) and become a new entity. In Qìgōng, this process is called Hùn Huà.

During metabolism, no matter whether it is anabolism or catabolism, a significant amount of enzymes are required. Enzymes are not readily available, they must be produced as needed. The production of enzymes is a very complicated process involving amino acids and genetic factors. In Qìgōng, enzymes are the concentrated Organ Hùn Yuán Qì and the production of enzymes is a "nothing to something" process. Metabolism is a process of merging Human Hùn Yuán Qì into a physical substance to become a new entity.

In catabolism, a complex substance breaks up and releases energy. This energy is the fuel for life functions/activities and is an energy source for anabolism. To form a more complex element, anabolism needs energy. Some of the energy released by catabolism will be re-integrated into and become part of the new substance. During metabolism, the energy and substance produced in different parts of the body has different purposes. The regular cells serve their own needs. For the inter-organ cells, besides serving their own needs, some of the substances, such as hormones produced by the endocrine gland and digestive enzymes from the digestive gland are for the needs of relevant body functions. For nerve cells, in addition to their own needs, they provide energy for mental activities. In other words, the Hùn Huà processes are not the same in the regular cells, the organ cells, and the nerve cells.

The Hùn Huà process is not just limited to the absorbed substances, it also includes the interaction with external substances. As long as there are interactions, there are Hùn Huà processes. For example, to pick up a glass, when the hand touches the glass, one's Qì and the glass's Qì will interact with each other; this interaction is a Hùn Huà process. A touched glass and a non-touched glass are not the same—a touched glass has one's Hùn Yuán Qì inside. The reason that most people feel comfortable with familiar things is that these things contain their information. Feeling, hearing, and seeing are all Hùn Huà processes. When a musician is concentrated on a piece of music, they and the music Hùn Huà (become) as one; even if someone calls them, they would not be able to hear the calling. But If their attention/concentration is no longer on the music, they will be able to hear the calling; they and the sound (calling) will Hùn Huà as one. There are many layers of the Hùn Huà process, and if one randomly pays attention to too many things, it is very easy to deplete Qì.

IV. The Formation of Human Hùn Yuán Qì

All human life functions, whether they are mental activities or life activities, are performed under the control of Hùn Yuán Qì. In other words, all human activities are Hùn Yuán Qì activities. These activities are carried out as metabolism, mental activities, and physical movements. These activities all consume Human Hùn Yuán Qì, but at the same time, they interact with External Hùn Yuán Qì, and Hùn Huà (transmute) the External Hùn Yuán Qì to become Human Hùn Yuán Qì to maintain the equilibrium of life functions.

In Traditional Chinese Medicine, the formation of Hùn Yuán Qì has two steps—they are Huà Qì 化氣 and Qì Huà 氣化. Huà Qì breaks down the physical substance into Qì. Qì Huà concentrates Qì to give birth to a new physical substance. In Qìgōng, the formation of Human Hùn Yuán Qì has two stages. In stage one, the Hùn Yuán Qì does not have consciousness (mental activities) and is called Life Stage Hùn Yuán Qì 生命層次混元氣. In stage two, the Hùn Yuán Qì has consciousness, can direct mental activities, and is called Human Stage Hùn Yuán Qì 人層次混元氣. When a baby is born, their consciousness is not fully developed and their Hùn Yuán Qì belongs to the "Life Stage." As soon as the baby begins to interact with the outside world, they will develop consciousness. Once the consciousness and Life Stage Qì Hùn Huà (are transmuted) as one, it becomes Human Stage Hùn Yuán Qì. The Hùn Huà processes, the formation of Life Stage Hùn Yuán Qì, and Human Stage Hùn Yuán Qì occur inside the body at all times.

A. The process of forming Life Stage Hùn Yuán Qì

The Hùn Huà (transmutation) process between a person's Hùn Yuán Qì and External Hùn Yuán Qì is the Life Stage Hùn Yuán Qì formation process. This Hùn Huà (transmutation) process occurs on both internal and external surfaces of the body.

1. The formation of Hùn Yuán Qì on an external surface

The external surfaces mainly refer to the digestive tract. This is a two-step process. The first step Huà Qì process breaks down the food into basic elements, and the second step Qì Huà process forms the Hùn Yuán Qì.

a) The Huà Qì process

As described in the Hùn Huà Movement section, before food can be absorbed into the body, it must first go through the Hùn Huà (also called Huà Qì) process in the digestive system to become "basic elements." As the Body Hùn Yuán Qì and the "basic elements" merge (Hùn Huà or Qì Huà), they will produce Life Stage Hùn Yuán Qì. From food to Life Stage Hùn Yuán Qì, there are two Hùn Huà processes.

- The Hùn Huà process between the digestive fluid and food.
  When the enzymes interact with food and break down food into basic elements, it is not just a simple digestive process; it is a complicated process involving concentrating Human Hùn Yuán Qì and then Hùn Huà with food. Every substance is a concentration of Hùn Yuán Qì and its surrounding surface has a Hùn Yuán Qì Field. The enzymes produced in the digestive system are the concentration of Human Hùn Yuán Qì which contain the body's whole (life function) information. During the process of digestion, the Hùn Yuán Qì of food interacts with Human Hùn Yuán Qì to break down food into basic elements that can be absorbed in the body. The Hùn Yuán Qì of food interacts with Human Hùn Yuán Qì via Hùn Huà (transmutation) process so that the food becomes compatible with Human Hùn Yuán Qì.
- The Hùn Huà process between the Hùn Yuán Qì Field and food (the basic elements) Hùn Yuán Qì.

The Hùn Huà process between the digestive tract's Hùn Yuán Qì Field and the compatible Human Hùn Yuán Qì will enable the digested food to obtain human information. Both Organ Hùn Yuán Qì and Body Hùn Yuán Qì's concentrating points are also located in the digestive system area. Hùn Yuán Qìào (混元竅), the concentrating point for Organ Hùn Yuán Qì, is at the center of the five inner organs. The Body Hùn Yuán Qì is concentrated in the area between the navel and Mìngmén. As noted in the section on the distribution of Body Hùn Yuán Qì, the Body Hùn Yuán Qì contains Reproductive Jīng, and Prenatal and Postnatal Qì. Together, these two groups (Body and Organ) of Hùn Yuán Qì have formed a very strong Qì Field. The Qì Field is like a magnetic field and food is like iron. When iron passes through the magnetic field, it will be magnetized. When food reaches the digestive tract, it will be affected by this Qì Field, and human information will be added into the food Hùn Yuán Qì.

b) The Huà Qì (Hùn Yuán Qì formation) process

As noted previously, all substances' Hùn Yuán Qì have their unique characteristics. Once a complex substance such as food is broken down into simple elements, the original Hùn Yuán Qì will be released in two ways. Some will be released as part of simple elements, and some will be released as formless Qì.

The simple elements are the digested food, such as amino acids and glucose. Although they are small, they are still physical substances with their unique characteristics. When food is broken down by enzymes, the simple elements retain their unique characteristics plus the addition of Human Hùn Yuán Qì. Although they are absorbed into the blood stream, they are not Human Hùn Yuán Qì. They have not become part of the body. They are the raw materials that can be used by Human Hùn Yuán Qì to transmute into Human Hùn Yuán Qì or the physical body. These simple elements are called "semi Hùn Yuán Qì." In Traditional Chinese Medicine, it is called Yíng Qì (營氣).

When simple elements transmute with Organ Hùn Yuán Qì (enzymes), some of them will not be able to maintain their original characteristics and become compatible with Human Hùn Yuán Qì, and exist as formless Qì. This formless Qì belongs to the Body Hùn Yuán Qì category and can be used directly by life activities. Normally, this formless Qì is stored in the membranes of the digestive system, and is present in the digestive tract, and participates in Qì Huà and Huà Qì (breaking down physical substance into Qì and concentrating Qì to give birth to a new physical substance). This formless Qì can also be moved by the mind intent—as the mind intent moves, the Qì follows, and the Qì moves very quickly. This formless Qì is called Wèi Qì (衛氣) in Traditional Chinese Medicine. It nourishes and protects the body. In addition to increasing the volume of Qì in the Dāntián area, Traditional Qìgōng practice cultivates this Qì so that it can be more responsive to the mind intent. This is the type of Qì that is referred to as Dāntián Qì in Qì healing, and is the Qì that is cultivated in Hard Style Qìgōng.

2. The Hùn Yuán Qì formed during the Hùn Huà processes in different parts of the body

When the nutrients (semi Hùn Yuán Qì or Yíng Qì), which are carried by the blood stream, reach different parts of the body, they will go through additional Hùn Huà processes with the Body Hùn Yuán Qì. After the additional Hùn Huà processes, they will lose their independent characteristics and will be absorbed into the body. Once they are absorbed into the body, their characteristics will be the same as that of the person and the Human Hùn Yuán Qì will be formed. During this process, energy will be released. Part of this energy will be consumed by human activities, and part of it will be used for the Hùn Huà processes.

There are many Hùn Huà processes (metabolism) happening inside the body simultaneously. There are Huà Qì processes of physical substances changing into formless Qì and Qì Huà processes of formless Qì changing into physical substances, and also the processes of concentrating and dispersing among the physical substances. All these Hùn Huà processes produce Hùn Yuán Qì that will become part of the physical body or will be used by human activities. This Qì is the Life Stage Hùn Yuán Qì.

B. The formation of Human Stage Hùn Yuán Qì

Because the Hùn Yuán Qì described above does not have any conscious activities, it is called Life Stage Hùn Yuán Qì. Only after mental activities are merged with this Qì can it then become Human stage Hùn Yuán Qì. Shén (mental activity) is the activity of Yì Yuán Tǐ (Upper Dāntián Qì). One of the characteristics of Yì Yuán Tǐ is that it can permeate every level of Hùn Yuán Qì in the body. When Shén merges with the Life Stage Hùn Yuán Qì, they will Hùn Huà to become Human Stage Hùn Yuán Qì. The Hùn Huà processes primarily occur in three ways.

1. Hùn Huà through the Nerve Cells

Human activities are controlled by the brain. All mental activities are transmitted to the responsive organs through nerve fibers and neurotransmitters. Every part of body has nerve cell receptors; therefore, the brain is connected with the body through the nerve cells. Shén (conscious activities) is the activity of Yì Yuán Tǐ (Upper Dāntián Qì). When mental information (Shén) is transmitted into the body, Yì Yuán Tǐ will merge with the body and transmute with Life Stage Hùn Yuán Qì to become Human Stage Hùn Yuán Qì. For the Yì Yuán Tǐ to merge with the body, it must overcome the barrier of Body Hùn Yuán Qì. The transmission of information depends on the chemical reactions and electrical pulses among the nerve cells, but under certain circumstances, such as stationary/fixed posture Qìgōng practice, Hùn Yuán Qì in the nerve cells and the Yì Yuán Tǐ can be connected directly. In conclusion, the Yì Yuán Tǐ connects with the body through the nerve fibers and Hùn Huà (transmutes) with Life Stage Hùn Yuán Qì through the nerve cells.

2. Hùn Huà through the secretions produced by Nerve Cells

Because the hormones produced by the brain (mainly from the Hypothalamus and Pituitary) are not only for the brain's own use but also for the whole body, the secretions belong to Organ Hùn Yuán Qì. The secretions referred to are the substances produced by the Yì Yuán Tǐ during mental activities. This is a "Wú (無 nothing) to Yǒu (有 something)" process. With mental activities, the structure of Yì Yuán Tǐ (Qì inside the brain) will change (go through the Hùn Huà process). When the change reaches a point at which it is no longer able to maintain balance, some of the Yì Yuán Tǐ will concentrate into physical (protein-like) substances. Some of these substances will be distributed to the body through the circulatory system, and some will be directly distributed to the cerebrospinal fluid by the brain's nerve cells. Through these distributions, the substances will Hùn Huà with Life Stage Hùn Yuán Qì.

3. **The direct Hùn Huà between Yì Yuán Tǐ and Body Hùn Yuán Qì**
Instead of relying on nerve cells or nerve fibers as intermediaries, Yì Yuán Tǐ will directly Hùn Huà with the Body Hùn Yuán Qì. This is a natural process, not a conscious process. This kind of Hùn Huà process is obvious and noticeable in our daily activities. When the mind (focus) moves, Qì will automatically follow. Also, this kind of Hùn Huà process shows up in the way that emotions affect Qì's movement.

Through the Hùn Huà processes, Life Stage Hùn Yuán Qì will have the characteristic of human information and will become Human Stage Hùn Yuán Qì. This is a gradual process. It starts from a fetus in the late trimester to the toddler stage. The formation of Human Hùn Yuán Qì follows the development of the physical body and its functions and consciousness. Because of the close relationship between mental activities and Body Hùn Yuán Qì, conscious activities, especially when one is in a serene state, can affect and change whole body functions.

Conclusion

This chapter primarily explains Human Hùn Yuán Qì's formation, characteristics, and its functions. Hùn Yuán Qì Theory considers that all human activities are Hùn Yuán Qì activities. Human Hùn Yuán Qì exists in three different forms: physical body (Jīng) is Human Hùn Yuán Qì's physical expression, formless Qì is Human Hùn Yuán Qì's normal existence, and the refined Human Hùn Yuán Qì is Shén. As a one-celled zygote, Jīng, Qì and Shén are transmuted as one. After birth, Jīng, Qì and Shén will undergo two stages of separation. The first stage which occurs from the period between birth and age three is the separation of Jīng, Qì and Shén. Stage two which occurs between age three and age six is the refinement of the separated Jīng, Qì and Shén.

As an adult, Jīng is the physical body. Qì is divided into Body Hùn Yuán Qì, Organ Hùn Yuán Qì and Brain Hùn Yuán Qì. Shén is the expressions/activities of Brain Hùn Yuán Qì. The fundamental difference between human beings and animals is that human beings have Shén. Shén is also called Yìshí. Yìshí means mental activities and social consciousness; it is the highest level of expression of Human Hùn Yuán Qì. Yìshí will be explained in detail in the next chapter.

第五章：意識論

Chapter Five: Yìshí Theory

Yìshí 意識 is usually translated into English as consciousness or mind activity. Zhìnéng Qìgōng defines Yìshí as a form of Hùn Yuán Qì movement of brain cells and is the activity process of Yì Yuán Tǐ. Yìshí is Yì Yuán Tǐ's response to the external environment, social information and internal life activities information. Yìshí is not only able to respond to the information it receives, it can also affect the external environment and bodily functions as well as dictate life activities

Consciousness is a form of activity that conceptualizes information. An object is a physical substance consisting of mass, energy and information. When the object is seen, it is a type of light stimulus which is converted into nerve impulses that are transmitted to the brain via the optic nerve. Because the mass cannot be transmitted to the brain, during the process, the mass is eliminated. The light stimulus activates the Hùn Yuán Qì of the brain cells, and Yì Yuán Tǐ analyzes and decodes the stimulus in the form of an image that contains energy and information. Once Yì Yuán Tǐ conceptualizes the image, the energy that forms the image is eliminated and what remains is the information—the concept of the object. Yìshí (consciousness) movement is to eliminate mass and energy and to conceptualize the information of the object. In order to understand Yìshí, Yì Yuán Tǐ will be described first.

I. Yì Yuán Tǐ

Yì Yuán Tǐ is a special Hùn Yuán Qì formed by the brain's nerve cells after the brain has achieved a certain degree of development. According to Hùn Yuán Qì Theory, a physical substance, which is surrounded by the uncondensed Qì, is its Hùn Yuán Qì in a condensed form. One of the characteristics of nerve cells is that they not only can absorb and excrete physical substances, they also can receive and send out information through energy during the metabolic process. This function enables the nerve cells to broadly receive and respond to the outside/external information, and also enables them to send out information to the external world. Because the nerve cells in the brain are very dense, when the brain is developed up to a certain stage, the uncondensed Qì surrounding the nerve cells will integrate as one. Consequently, the partial information received by the individual cell will be integrated as a whole. This new entity is able to receive and reflect information. Once it develops the ability to have logical reasoning, it is called Yì Yuán Tǐ.

Yì Yuán Tǐ contains all the information of the person. It has the ability to receive, reflect, store, integrate, analyze, and extract information. Also, it has the ability to send out information and instructions. When Yì Yuán Tǐ is not interfered with by external factors, it maintains its original even state, and if it is stimulated, it will produce responses to the stimuli. Yì Yuán Tǐ is both subjective and objective; it is the source of all mental activities.

A. The characteristics of Yì Yuán Tǐ

Yì Yuán Tǐ is a substance that is formless, shapeless, and is evenly distributed. Under normal circumstances, it cannot be seen or be touched. It co-exists with the physical brain but does not occupy any physical space. Its center point is located at the center of the cerebrum, and it is distributed all over the brain and the entire body. Yì Yuán Tǐ is a transmuted state of the functions in all of the nerve cells in the nervous system. Although its existence is primarily based on the physiological, chemical, and biological changes in the cells of the brain, it has a certain degree of independence, and can affect the functions of the nerve cells. The following are characteristics of Yì Yuán Tǐ.

1. Yì Yuán Tǐ is evenly distributed

Yì Yuán Tǐ is a transmuted state of the functions of the nerve cells' Hùn Yuán Qì. It is a special kind of Hùn Yuán Qì and its characteristics are defined by the unique functions of the nerve cells. All cells have a normal metabolism of substance and energy. The basic difference between the nerve cells and the regular cells is that only the nerve cells have information metabolism. Nerve cells can receive and send information directly, such as visual, auditory, taste, smelling, and skin sensations. Regular metabolism changes substances into energy or one substance into another substance to power life functions. Information metabolism in the brain is used directly by Yì Yuán Tǐ since information does not change into energy or physical substances. All metabolisms inside the brain serve the information metabolism.

Even distribution of Yì Yuán Tǐ occurs because of the functional and structural characteristics of nerve cells and the high degree of density among the brain cells, allowing the Hùn Yuán Qì from each cell to permeate and merge to create an evenly distributed field. For example, a marble jar with only a few marbles inside is not even distributed throughout the jar, but when full, the jar is densely packed with marbles and evenly distributed. There are billions of cells in a human brain, and they are connected with dendrites; this structural characteristic enables Yì Yuán Tǐ to function as one unit. When one cell moves, it can activate Yì Yuán Tǐ to move. The brain cells do not regenerate new cells; this property allows Yì Yuán Tǐ to function with minimum interference and to maintain its stability and evenness.

2. The Reflectiveness of Yì Yuán Tǐ

When a substance with a slightly different structure enters a homogeneous object, it will become noticeable. If the information the nerve cells receive is not synchronized with Yì Yuán Tǐ, it will create changes in the Yì Yuán Tǐ and the information becomes noticeable. This is called reflectiveness of Yì Yuán Tǐ. This reflectiveness is similar to a mirror reflecting a substance's physical appearance and color. But the reflection in the mirror is only the result of the optical difference of the subject which is its external surface and not the entire subject. Yì Yuán Tǐ has numerous layers and its reflection is three dimensional. What is reflected in Yì Yuán Tǐ is the entire information of the subject. In addition to reflecting external objects, Yì Yuán Tǐ also reflects its own internal conditions.

The reason the mirror can reflect the external subject is because it is very flat and even; if the surface is rough, it will lose its effectiveness. Because Yì Yuán Tǐ is extremely even, if the information the nerve cells receive is slightly different or uneven, Yì Yuán Tǐ will be able to reflect it. The ability to reflect things is different from person to person and depends on the conditions of the Yì Yuán Tǐ in each person. If the mind is agitated, it will be very difficult to reflect things. When water is calm, it can reflect things; when it has ripples, the reflection will be distorted. Also, if the water is clean, it reflects much better than when it is dirty. Yì Yuán Tǐ behaves the same way.

To improve the clarity/reflectivity of objective substances, one must improve the reflectiveness of Yì Yuán Tǐ. There are three major methods to improve the reflectiveness of Yì Yuán Tǐ. One method is to cultivate Qì to nourish the nerve cells that will gradually improve the evenness of the Yì Yuán Tǐ. It is a slow and long process. Another method is to eliminate agitation. Some Qìgōng methods require the practitioners to isolate from the outside world to eliminate its influence. These methods cultivate quietness/serenity to improve the clarity of Yì Yuán Tǐ. The last method is to produce a slow rhythmic movement inside the Yì Yuán Tǐ. This method does not focus on cultivating quietness. In this method, the mind intent moves in a slow rhythmic way. With slow rhythmic movement, all mind activities will be gradually merged as one and agitations will be eliminated. It is Yì Yuán Tǐ that cultivates quietness/serenity through movements.

3. Mobility of Yì Yuán Tǐ

Yì Yuán Tǐ has mobility and is dynamic. Once the Yì Yuán Tǐ is formed, all life activities such as time Information (functions) and space Information (structures) are reflected (presented) inside the Yì Yuán Tǐ. Because human functions are not static but are dynamic, Yì Yuán Tǐ reflects their mobilities. Yì Yuán Tǐ receives information as soon as it is formed. When information enters Yì Yuán Tǐ, the entering movement becomes a driving force that enables Yì Yuán Tǐ to have mobility, and this mobility enables Yì Yuán Tǐ to perform movements such as In-Out, and Open-Close.

a) Concentrate and Disperse

Hùn Yuán Qì has In-Out, and Open-Close movements, but these movements are passive; they are the result of metabolism and interaction with external substances. Yì Yuán Tǐ's movements are active movements. For example, when focusing on listening, Yì Yuán Tǐ's force is focused on the sound and is connected to the ears; when focusing on seeing, the attention will be on the eyes. All of these are "concentrate" movements of Yì Yuán Tǐ, and are active movements. When attention is distracted and a person is no longer concentrating on something, this is a "disperse" movement of Yì Yuán Tǐ.

b) Movement

The movement referred to is the special Yì Yuán Tǐ movement that can be either a "micro" movement of the basic information or a "macro" movement of conceptual information. The "micro" movement is an unconscious or an unintentional movement such as the integration of information in the process of forming a concept. A concept does not just appear but goes through an extremely complicated process to be formed. There is weak and scattered information throughout the brain; to form a concept, the information has to connect and act as one. To connect trillion of cells in an instant requires extremely high speed; therefore, the "micro" movement operates at the speed of light.

The "macro" movement of conceptual information refers to a movement that can be controlled such as mental activities. Once a concept is formed, the speed of the movement can be controlled. The "macro" movement is a conscious movement. In a controlled low-speed movement, one can use concentration to strengthen mental activities. But in an uncontrolled high-speed movement, it is very difficult to force-stop mental activities. For example, when distractions appear during Qìgōng practice, a person can guide mental activities without force and can easily remain focused. But if one keeps focusing on getting rid of the distractions, the result will be quite the opposite.

Unlike life activities having movements that are either active (self-initiated) or passive in reaction to outside stimulation, the movements of Yì Yuán Tǐ are processes that collect and analyze information which are neither active nor passive. When a person receives information (passive) or has a thought (active), Yì Yuán Tǐ treats both in the same way; it "scans" the information and goes through a series of collecting and processing actions to form a conclusion/pattern. Once a conclusion is formed, conceptual instructions will be issued, and movement will occur.

B. The Functions of Yì Yuán Tǐ

The functions of Yì Yuán Tǐ are the following: receiving information; storing, processing, and extracting information, and sending information.

1. Receiving information

One of the characteristics of Yì Yuán Tǐ is "reflectiveness." What is "reflectiveness?" It means to receive information. Receiving information is the function of "reflectiveness." It is a process of changing (internalizing) the information from the outside (the objective world) into the subjective world. There are two ways to receive information.

a) Receiving information through sensory organs

Most of the information received by human beings is through their sensory organs. When the sensory organs are stimulated by or contact with the external materials, they will receive and distribute information and energy. When the information reaches the brain, the brain will respond, and subsequently creates changes. Because all things have their own Hùn Yuán Qì, when the Hùn Yuán Qì of the brain cells changes, Yì Yuán Tǐ will reflect these changes. A single stimulation will produce a sensation, and multiple-related stimulations will produce perception. When a subject's whole information enters the Yì Yuán Tǐ, an image of the subject can be formed. Once the image is formed, one can recall the whole original image based upon the characteristics of parts of the image.

Every substance has many different characteristics. When a substance sends out information that is received by different sensory organs, it will stimulate the nervous system and cause different physiological changes. The information of the substance is disintegrated and is partially received by different sensory organs. The partial information received by the sense organs will be integrated once it enters the Yì Yuán Tǐ and the original information will be restored. In other words, Yì Yuán Tǐ will reflect/show all the information it receives from the sensory organs.

b) Receiving Information through extraordinary sensory perception

Yì Yuán Tǐ can receive and reflect/show the information from the sensory organs and other organs and also directly receive and reflect/show information. Unlike the partial information received through each sensory organ that must go through the logical processing to be restored as whole information, Yì Yuán Tǐ can instantly receive and process the whole characteristics (space and time) of the substance. This ability to directly receive information is usually referred to as the "extraordinary sensory perception method."

Whether the information is delivered through normal sensory organs or through the extraordinary sensory method, receipt by the brain depends on the evenness and the reflectivity of Yì Yuán Tǐ. Once the information is received, the important thing is to retrieve it. The empty space in the universe is full of information. Since most people cannot sense or retrieve the information, the space is considered empty. If the information from Yì Yuán Tǐ cannot be retrieved, it will remain inaccessible and Yì Yuán Tǐ is considered "empty." When a person receives the information, they should be able to sense it; otherwise, they have not received the information. The information that both sensory organs and extraordinary sensory perception receive is the information that one can sense.

2. Processing, storing, and extracting information

a) Processing information

Once the information is received by the sensory organs, it needs to be processed. For example, no one can remember how many cars were seen on the way to work two weeks ago. The information exists, but it is not processed, so it cannot be extracted. The reason a human being has the ability to recognize things and perform mental activities is because of Yì Yuán Tǐ's ability to process the information it receives. It is a two-step process.

Step one. When the sensory organs receive information from an object, the information will be reflected in Yì Yuán Tǐ. Yì Yuán Tǐ will process the partial information from each sensory organ and rearrange the information in a way that reflects the original state. This process is performed automatically—no mental activity is involved. For example, a significant amount of information is received from a person's sensory organs when looking at a water bottle, e.g., color, shape, volume, and water. Information such as color and shape will activate different nerve cells and will cause changes in Hùn Yuán Qì in the brain cells. Because the information is received separately, the change occurs separately. When the information received by different nerve cells reaches Yì Yuán Tǐ, it collects and processes the information, and integrates the space, time, and information into a whole. The space, time and information is the unified whole of the substance (water bottle).

Step two. This step condenses the whole, which has complex information, into simple information and presents it as a verbal phrase. This is a process of forming concepts that includes analyzing, interpreting, subtracting, and synthesizing the substance's information, and changing it from a solid image to an abstract form. Once the image/information becomes abstract and is given a name, it no longer occupies the original space but will enter another part of the Yì Yuán Tǐ, and will establish other systematic connections. Forming concepts is called the second step of processing information.

When we see a substance (i.e., fruit), our Yì Yuán Tǐ will collect the information from sensory organs. Yì Yuán Tǐ will reconstruct and reflect the information and the image of the fruit. As soon as the fruit disappears, the image will be gone. If we give the fruit a name, e.g., apple, although the fruit is not in front of us, when we hear the word "apple," the information of the apple will appear. Processing the information in its original form is step one; changing it to an abstract form is step two.

b) Retaining information

Hùn Yuán Qì has the characteristic of retaining information. Once information appears, Hùn Yuán Qì can retain it. For example, the air surrounding us has retained numerous amounts of information. All information that enters Yì Yuán Tǐ can be retained. The way Yì Yuán Tǐ stores information is slightly different from Nature (External) Hùn Yuán Qì. Nature Hùn Yuán Qì can retain information, but its concentrate-disperse functions are passive, it must interact with external subjects to retain the information. The concentrate-disperse functions in Yì Yuán Tǐ are active, no interactions with an external subject are needed. Once the subject (information) reflects on Yì Yuán Tǐ, the information will be conceptualized and stored by Yì Yuán Tǐ. Yì Yuán Tǐ and information do not occupy space and time; the information that can be stored is limitless. The information that is sensed or that one is aware of can be received and stored; the unsensed information that enters the Yì Yuán Tǐ also can be stored. The difference between the two is that the former is obviously present and can be easily retracted; the latter is hidden and is not readily available.

When information enters the brain, it will stimulate the Hùn Yuán Qì in the brain and will cause movements and changes. These movements and changes will be reflected on the Hùn Yuán Qì of Yì Yuán Tǐ and will lead Yì Yuán Tǐ to focus on the information. Consequently, the volume of information will be increased and strengthened; therefore, the Yì Yuán Tǐ is able to reflect the information more clearly and causes bigger changes in its Hùn Yuán Qì. When the changes in the Hùn Yuán Qì of Yì Yuán Tǐ reach a certain point, the information in Hùn Yuán Qì will be concentrated into a point and becomes a physical substance. Once the physical substance is formed, the information will disappear from the Yì Yuán Tǐ; it is concentrated into the brain cells and becomes part of the cells.

c) Extracting information

Yì Yuán Tǐ contains and stores all kinds of information which is received and stored both consciously and unconsciously. Conscious activity, such as a thought, connects a series of related information about a subject in the brain. For example, when we have a thought about John Doe, consciousness will scan, connect, and reconstruct a series of information about John Doe in the brain. Because Hùn Yuán Qì in Yì Yuán Tǐ has the complete information about John Doe, when consciousness concentrates to extract the information, the concentration will increase the volume of information it is able to extract; thus, it can extract the whole information about John Doe.

Extracting information is an active activity. It involves mind activities (thoughts), scanning and concentrating processes, and it also has directions and purposes. Yì Yuán Tǐ has initiative and mobility. The content of the activity of Yì Yuán Tǐ is to give commands (purpose). For example, if the purpose is to search for certain information, once the purpose is defined, the Yì Yuán Tǐ gives the command to search. Its searching speed is extremely fast and readily extracts the information from Hùn Yuán Qì and brain cells.

The degrees of effectiveness in receiving, storing, processing, and extracting information mainly depend on the sensitivity of Yì Yuán Tǐ. How the information is stored also plays a role. Information that is received and stored unconsciously is normally hidden and is difficult to process and retract.

3. Sending information to interact with objects or subjects

Yì Yuán Tǐ contains large amounts of information. In order to send out any information, the information first needs to be concentrated. This requires conscious/mind activity. Once a thought is formed, the information can be sent out by this conscious/mind activity. There are two ways to send out information.

a) By sensory organs

Human beings normally send out information through the nervous system. When a sensory organ is stimulated, Yì Yuán Tǐ scans the information and concentrates it to become a response/command. Then the information is sent out via the nervous system to interact with external subjects. But the nervous system cannot interact with external subjects directly, it relies on the sensory organs such as the muscular system, eyes and ears to carry out the interactions. Because the information the sensory organs sends out and receives is partial, the information the external subject receives is also partial.

The information the external subject receives is the information sent by a particular organ. Therefore, the interaction between the information and the external subject occurs in an area related only to that particular organ. If the information one receives is physical in nature, the interaction will be physical in nature. If it is chemical, the interaction will be in chemical in nature. The interaction will form a physical or chemical level of Hùn Yuán Entity.

b) By extraordinary sensory perception

In extraordinary sensory perception, a human being receives and sends whole/wholistic information between the person and an external substance directly. Extraordinary sensory perception does not rely on any physical organs. One sends out the wholistic information to interact with the external substance. This kind of interaction transcends the physical or chemical level of Hùn Yuán Entity; it belongs to the fiber of space and time of the Hùn Yuán Entity. Abilities such as see-through ability, emitting external Qì, and moving objects with the mind belong to an extraordinary sensory perception way of sending information. Technically, see-through ability belongs to receiving information, not sending information, because one must send information out first before one can receive information. In order to be able to see through an object, one must establish the connection with the object first, and then retrieve the information.

C. The formation and development of Yì Yuán Tǐ

1. The formation of Yì Yuán Tǐ

Yì Yuán Tǐ is the foundation of conscious/mind activities. It is the product of the continuous evolution of Primal Hùn Yuán Qì. As the Primal Hùn Yuán Qì evolves and develops, animals with a cerebral cortex that has special structures and functions will emerge. Yì Yuán Tǐ is the special form of substance movement within the cerebral cortex. Yì Yuán Tǐ also is the Hùn Yuán state (wholistic state) of the nerve cells when they develop highly specialized functions. When Yì Yuán Tǐ is formed, it is empty, does not contain anything and is extremely even and uniform.

Based on the history of evolution, human beings have evolved from animals. However, the structures of the organs in human beings are more advanced and complete and their functions are more specialized and refined. The cerebral cortex is highly developed, and the amount of brain cells and their structures are obviously different from that of normal cells—especially the connections between the cells. With the development of numerous connectors (dendrites and synapses) between the brain cells, human beings dramatically increase the volume of information in their brains. Brain evolution allowed the brain cells to connect and to form a wholistic entity. Once the entity is formed, it will allow the Hùn Yuán Qì from both inside and outside the brain cells to permeate and merge with each other to form Yì Yuán Tǐ. With the emergence of Yì Yuán Tǐ, the nervous system develops at a higher level and creates a foundation for individuality.

Animals can have memories and brain activities (thinking). Without the brain activities, animals would not be able to develop the ability to reflect/react to the outside world and to survive. Animals also have a cerebral cortex but it is very simple and only able to reflect the outside world in a non-specific way. Animals have the capacity of simple analysis and synthesis but most of them do not have advanced skills in language, conceptual or logical thinking. This kind of brain activity is called "Nǎo Yuán Tǐ" (腦元體). Although brain activities in animals are very primitive and simple, they form the foundation for the evolution of Yì Yuán Tǐ. Human beings have languages and conceptual thinking that evolve into logical activities and concepts and then abstract conceptions. The ability to abstract a concept allows human beings to separate from the individual concrete object. When a "car" is mentioned, it can be a "Ford," a "VW," a "GM", or none of the above; the word "car" is not a concrete object, it is an abstract concept. With logical thinking and abstract concepts, brain activity is no longer called "Nǎo Yuán Tǐ," it becomes "Yì Yuán Tǐ."

2. The development/changes of Yì Yuán Tǐ

Following its genetic blueprint, a fertilized egg develops into a fetus. At about the seventh month, the brain cells will be mature enough to have enough connectors to form an entity. As the brain cells develop and their Hùn Yuán Qì concentrates, the concentrated brain cell Hùn Yuán Qì is called Yì Yuán Tǐ. The fetus in the womb is in a developing stage with organs growing according to their genetic blueprint. This genetic blueprint is the result of the evolution of human beings from animals. Once Yì Yuán Tǐ is formed, the whole information from evolution will be reflected inside Yì Yuán Tǐ. Therefore, Yì Yuán Tǐ has the wholistic life information. The functions of the brain in the fetus are very low and have not established the functional connections with each part of the body. In other words, the fetus's brain is basically in a low-active state and is not able to fully reflect the existence of other things. Although it contains the whole life information, this information and its functions have not been expressed; Yì Yuán Tǐ is in the most primeval balanced state, which is basically "empty." At this stage, the Yì Yuán Tǐ is called "the Beginning Yì Yuán Tǐ."

After birth, the baby interacts with Nature and the outside environment and the functions of the infant's organs and body parts will gradually mature and establish a more independent life. With new life activities, Yì Yuán Tǐ will no longer be pure/empty, it will go through a series of changes.

a) The first change is from "the Beginning Yì Yuán Tǐ" to "I Yì Yuán Tǐ"

When the Beginning Yì Yuán Tǐ begins to accumulate information, it first forms "I" (oneself) and it divides the world into "objective world" and "subjective world." This "I" is the awareness of one's own existence. It is a function of self-consciousness. For example, when we self examine our behavior, the mental picture of ourselves is "I."

Once the baby is born, the external environment is completely different from the womb. The stimulations the baby receives are different for each part of the body. For example, the parts that touch the bed will be different from the parts that contact with air. These stimulations will leave objective impressions such as solid and emptiness in the brain. In the meantime, the functions of the inner organs begin to occur and all of these changes will be reflected in Yì Yuán Tǐ.

Shortly after birth, the information in the baby's Yì Yuán Tǐ will be increased significantly. Part of the information is the baby's own life information. Each body part has its unique life information, e.g., the hands' information is different from the heart's, and each organ has different information. The other part of the information is from the surrounding environment (Nature); the surrounding environment includes air, physical substances and other human beings. This is the first stage of "I" (Self) Yì Yuán Tǐ – It is the beginning of internalizing the external (objective) world.

At this stage, Yì Yuán Tǐ has not established the connections between itself and life activities, therefore, it is not able to function subjectively. It is basically in a reflecting stage – Yì Yuán Tǐ reflects/mirrors life activities. Although it has the capacity to receive and distinguish information such as good or bad, and right or wrong from objective world, it does not have the ability to direct life functions. In order to establish the connections with life activities and to be able to function subjectively, the Yì Yuán Tǐ has to go through a process. Yì Yuán Tǐ has to retain more information and becomes more complex. With increased information, one can slowly and gradually establish the subjective (conscious) world and give commands. It is only when one can use Yì Yuán Tǐ's functions that one can direct life activities. With only "the Beginning (empty) Yì Yuán Tǐ," one cannot direct the life functions.

Inside Yì Yuán Tǐ, the internalized external information (the reflection of the environment) is different from the reflection of one's life information, therefore, the reflection will be composed of subjective and objective information. But at the first stage of "I" Yì Yuán Tǐ, this information is merged as one and the distinctions between the internal and external word are blurred. When the baby begins to interact with the outside world, the subjective and objective worlds will gradually separate. This separation occurs automatically and unconsciously. When the baby looks at an object, their attention will go outward, creating the difference between the subjective (self) world and the objective (outside) world. When the baby touches the object, they will establish a relationship between the two worlds. This relationship will be reflected in the brain and will establish the subjective world (self) and the objective world. At this point, the Yì Yuán Tĭ is different from the "Beginning Yì Yuán Tĭ". It begins to have subjective movements and the "Beginning Yì Yuán Tĭ" is no longer empty/pure. The "Beginning Yì Yuán Tĭ" has evolved to become "I Yì Yuán Tĭ."

This "I Yì Yuán Tĭ" is not fixed, it is continuously evolving. It is a transitional phase from "Beginning Yì Yuán Tĭ" to "Partial/Biased Yì Yuán Tĭ," and the contents of "I" also are evolving. Strictly speaking, the existence of the "Beginning Yì Yuán Tĭ" and the "I Yì Yuán Tĭ" is very brief. Once the Yì Yuán Tĭ is formed, it will reflect the external information; it is no longer "empty/pure." Also, this external information is personalized as soon as it enters Yì Yuán Tĭ. Once that happens, "Beginning Yì Yuán Tĭ" will become "Partial/Biased Yì Yuán Tĭ."

b) Partial Yì Yuán Tĭ

As the baby grows, the development of the organs, especially the functions of the nervous system, will gradually become mature and complete, and the abilities for self-control and self-independence become stronger. With better understanding of the external world, the young child will gradually distinguish the difference between oneself and the rest of the world. As the distinction becomes clearer, the young child will know the difference between "me" and "them;" and gradually the surrounding world will be centered on "me." When the young child understands the meaning of "mine" and "theirs," the surrounding world will become secondary and will play a supporting role to the primary existence of "I (me)." In Chinese Buddhist philosophy, the surrounding world refers to "I belong to or my surrounding," and "I belong to" supports "I (me)."

Normally, the way human beings understand (connect with) the external world is through sensory organs and language. Because the information the brain receives from the sensory organs is partial, the reflection in Yì Yuán Tĭ is also partial. The information from language is the integration of language and substance by someone, and it is also partial. Therefore, the relationship between "I" and "the surrounding" is also partial. The Yì Yuán Tǐ in this stage is called "Partial Yì Yuán Tǐ."

Yì Yuán Tǐ itself is whole. It should reflect all the information from the surrounding environment. Why is it biased or partial? As mentioned earlier, Yì Yuán Tǐ receives information in two ways: by extraordinary sensory perception and by ordinary sensory organs. After a baby is born, they will be stimulated by the surrounding environment. The infant receives the wholistic information but will not be able to hold on to it. On the other hand, the information that sensory organs receive not only contains information, it also contains energy. It is much stronger than the wholistic information and leaves a bigger imprint in the brain. The development of a baby's life functions and consciousness are parallel to one another. Most activities are conducted under the direction of consciousness and verbal instructions. When adults use language to communicate with the baby, the information will be strengthened with energy. This is a normal human development, but from the perspective of Qìgōng, it is partial and biased.

In a sense, the name "Partial Yì Yuán Tǐ" is inappropriate. It is not the functions of Yì Yuán Tǐ, such as evenness, extremely fine and reflections, that have changed, only the information that enters Yì Yuán Tǐ is partial. Furthermore, this partial information will evolve to become the foundation or background for understanding the external world. Thus, the way a human being understands the world will be partial/biased and will remain as non-wholistic. This is called "Partial Yì Yuán Tǐ." In Chinese Buddhism, this partial/biased view is call Wúmíng (無明 cannot understand); it means that one will not be able to understand unless one becomes a Buddha.

It is not going backward when Yì Yuán Tǐ becomes biased, it is the result of continuing development. When a baby is born, they do not have any mental activity, their brain is "pure/empty." Through development, the "I" is formed. As a young child, the "I" is the center of the universe. Once the young child understands the meaning of "mine" and "theirs", the functions of Yì Yuán Tǐ and life activities will be separated, and will become independent from each other. As the "I" evolves, it will include all the "I" in physiological needs and rational needs, ideological "I" (subjective beliefs) and realistic "I" (rational thought). Yì Yuán Tǐ no longer just reflects the objective world or just functions according to physiological needs; the logical, subjective world is gradually formed, and Yì Yuán Tǐ begins to have certain degrees of logical thinking. This logical thinking is based on normal development and differs from person to person. The essence of Partial Yì Yuán Tǐ is that one uses sensory organs to interact with Nature. The information that one receives from the organs is reflected in Yì Yuán Tǐ, and is occupied by it. This information is not wholistic, it is partial.

c) Complete Yì Yuán Tǐ

One of the important aspects of Partial Yì Yuán Tǐ is that it does not utilize extraordinary sensory perception (commonly called Extraordinary Intelligence). Complete Yì Yuán Tǐ occurs after one has developed extraordinary sensory perception and utilizes it to interact with Nature. The information one receives from extraordinary sensory perception is wholistic; therefore, one can interact with Nature more comprehensively. Once the information is received by the brain, the Yì Yuán Tǐ will have/reflect two types of information, one from ordinary sensory perception and the other from extraordinary sensory perception. Both types of information can naturally interact with Nature. Since Yì Yuán Tǐ in this stage has/reflects both types of information, it is no longer partial, it is called "Complete Yì Yuán Tǐ." "Complete Yì Yuán Tǐ" does not occur automatically, it must be obtained by Qìgōng practice.

d) Integrated Yì Yuán Tǐ

Once Complete Yì Yuán Tǐ is established, the extraordinary sensory perception wholistic information in Yì Yuán Tǐ can be sent out to interact with Nature and/or oneself. This ability will change one's life functions from following sensory information nature to extraordinary sensory perception nature. Because the extraordinary sensory perception wholistic information in Yì Yuán Tǐ commands the physical body, life functions and Yì Yuán Tǐ will have the same characteristics. Yì Yuán Tǐ in this stage is called Integrated Yì Yuán Tǐ.

Yì Yuán Tǐ's change from "Beginning" to "I" to "Partial" to "Complete" and finally to "Integrated" is a process. The original Yì Yuán Tǐ is "pure/empty" — it can reflect millions of things. Once things enter it, it begins to have "I." This "I" can evolve in all directions and in human beings, this "I" becomes "Partial." From "Partial" to "Complete," it becomes "Integrated." Although there seems to be many stages in Yì Yuán Tǐ development, Yì Yuán Tǐ itself has not changed. The changes are actually different levels of information reflection that are also called frames of reference.

There must be a reference standard in the subjective world in order to make a decision or to change the objective world. When the subjective world (Yì Yuán Tǐ) interacts with the objective world, the information will be imprinted (stay) within Yì Yuán Tǐ. These imprints of information become the background and reference points for understanding and interacting with the objective world. The information that is received primarily through sensory organs and language takes time to accumulate; therefore, the reference point will change accordingly. Consequently, Yì Yuán Tǐ will reflect different information. A different frame of reference creates a different reflection of information To understand Yì Yuán Tǐ, one must first understand the frame of reference.

D. The Frame of Reference of Yì Yuán Tǐ

A frame of reference normally refers to the standard of an object or system with which others are compared to. In Yì Yuán Tǐ, its meaning is different, and its definition is the following:

The frame of reference represents the different characteristics of the objective world that are internalized by sensory organs and that become parts of the overall space and time structure of Yì Yuán Tǐ. The frame of reference of Yì Yuán Tǐ is the internal prescriptive standard for all the activities of consciousness and is the standard by which the objective world is measured, evaluated and compared by consciousness. The frame of reference is the foundation that human beings rely on for their knowledge, judgment and behavior. It is the background for all human consciousness/ logical activities.

1. The formation of the Reference System of Yì Yuán Tǐ

Nature contains all types of information. Once the Yì Yuán Tǐ is formed, it will receive, store and reflect all the information that enters it. This information will remain in hibernation until it is unlocked by experience and knowledge as one evolves.

Yì Yuán Tǐ receives information from ordinary sensory perception and extraordinary sensory perception. As information from the environment, human relationships, language and consciousness repeatedly enters Yì Yuán Tǐ, it will be strengthened and activated. The strengthened information will be changed/ internalized from general to specific, from simple to complex in Yì Yuán Tǐ, and will become the contents of the subjective world. When the information is internalized to a point at which it is no longer able to maintain balance, it will concentrate into a physical substance and changes will occur in the brain's nerve cells; therefore, the internalized information will be fixed in Yì Yuán Tǐ. Once the internalized information is fixed, it will become a form of Hùn Yuán Qì and a new addition to the existing content of Yì Yuán Tǐ. These contents will become the blueprints for recognizing things in the objective world and will serve as the background for all newly acquired information.

The reference system in Yì Yuán Tǐ is not absolute or fixed; it evolves with the continuing development of Yì Yuán Tǐ. For a child, the reference system is very simple. As one gains experience and knowledge, the contents in the reference system will grow. It is the reflection of the objective world in Yì Yuán Tǐ, and is the result of the objective world being internalized in the subjective world. It contains the most basic information about Nature, and the information on relationships and interactions between all things. Because ordinary sensory perception is used to interact with Nature (space and time), the brain will have the concept of space and time, and will use this concept as a reference point when interacting with the environment. The information that enters first will serve as background/reference for future information and interaction with environment. Because the background, experience, and the internalized information are different from person to person, the reference system will vary in each person.

The concept of a Reference System is like a glass (mirror). When Yì Yuán Tǐ is formed, it behaves like glass, empty with no reflection. As information enters Yì Yuán Tǐ, Beginning Yì Yuán Tǐ will behave like a glass (mirror) with mercury in the back and it will reflect all things as they appear. In Partial Yì Yuán Tǐ, the back of the glass is no longer mercury, it will be material with different colors, which are dictated by the frame of reference (background) of the person. A mirror with tinted color on the back will reflect things with tinted color, and the appearance of things will all be based on the color and will be different from the actual appearance.

2. The relationship between Yì Yuán Tǐ and the Reference System

Yì Yuán Tǐ is like a mirror—it is even, fine, reflective and empty, but it also has mobility. Once it moves, it will have content. The contents are the background of the movements and belong to the Reference System. In other words, information entering Yì Yuán Tǐ is a movement, once it enters, it becomes content. The control of movements belongs to the Reference System and follows the protocols in the Reference System. For example, stealing food in order to survive may be considered by some to be reasonable, but to people who have plenty to eat, it may be considered illegal. Two different Reference Systems with the same content may result in different conclusions. Different conclusions reflect the event differently.

Deciding what to do or how to evaluate a thing is controlled by the Reference System. For the hungry, the reference point is for survival, therefore, taking food from other people is considered a necessity. For the well-fed, the reference point is stealing—it is illegal. In a sense, the "emptiness" characteristic of Yì Yuán Tǐ is replaced by the Reference System. When Yì Yuán Tǐ is empty, it does not distinguish between conditions but only reflects them. All movements, all decisions are decided by the Reference System. The relationship between Yì Yuán

Tǐ and the Reference System is that Yì Yuán Tǐ is primary and the Refence System is secondary when there is no movement/decision. Once distinguishing movements/decisions are made, then the Reference System becomes primary and Yì Yuán Tǐ becomes secondary.

Although Yì Yuán Tǐ is divided into four stages according to its development, there are very few changes in Yì Yuán Tǐ itself. The changes mainly occur in the Reference System. The Reference System in "the Beginning Yì Yuán Tǐ" is like a sheet of blank paper. In "I Yì Yuán Tǐ," it has simple "subjective" and "objective" worlds, but they are the same and indistinguishable. In "Partial Yì Yuán Tǐ," the "subjective" and the "objective" worlds are defined and become biased. In "Complete Yì Yuán Tǐ", it has "Ordinary" and "Extraordinary" perceptions. In "Integrated Yì Yuán Tǐ", it merges Man and Nature as one. Yì Yuán Tǐ reflects the subjective world; once the Reference System changes, it will change. It is the contents of the Reference System that are added into the "empty/pure" Yì Yuán Tǐ, and the changes in the Reference System that will create the "changes" in Yì Yuán Tǐ.

II. Yìshí and Yìshí Activity

A. The Definition of Yìshí

Yìshí 意識 is usually translated into English as consciousness or mind activity. To most westerners, the word "consciousness" connotes the relationship between the mind and the world, or the relationship between the mind and deeper truths that are thought to be more fundamental than the physical world. In his book, *Cosmic Consciousness: A Study in the Evolution of the Human Mind*, Psychiatrist Richard Maurice Bucke distinguished between three types of consciousness: "Simple Consciousness," an awareness of the body, possessed by many animals; "Self Consciousness," an awareness of being aware, possessed only by humans; and "Cosmic Consciousness," an awareness of the life and order of the universe, possessed only by human beings who are enlightened.

In Chinese culture, depending upon the context, the name and definition of mind activity (neural activity or consciousness) is different. Traditional Chinese Medicine calls it Xīn 心 (Heart), Buddhism calls it Shì 識, Daoism calls it Shén 神, and philosophy and general science call it Yìshí. Nowadays, Yìshí is an acceptable term to describe mind activity, but each school maintains its unique definition.

1. Traditional Chinese Medicine

Traditional Chinese Medicine (TCM) defines Yìshí as the entire thinking process, which includes perception of, response to and reasoning about the external environment. TCM calls this process "mind activity." According to The Yellow Emperor's Classic of Internal Medicine, this process has six levels/steps.

- Xīn 心: the ability/function that can reflect things. Xīn does not perceive, it only reflects.
- Yì 意: the ability/function that can recall or remember what is reflected in Xīn.
- Zhì 志: the ability/function that can maintain things (thoughts) in Yì.
- Sī 思: the ability/function that can consider and follow changes in Zhì.
- Lǜ 慮: the ability/function that can follow Sī to think in detail.

所以任物者謂之心, 心有所憶謂之意, 意之所存謂之志, 因志而存變謂之思, 因思而遠慕謂之慮, 因慮而處物謂之智.

黃帝內經

Xīn, Yì, Zhì, Sī, Lǜ and Zhì are all mind activities and collectively are called Yìshí or Yìshí activities.

Note: Xī 心 has two meanings, one is the heart, the other is the mind (consciousness and thought) with emotion or feeling. Sī 思 is regular consideration, Lǜ 慮 is detailed consideration, much deeper and broader. Zhì 智: the behavior and/or action one takes after Lǜ is Zhì. (Both 志 & 智 have the same Pīnyīn.)

2. Buddhism

The term Yìshí originated from Chinese Buddhism. Yìshí consists of two words, Yì 意 and Shí 識. Yì means thinking, pondering and considering; Shí means differentiating, comprehension and understanding. Both Yì and Shí are the function of Xīn 心 and the reflection of the mind. Although Xīn, Yì and Shí are slightly different, they are embodied as one. Xīn is divided into eight Shís, and the eight Shís are the eight kings of Xīn 八識心王. The Eight Shís (Eight Consciousnesses) are:

- Eye Shí 眼識
- Ear Shí 耳識
- Nose Shí 鼻識
- Tongue Shí 舌識
- Body Shí 身識
- Yì (Mind) Shí 意識
- Root Shí (mānas-vijñāna) 末那識 (意根)
- Alaya Shí 阿賴耶識

Chinese Buddhism considers human beings and Nature to be united in Xīn. The first five Shís are receptive Shí. They receive/reflect partial information but cannot interpret information. For example, eyes can see but cannot distinguish the difference between existing and non-existing; things do not exist until the eyes and Xīn and united. All the colors and shapes one sees are the functions of the eyes; nothing exists until the eye functions are united with Xīn. Substances do not have any meaning until they are interpreted by Xīn. When one interprets things, it is the function of Yì Shí (the sixth Shí).

Yì Shí has the function of logical reasoning, it can distinguish the difference among substances. Once any of the first five Shís is activated, Yì Shí will follow. The first five Shís are externally oriented and Yì Shí is internally oriented. Root Shí and Yì Shí are connected; Root Shí is the root of Yì Shí. Root Shí's function is to consider/contemplate; it is always self-centered, and it is the commencement (activation) point for Yì Shí. Alaya Shí controls all Shí and it contains the seeds of the universe. A tree is used as an example to illustrate the relationship among the Eight Shís. The first five Shís are the leaves and branches. Leaves and branches depend on the trunk which is Yì Shí (sixth Shí). Leaves, branches and trunk depend on the root which is Root Shí (seventh Shí) to survive. The eighth Shí is the seed. The seventh and eighth Shí are in a hidden state, only the Buddhist can see it.

Chinese Buddhism considers that the physical realm is the phenomenon of consciousness. It summarizes the relationship between Yìshí and the universe as:

> Ten thousand Fǎ 法 begins with Yuán 缘, all are created by Xīn.
> 萬法從緣起,一切唯心造.
>
> *Fǎ 法 means substances with forms and shapes. Yuán 缘 is the conditions/environment that enables the formation of a substance. Xīn means the mind. Therefore, the sentence means that all things are created by Yìshí.*

3. Daoism

Daoism does not use the term Yìshí, it calls consciousness Shén 神. Shén can be divided into Yuán Shén 元神, Shì Shén 識神 and Zhēn Yì 真意.

- Yuán Shén 元神: Manuscript Mài Wàng 脉望 explains that *"What is Yuán Shén? When there are no thoughts that arise from within and no thoughts that enter from without, and that the mind is fully independent, it is called Yuán Shén."*
  何為元神? 內念不萌,外想不入,獨我自主,謂之元神.

Yuán Shén is the state in which the mind is empty, and there is no mental activity, no distractions from desire, thinking and reasoning. Yuán Shén is innate and all mental activities are based on it. Yuán Shén corresponds to Alaya Shí in Buddhism or the Beginning Yì Yuán Tǐ in Zhìnéng Qìgōng.

- Shì Shén 識神: It refers to all mental activities including emotions. Shì Shén is learned behavior. Qìgōng master Huáng Yuánjí 黃元吉 says that: *Shì Shén has mind intent, Yuán Shén has no mind activity.* Shì Shén corresponds to Yì Shí in Buddhism or to the Partial Yì Yuán Tǐ in Zhìnéng Qìgōng.
- Zhēn Yì 真意: It is the ability to be aware of Yuán Shén. When one is aware of Yuán Shén, the mental activity following the awareness is called Zhēn Yì.

Shì Shén is the activity of the brain. Once Shì Shén exists, it occupies Yuán Shén and its activities rely/depend on Yuán Shén. Water will be used to explain the relationship between Yuán Shén and Shì Shén. Calm water is Yuán Shén. When the wind blows (thoughts arise), the water will have waves and the waves rely/depend on water; and the wave is Shì Shén. With or without waves, the water (Yuán Shén) does not change, it remains the same.

4. Zhìnéng Qìgōng

In Zhìnéng Qìgōng, Yìshí is defined as a special form of substance movement. It is the state/condition of Yì Yuán Tǐ's activity, and the content and process of Yì Yuán Tǐ's activity. Zhìnéng Qìgōng defines Yìshí in three classifications.

- Narrow sense: Yìshí is the conceptual activities in a subjective world. It is the logical reasoning and vocabulary that one uses when contemplating a question/problem.
- Broad sense: Yìshí is all life activities in a subjective world. There is no conceptual reasoning in the movement. For example, when needled by a sharp object in the hand, a human being will feel pain and will withdraw the hand automatically. Zhìnéng Qìgōng considers this kind of life activity a Yìshí activity.
- Extraordinary sense: Yìshí is the wholistic function of Yì Yuán Tǐ, only people with extraordinary abilities have this kind of Yìshí activity.

Yìshí is the reflective response to the internal and external information that one encounters during the activity/process of life. Therefore, Yìshí's contents and expressions are different in each stage of life. For example, although a baby is unable to use concepts, their Yì Yuán Tǐ is able to command movements of the body and has the ability to distinguish among the senses. The contents and expressions of the baby's Yìshí are mainly movements and tactile sensations. For a young child, thinking will be based on "imagery thinking" and for an adult, it will be based on logical thinking. In Qìgōng practice, when a practitioner reaches a certain level of proficiency, they will be able to change from logical thinking to wholistic thinking—using Yì Yuán Tǐ to directly observe and direct life activities.

B. The Classification of Yìshí

In the preceding section, Yìshí was briefly described according to the definitions of various schools. To better understand Yìshí, it will be classified into two categories.

1. Classification based on the contents of Yìshí

This category can be divided into five sub-categories.

a) Intuitive movement and intuitive sensorimotor movement

- Intuitive movement: It is the body movement directly integrated with mental activity without the involvement of conceptual or logical thinking/ reasoning. When a child learns to walk, they may be able to say the word "walk", but they do not have the concept of walking. Therefore, when the child hears the command "walk," the mental activity "walk" will become movement; there is no concept of walking nor logical thinking involved. While being chased by a dog, if confronted by a ditch, a person would not ponder whether they are able to jump over it or not, they would just jump because their mental activity is to jump. Mind and movement are integrated, it is an intuitive movement.
- Intuitive sensorimotor movement: When the hand touches a hot object, a person would automatically withdraw the hand. The sense/thinking at that instant is "hot," and action follows. The concept of hot that may lead to burning would not occur.

Some people may consider intuitive movement and intuitive sensorimotor movement very elementary but in fact, these movements are the most basic, economical (energy sufficient) body and mind integration method. One of the purposes of Qìgōng cultivation is to obtain body and mind integration.

b) Imagery thinking

The process of a baby familiarizing with something begins with the sensation of touch, then the awareness of existence and finally to the thought of image/ imagery. An image is a substance's complete picture/shape with many types of information merged together. Before the baby develops logical thinking, their primary mental activity is imagery thinking. The characteristic of imagery thinking is that it consists of distinctive imagery which has collective information and is relatively easy to activate and to follow. For example, to meet someone at a certain place, logical thinking will involve logistical thinking that becomes complicated. In imagery thinking, one merely imagines getting there and the process is much simpler. One of the main tool artists and Qìgōng practitioners use is imagery thinking. Imagery thinking can activate Qì quickly.

c) Conceptual thinking

Conceptual thinking is the normal way of thinking, e.g., should I take a vacation or what is the best way to do this? In most abstract reasoning such as mathematics, theoretical theories are based on conceptual thinking. This type of thinking does not have imagery, it conceptualizes the physical substance. Because conceptual thinking is separated from the physical substances (imagery), its effect on Qì is limited.

d) Observation

Observation means to observe the life activities/changes inside the body. In Qìgōng, observation is different from that of psychology which only observes changes and does not intervene in the change process. In Qìgōng, the process of observation is to observe and to sense/perceive, and the focus is on the life activities that are related to Qìgōng practice. The objective is to observe life activities (movement) and the changes created by life activities. This type of observation is called inward-focusing Yìshí motion. Therefore, the purpose of observation in Qìgōng is to be aware of the life activities inside the body so that one can change or improve them. There is no logical thinking involved. In Qìgōng observation, one remains quiet and calm to feel/sense the internal movements and one does not use the eyes to observe but uses the senses to "see" inside the body. This observation process is called "internal vision 内視" and the feeling that one senses is called "internal phenomenon 内景." Logical judgment is not involved in this process.

e) Specific Yìshí activity

Specific Yìshí activity refers to the specific Yìshí functions possessed by high level Qìgōng practitioners or people with extraordinary ability. Normal Yìshí activity (conceptual thinking) is restricted to space information. Specific Yìshí activity is time and space information. This Yìshí activity is based on Integrated Yì Yuán Tǐ that can directly capture the wholistic information of an object. For most people, the inspiration of an idea that is experienced or that is received from a dream belong to Specific Yìshí activity; however, this type of information is unconscious and cannot be controlled. One of the objectives of Qìgōng cultivation is to find the rhythm of the Specific Yìshí activity and to learn how to control it.

All of these sub-categories exist in adults and can be expressed in certain circumstances.

2. Classification based on the direction of Yìshí

This category refers to the direction of mental activity or thinking that one has during Yìshí activity. It is divided into two sub-categories.

a) Outward Yìshí activity

Outward Yìshí activity refers to mental activity that is not related to internal life functions (activities). It is the normal Yìshí activity for most people. For example, when we look at a glass, our Yìshí activity is on the glass. The glass and life function are not related; the glass is not part of life functions, it is "outside" or external to internal functions. Therefore, as soon as we think (are aware) of the glass, Yìshí activity will migrate to outside of the body. This is call outward Yìshí activity. Strictly speaking, all Yìshí activities outside of Yì Yuán Tǐ are outward Yìshí activity. For example, in Qìgōng practice, when the focus is on the body, it is an outward Yìshí activity because the body is not part of Yì Yuán Tǐ.

When one focuses on or thinks about something, the mind always expands or diverges outward from the core issue. For example, when working on a construction project, one's mind does not only focus on the project, the mind also expands to the related issues such as materials and labor. Materials and labor are an extension of the core issue. All judgement, logical reasoning and memory are outward focusing. Qì follows the mind intent; therefore, from the perspective of Qìgōng, the disadvantage of outward Yìshí activity is that it leads Qì to move out of the body. If one focuses on the external objects too often, this outward Yìshí activity may lead to draining one's Qì. One of the reasons that there is more Qì on the skin is because of outward Yìshí activity.

b) Inward Yìshí activity

Inward Yìshí activity is the opposite of outward Yìshí activity because during Inward Yìshí activity the focus is on the awareness of internal conditions in the body. During Inward Yìshí activity, consciousness focuses on the activity and merges the Yìshí activity (mind intent) with life functions. Most Qìgōng practitioners use Inward Yìshí activity to cultivate Qì. For example, in Qìgōng breath cultivation practice, the practitioner uses breathing techniques to focus on the movement of breath, and some practitioners may follow the breath to listen to heart beats, in order to allow Yìshí activity and life activity to merge as one; consequently, Yìshí activity will stay within the body. At the beginning, a practitioner merges Yìshí activity with Xìng 形. With further development, the practitioner progresses to merging Yìshí activity with Qì. At an advanced level of practice, the practitioner progresses to merging Yìshí activity with Yì Yuán Tǐ (Shén 神). To merge Yìshí activity with Yì Yuán Tǐ is extremely difficult, Yì Yuán Tǐ is formless, once the mind thinks of it as something with form, it is no longer Yì Yuán Tǐ.

Concentrating scattering thoughts into a single area/point or simplifying complex thoughts into a simple one also can be considered as inward Yìshí activity. When working on a project, one would look at situations from all angles, and the project can become very complicated. For example, when preparing dinner, one needs recipe, ingredients, and needs to consider dietary restrictions. During the preparation, it is an outward Yìshí activity but once one begins to cook, focus is on one task at a time and it becomes inward Yìshí activity. Some Qìgōng practices use repetitive movements/ patterns to concentrate the mind. Focusing on body movements is Yìshí merging with life activity; by focusing on body movements, Yìshí can strengthen life functions. Also, when the mind is inward focusing, Qì will automatically concentrate in the body and will merge with life activity; consequently, it will strengthen the function of Shén. Buddhist Chán (Zen) Qìgōng 禅宗 uses the "substitute thousand thoughts with one" technique to achieve inward Yìshí activity. Chán (Zen) Qìgōng emphasizes Shén (mind) so that inward Yìshí activity contributes to tranquility much faster than most other types of Qìgōng; however, because the focus is on Shén, inward Yìshí activity does not merge with life activity, and the changes of Qì inside the body are not very obvious. Therefore, Chán (Zen) Qìgōng's effects on the physical body are relatively slow. Some Daoist Qìgōng use techniques that focus on the life functions (internal feelings) while merging Shén and Qì. These practices can strengthen the body but are difficult to do. Zhìnéng Qìgōng uses a simpler technique, one that focuses on just Xíng, or Qì or Shén—as long as one can focus on one of these three, one can achieve inward Yìshí activity.

C. The formation of Yìshí

As noted previously, all formations are Hùn Huà processes, and Yì Yuán Tǐ is a special type of Hùn Yuán Qì formed by the brain's nerve cells after the brain has achieved a certain level of development, and Yìshí is Yì Yuán Tǐ's activity process (special Hùn Yuán Qì movement). Therefore, Yìshí's formation is a Hùn Huà process that can be Prenatal and Postnatal Yì Yuán Tǐ hùn huà (transmutation) or the brain and Yì Yuán Tǐ hùn huà.

1. Prenatal (pre-existing) and Postnatal (post-existing) Yì Yuán Tǐ transmutation

In this context, Yì Yuán Tǐ is both Prenatal and Postnatal. In human beings, Yì Yuán Tǐ, which provides the conditions for Yìshí to exist, is formed around seven months after conception—Yìshí does not exist at this stage of fetal development. Yì Yuán Tǐ's characteristic/function is to reflect, receive and process information, and then deliver the information to interact with the external environment. Since these functions already exist by the time Yìshí is formed, Yì Yuán Tǐ is prenatal as it relates to Yìshí. How does this prenatal existence come about? It is through evolution. From an evolutionary perspective, Yì Yuán Tǐ exists at the postnatal stage. Once Yì Yuán Tǐ is formed, it will reflect external substances and will establish a reference system. As the person evolves, any substance that enters Yì Yuán Tǐ will be measured/compared with the contents in their reference system and that action is Yìshí activity. The reflection in Yì Yuán Tǐ exists postnatally. In other words, Yìshí activity is the product of transmutation between Yì Yuán Tǐ's prenatal existing features and postnatal reflected information.

Transmutation is a process. When Yì Yuán Tǐ becomes functional, it establishes pre-existing conditions for Yìshí activity. As the external substances enter and reflect inside Yì Yuán Tǐ, repetition causes a "groove/routine" to develop in Yì Yuán Tǐ. The "groove" and Yì Yuán Tǐ transmute to form a reference system. In the beginning, the process of forming a reference system is automatic and natural. When the initiative nature of Yì Yuán Tǐ analyzes the contents inside the reference system, it becomes Yì Yuán Tǐ activity. The process is Sensorimotor Thinking analysis first, then it is Imagery Thinking analysis, and finally it is Language analysis. These analyses are the Hùn Huà processes between Yì Yuán Tǐ's pre-existing functions and the external information that entered into Yì Yuán Tǐ. Therefore, Yìshí activity is the expression of Yì Yuán Tǐ's function; it is a Hùn Huà process.

In Yìshí, the relationship between Prenatal and Postnatal is dialectical. Compared to Yìshí, Yì Yuán Tǐ is Prenatal; Yì Yuán Tǐ is the result of long periods of evolution. Human beings evolved from animals; from the perspective of human beings, animals are Prenatal and human beings are Postnatal. After transmuting with life activities, the human being becomes Prenatal for the next generation.

Social Yìshí and Individual Yìshí behave the same way. Social Yìshí refers to the common Yìshí characteristics of a society. Each society has its common ideas of ethics, sciences and the arts—these common characteristics are Social Yìshí. Social Yìshí is expressed through individuals. When a child follows the instructions from an adult on how to behave, the child is accepting Social Yìshí. Once Social Yìshí enters an individual, it becomes their Individual Yìshí. The Individual Yìshí and Social Yìshí that interact may create new thoughts. If these new thoughts have commonality with society and are accepted by many people, they will become Social Yìshí. For example, when Albert Einstein studied science, Social Yìshí (science) entered him and became his Individual Yìshí (knowledge). At the beginning, the Theory of Relativity was Albert Einstein's idea, it was an Individual Yìshí. Once it was accepted by the scientific world, it become Social Yìshí. As an Individual Yìshí, the Theory of Relativity was very difficult to accept, but once it became Social Yìshí, it was accepted by most people.

2. The brain and Yì Yuán Tĭ hùn huà (transmutation)

Throughout one's life, Yì Yuán Tĭ and the brain's cells continuously affect each other and the transmutation between them is nonstop, but Yìshí activity is relatively independent. There are numerous cells inside the brain and the Hùn Yuán Qì of these cells forms Yì Yuán Tĭ. Yìshí activity relies on these cells to function. When the sensory organ receives information from the outside (externally), it will stimulate the Hùn Yuán Qì of the surrounding brain cells and will cause the Hùn Yuán Qì to change. Because Yì Yuán Tĭ (Hùn Yuán Qì) is very evenly distributed, one small change/stimulation will be felt by and will affect the whole Yì Yuán Tĭ. Information is reflected on Yì Yuán Tĭ via the changes of sensory centers' nerve neurons. Once the Hùn Yuán Qì of the nerve neurons enters Yì Yuán Tĭ, it becomes part of Yì Yuán Tĭ. The Yìshí activity created by the information from the localized center will become Yì Yuán Tĭ activity. For most people, these changes can affect only Partial Yì Yuán Tĭ. The reason is that the brain has many centers such as those for visual, hearing and language, and each center has its own functions, and information is reflected on Yì Yuán Tĭ via these centers. Information can move freely inside Yì Yuán Tĭ but not in the centers. Only when one is in a very calm and in a concentrated state can the stimulation affect the whole Yì Yuán Tĭ. For example, normally, a sound might not startle a person but when that person is concentrated on reading, an external sound might cause that person to jump or be startled. The reason for this is that normally the brain functions are fragmented but with concentration, all brain centers are very calm, and when sound occurs, these centers react as a single unit.

The relationship between the brain and Yì Yuán Tĭ mentioned above is the brain affecting Yì Yuán Tĭ Hùn Huà (transmutation) process. Another form of Hùn Huà process is Yì Yuán Tĭ affecting the physical brain. When the changes in Yì Yuán Tĭ reach a point where it is no longer able to maintain balance, some of its Hùn Yuán Qì will be condensed into physical form. This "from formless to form" process occurs and is accomplished at the center of Yì Yuán Tĭ. This process is a crucial step for information reflected in Yì Yuán Tĭ to establish the "groove" and to be stored. The substance produced by the "formless to form" process can create the protein particles in nerve cells, and the substance also can form the dendrites of nerve cells. This is the process that enables memory to form and is the first step that establishes long term memory.

D. The generating process of Yìshí activity

Yìshí activity is a general term for all mental/conscious activities such as cognition, memory, reasoning, emotion and the formation of instructions. In this section, we will focus on the formation of mind activity and emotion (activity).

1. Mind activity

For most people, mind (brain) activity (thought) never stops, it just happens and no one can control it. How do thoughts occur? The brain (Yì Yuán Tǐ) and life functions are connected via the endocrine system, nervous system and Qì. Yì Yuán Tǐ connects with Nature either directly and/or through the sensory organs. Yì Yuán Tǐ is the central point of the objective world. Therefore, Traditional Qìgōng says "one's mind is the mind of the universe 人心者, 天地之心也." This concept means that the mind is the center of the universe and the congregation point of the various types of information. The information in the mind (brain) is Yì Yuán Tǐ's reflection of the information that it receives. When there are changes in Nature, Yì Yuán Tǐ will reflect the changes accordingly. Nature is dynamic—therefore information inside Yì Yuán Tǐ is dynamic.

Most of the information received by the brain is weak. Within Yì Yuán Tǐ, some information is stronger than others. Strong information becomes prominent and weak information becomes irrelevant. Because information is dynamic, Qì will congregate in the area of the brain with strong information and Yì Yuán Tǐ will become uneven. As strong information groups together to form a sequence called "Information Sequence," the chaotic state of information becomes ordered. When several Information Sequences combine, the volume of information will become large and will temporarily become an information center. Large amounts of information will create energy which will affect Yì Yuán Tǐ. Consequently, Yì Yuán Tǐ will affect the brain cells and the brain cells will transmit the information to corresponding organs. In turn, the brain cells will affect Yì Yuán Tǐ and strengthen the Information Sequences simultaneously. If the information from the temporary information center and the brain cells reaches the corresponding organs, it will create a natural and fitting (following the information's command/requirement) movement. Once there is movement, information will be sent to the brain via the corresponding organs. Then Yì Yuán Tǐ will summarize the information to correct, improve and change the contents of the information before repeating the cycle. All these processes are extremely fast and create thoughts (mental activities). Once a thought occurs, it will act upon the life activities. The process of thought formation is similar to how ice is formed on the surface of water. When the temperature drops, ice will form on an area of a surface and as more ice is formed, the area will become larger; then suddenly, the entire surface will be covered with ice.

Whether or not conscious activity occurs due to external stimulation or on purpose, the activity occurs inexplicably in the beginning. For example, suddenly, one may have a thought about XYZ. How does the thought come about? The thought may occur because of seeing a certain event or object or because someone has mentioned something which is the reflection of information received by Yi Yuán Ti, and occurs automatically.

There is a significant amount of information in Nature that is interacting with all people, even under the same circumstance, so why are the mental activities in two people not the same? This difference is because each person receives information in a very distinctive way. Due to each individual's background, the Reference System in each person's Yì Yuán Tǐ is different; therefore, the reflection and reaction to the information are not the same. For example, when looking at a tree, some may think "it is a perfect place to relax," some may think "it is a perfect rest area for the birds," and others may think "it is a perfect material for a table." Mental conditions of the individual can also affect the outcome of Yì Yuán Tǐ's reflection. Hearing the same music may create happy thoughts or feelings of sadness.

All Yìshí activity formations have background that is related to its activity. Chinese Buddhism calls this background Yīn Yuán 因緣 (cause). The primary cause is Yīn, the secondary/assistant cause is Yuán. All existences are the merging of Yīn and Yuán. For example, seed is Yīn, and soil, water and labor are Yuán; fruit is the result of merging Yīn Yuán. When an inexplicable thought (Yīn) arises, it will look for related information which is called Pān (connect) Yuán 攀緣 in Chinese Buddhism. When Yīn and Yuán merge, existence (substance or thought) is created. Chinese Buddhism believes all things are created by Xīn 心 (heart) 一切唯心造.

2. Emotion

Mind (activity) and emotion (activity) are the two most basic elements of Yìshí. Mind activity is Yì Yuán Tǐ's conceptual reflection of life activity. Emotion is an expression/response of a psychological state experienced by an individual internally, and it is normally expressed via facial expressions in the form of happiness, anger, fear or sadness.

Emotion does not occur randomly, it needs stimulation, which can be either external or internal (physical and/or mental condition of an individual). Emotion is one's mental response to stimulation. Under normal circumstances, an individual's mental state is balanced. Once an individual is stimulated, their mental state will lean toward the stimulated area and is no longer balanced. Because the mental activity guides the life activity, a state of imbalance will occur in the life activity. Emotion is directly related to "I" (self) Yì Yuán Tǐ, and uses "I" Yì Yuán Tǐ as a reference point to measure the stimulation. Changes in emotion will be reflected in Yì Yuán Tǐ and in turn, will affect the life activity. When life activity is changed, there will be a physiological reaction. With emotion, this physiological change would be primarily reflected as a change in facial expression.

According to Hùn Yuán Qì Theory, emotions are the expression of internal feelings when Body Hùn Yuán Qì transmutes with Nature Hùn Yuán Qì. In other words, when stimulated, one's Internal and External Hùn Yuán Qì merge, which creates changes. With changes, there are internal feelings/sensations and external physical expressions which when combined are called emotions. In Qìgōng and Traditional Chinese Medicine, there are two major driving forces or circumstances that enable the formation of emotions.

a) United Qì creates emotions 氣一而動志

When Qì's movements are united and formed a pattern or are moved in the same direction, this movement will be reflected on Yì Yuán Tǐ. In turn, Yì Yuán Tǐ will affect mental activities (emotions). For example, if Qì moves upward or outward at a relatively fast pace, when it is reflected on Yì Yuán Tǐ, Yìshí will have a feeling of anger. If Qì moves downward or inward, Yìshí will have a feeling of fear. If Qì moves naturally and smoothly, the feeling will be happiness. If Qì movement becomes stagnant, the feeling will be sadness. If Qì concentrates, the mind will become pensive or persistently thinks about a certain subject. If Qì disperses, the feeling will be sadness or fear. All of these emotions are caused by the change of Qì movements inside the body and are called *united Qì creates emotions.*

Normally when Qì moves, muscles will follow and the body appearance (facial expression) will change. Muscles are Jīng, expression is Shén, therefore, emotion is the expression of Jīng, Qì and Shén's transmutation. Qìgōng practitioners can use muscle expressions (physical movements) to adjust Qì movement to change emotions. The Five Element Method 五元庄 of Zhìnéng Qìgōng uses movements and sound to move Qì to certain areas (Liver, Heart, Spleen, Lung and Kidney). Without proper instructions, practitioners may experience mood swings that are related to the affected organ. For example, the Section Eight of Five Element Method of Zhìnéng Qìgōng that moves Qì to/from the liver may cause anger.

b) United mind intent (emotion) creates Qì movement 志一而動氣

When the mind intents are united, it will create changes in the Reference System that will cause changes in Body Hùn Yuán Qì. When information (stimulation), which can be either physical substance (external) or mental activity (internal), enters Yì Yuán Tǐ, the Reference System will be activated. With the stored information as reference, the Reference System will give Yì Yuán Tǐ responding information (judgment) about the physical and mental impact that stimulation would have on the body to create a response. The responding action will produce internal sensation/feeling that will cause changes in Qì and in the appearance of the body. If the internal sensation is emotional, it will create changes in Qì movement according/related to the type of emotion. Traditional Chinese Medicine utilizes the relationship between Qì and emotion in diagnosis and in treatment of health conditions. According to TCM, anger causes Qì to move upward and happiness causes Qì to move slowly and evenly. Deliberating/thinking causes Qì to become stagnant, sadness causes Qì to disperse, fear causes Qì to sink, and being startled causes Qì to scatter.

These two driving forces (United Qì creates emotions and United mind intent creates Qì movement) do not exist in isolation—they are closely related and keep replacing each other in a looping manner. When Qì changes inside the body, normally it will be accompanied by some changes in physical/facial expressions. The movement of physical/facial expressions will further facilitate Qì and blood's movement and the changes in their concentrate-disperse functions can either strengthen or weaken the internal feeling of emotions. The change of internal feeling will affect Yì Yuán Tǐ and will affect the appearance of the body and Qì movement that, in turn, will affect emotion.

Emotions are very complicated. Only after mind intent (Shén), physical movement (Jīng), and Qì are merged as one can the emotion be true. In theaters, actors perform all kinds of emotional acts with which the audiences can clearly identify, but the actors' mental states are very stable because they know they are acting and therefore, Qì is not affected. These emotions are not true emotions. When nonprofessionals act during a play, they may actually become emotional because movements and facial expressions activate Qì. If Shén is not stable, Jīng, Qì and Shén will merge as one—then the emotions become true.

E. Yìshí Movement

Yìshí activity/movement is a special kind of space-time structure (information) movement. Yìshí does not have energy or mass, it relies on the energy of other substances, physical or non-physical substance, such as light, electricity, magnetism, and heat to convey its information. To assist its functions, Yìshí (activity/movement) utilizes Yì Yuán Tǐ internally and Primal Hùn Yuán Qì externally.

According to Zhìnéng Qìgōng, Yìshí, in a narrow sense, is the conceptual activities in a subjective world. As noted previously, concept formation involves the following: an external substance reflects on Yì Yuán Tǐ; Yì Yuán Tǐ extracts its mass and energy, and what remains is information that becomes a concept. For example, when seeing a cup, the cup's characteristics and energy will enter the eyes, and will be reflected on Yì Yuán Tǐ. During this process, mass will be extracted, and only energy and information remains. Once Yì Yuán Tǐ processes the information, the energy that maintains the image of the cup will be extracted and the cup becomes a concept. The concept does not contain the cup's mass and energy, it only contains the information's space-time structure information. Therefore, one defines the changes of space-time structure (contents) inside Yì Yuán Tǐ as Yìshí activities.

Yìshí activity is formless and does not exist in the objective world. Yìshí can eliminate/extract mass and energy and conceptualize information. It also can retract information to recreate the image, and can concentrate energy (Qì) to form a physical substance (third level of extraordinary ability). It can interact with and/or change the space-time structure of another substance (Yìshí healing).

Since Yìshí is Yì Yuán Tǐ's activity, its characteristics are very similar to Yì Yuán Tǐ's. It has the following characteristics.

1. Yìshí activity contains wholistic information

All Yìshí activities contain wholistic information. For example, the concept of John Doe will contain all the information about him. Before John Doe is a concept, his Hùn Yuán Qì, which contains his wholistic information, reflects on Yì Yuán Tǐ. Once John Doe is conceptualized, his mass and energy are extracted but the wholistic information remains. When one thinks (thinking is a Yìshí activity) about John Doe, the concept (image) of John Doe will contain the wholistic information. Because human beings receive information through sensory organs, the information entering the brain is partial; therefore, information is there, but the connection is partial. To unite all the information as one is not that easy. The wholistic information that Yìshí contains is not prenatal, it is postnatal and is formed during the Hùn Huà (transmutation) process between Yì Yuán Tǐ and external substances.

2. The unrestricted/variable function of Yìshí activity

The unrestricted/variable function of Yishi activity refers to functions of speed, selection and change. Yìshí activity is decided by "I" (self) Yì Yuán Tǐ and follows the command of "I" (self) Yì Yuán Tǐ, and it is not restricted by speed, selection and change. Previously, it was mentioned that the formation of mind activity is random and that no one can control it. But once a mind activity is formed and the brain is able to sense it, it becomes Yìshí activity. Yìshí's formation cannot be controlled but Yìshí activity is controlled by "I" (self) Yì Yuán Tǐ.

a) Speed

The speed of Yìshí activity can be controlled. Uncontrolled or unrestricted (free form) Yìshí activity is nonlocal and travels faster than light. Normally, this type of activity does not carry energy. For example, the North Star is about 430 light-years from the Earth; when one thinks of it, one's Yìshí connects with it right away. Controlled Yìshí activity is usually at sub-light speed and is more detailed/specific or concrete. In order to be more specific, energy must be added; therefore, strictly speaking, controlled Yìshí activity is not pure Yìshí activity. It is an activity that involves mental activity and Qì. For example, emitting Qì for healing is a controlled Yìshí activity.

b) Selection

The target for Yìshí activity is not restricted by its location. Once a thought (Yìshí activity) is formed, it can choose to interact with any target regardless of its location. For example, in the experiment of Qì affecting matter or Qì healing, as soon as the target is chosen, Yìshí activity can affect the target immediately, whether it is nearby or faraway, distance or location is irrelevant. But the way Yìshí activity affects the Qì experiment (non-living subject) and Qì healing (living subject) is slightly different.

In Qì healing both the distance and the location are irrelevant, the healer does not even need to know the target as long as someone can relate the target's information to the healer. For example, John Doe's leg has problems and his friend Jane Doe comes for help. As she describes John Doe's condition to the healer, her Yìshí activity has selected John Doe's leg (target) and the leg's information will be very strong and becomes a target for the healer. The healer's Yìshí activity (healing/wellness thought) will merge with Hùn Yuán Qì and will affect John Doe via Jane Doe's Yìshí activity (target). In remote healing, the healer does not need to know the target, but they need a connection to the target.

In a Qì experiment with a non-living subject, the facilitator needs direct specific information about the subject. For example, if John Doe asks the facilitator to emit Qì to the water in his house, this process is very difficult to do without being familiar with the house. If the facilitator uses John Doe's Yìshí activity to connect to the water, John Doe's mind (brain) has to reflect the floor plan of the house and the location of the water. The more information John Doe has to reflect, the weaker the information becomes. If John Doe shows the pictures of the room and the location of a particular glass of water to the facilitator, then the facilitator's Yìshí activity can target that particular glass of water without affecting the other water in the room.

c) Change

Yìshí activity contains wholistic information, therefore, Yìshí can change or construct space-time structures. Changes in space-time structures can cause changes in Hùn Yuán Qì's concentrate-disperse functions and changes in concentrate-disperse functions will lead to structural changes. The way one arranges Yìshí will determine how Yìshí organizes Hùn Yuán Qì and in turn it will determine how a substance changes. Therefore, change needs to have an intent, a standard, and Yìshí activity follows the intention. For example, to change the physical condition of a paralyzed person, whether the person's intent is to be able to stand up or to be able to walk, Yìshí activity follows the intention. It is called "Use Yìshí to change Qì, Qì to change Xìng 以意會氣, 以氣會形" in Traditional Qìgōng.

3. Ability to Permeate

Yìshí activity is a special type of movement that can permeate all substances. Because Yìshí does not contain mass or energy, it contains only information that is the most basic space-time structure, and is very similar to Primal Hùn Yuán Qì; therefore, it can permeate and co-exist in every level of Hùn Yuán Qì. The permeating function of Yìshí is the result of the selective function of Hùn Yuán Qì to be combined with a co-existing function. Whatever Yìshí focuses on (selects), Yìshí permeates. If there is no target (selection), Hùn Yuán Qì co-exists with a substance, and they are within each other and co-exist naturally. Permeation is initiative and has substance. For example, in Qì diagnosis, Yìshí selects an area and penetrates inside that area. Once Yìshí is inside, energy will be reflected back to the brain. Information is delivered to the facilitator as Yìshí moves in and out of the target. It is similar to radar, where radio waves are delivered and bounced back. When a facilitator looks at a substance (e.g. John Doe's heart), Yìshí will automatically permeate inside. If the facilitator looks at the heart and then analyzes how to penetrate inside, Yìshí will have the substance "fixed/secured" and it becomes impenetrable.

4. Ability to be Independent

Although the activity formation process of Yìshí is affected by the person's internal and external environment and is restricted by the neurons' activity, Yìshí activity has a certain degree of independence. The relationship between Yìshí activity, environmental stimulation and brain (cells) activity is not linear. It is similar to the relationship between electric current and magnetic waves. In a sense, they are directly related. If the current is strong, the magnetic field is strong and the reverse also is true; although the magnetic field exists because of electric current, these two are not the same and the magnetic field has a certain degree of independence. By the same token, the chemical and physical changes inside the brain cells produce energy to support/power the activities inside Yì Yuán Tĭ, and these activities are independent. Under normal circumstances, most people can use Yìshí to control themselves. When stimulated, Yì Yuán Tĭ receives all types of information. If one remains calm, no matter what kind of environment one is in, Yì Yuán Tĭ still can remain balanced. In other words, Yìshí activity can be independent from life activities and from the changes in brain functions.

III. The functions of Yìshí

A. The effects of Yìshí on human beings

As noted previously, Yìshí (activity) is the movement and movement process of Yì Yuán Tĭ; Yì Yuán Tĭ can control/direct a person's life functions and can change Hùn Yuán Qì's functions. In this section, focus will be on the conceptual activity (concentration) aspect of Yìshí activity.

Life activity and Yìshí activity are two different functions. Human beings receive external information through sensory organs, and send corresponding information via various systems to adjust the balance between life activity and the surrounding/external environment. In science, this process is carried out via the central nervous system; in Qìgōng, it is a process of receiving and delivering information in Yì Yuán Tĭ. Some contents of this process become overt Yìshí activity, and some will become latent Yìshí activity.

The ability of Yìshí to control and direct life functions is not accessible at birth—it is a learned behavior. Yìshí has to go through the process of integrating with life activities. Normally, Yìshí activity is formed through language and feeling. Language is a concept involving physical substance and it references numerous life functions and information. Therefore, Yìshí activity directly affects life activity. When there is activity in the brain, there will be changes in the body. Life activities are directed by Yìshí, and they are the tools to perform the commands directed by Yìshí. Although the connection between Yìshí activity and life activity is formed automatically and unconsciously, the connection with learned behavior needs to build up slowly. In order to perform a certain task, the connection between Yìshí activity and life activity must be established first. All life activity is an integrated activity—integrated activity needs coordination among different parts of the body in order to form abilities in the brain. For example, swimming needs to be coordinated throughout the various parts of the body. If one does not know how to swim, even after learning numerous instructions in books, one will probably sink upon entering water. A coherent unit and reference point will be formed only after Yìshí directs the movements/practice in a repetitive and coordinated manner using the appropriate muscles, limbs, and other body parts required to swim. Once swimming becomes a reference point in Yì Yuán Tǐ, Yìshí gives a command to swim and the body will swim as a coherent unit.

In human life, Yìshí activity affects Qì, forces (energy) and matter. If Yìshí concentrates, Qì will concentrate. When Yìshí focuses on a certain area such as the hands, Qì will follow. As soon as Qì arrives, it will change to become the force that moves the hands. This process is called Yìshí leads Qì, Qì leads Xíng (body) in Qìgōng. Qì in our body is not evenly distributed so that some areas have more Qì than other areas. Therefore, when a certain part of the body is used, Qì needs to be concentrated there and requires Yìshí concentration. Highly concentrated Yìshí can concentrate Qì in the body to the point that a knife cannot penetrate that area. This is routinely demonstrated in Hard Style Qìgōng. The key is the extent of Yìshí concentration. The Qì that one concentrates is from Dāntián. An accomplished Qìgōng master can accumulate enough Qì to reach the "everywhere is Dāntián" state and no longer needs to draw Qì from the Dāntián.

One of the musculoskeletal system's functions is to produce energy (force) to power daily activities such as walking, eating and moving. The amount of energy (force) that one can produce is limited to the strength of their musculoskeletal system. But under certain circumstances, Yìshí can alter the strength of the force that the musculoskeletal system can produce. Normally, when the Yìshí is highly concentrated or one is extremely excited, the musculoskeletal system can produce force beyond its capacity. When Yìshí is out of focus or a person is depressed, the musculoskeletal system will not be able to produce force up to its capacity. For example, in an extremely excited state, a small person having highly concentrated Yìshí can lift a car to free a person underneath it. An accomplished athlete cannot perform a common movement when their Yìshí is not focused, or a strong person cannot stop shaking when a gun is pointed at them.

Yìshí can alter the metabolism inside the body. For example, when one is hungry and sees something delicious, saliva will be formed in the mouth. Also, Yìshí can alter the metabolism inside the body to cause a pathological condition. When diagnosed with cancer, a worried person may die quickly; a positive person may recover without any interventions. Worry can age a person overnight. Yìshí plays a key role in one's health. In medicine, all placebo and nocebo effects are the products of Yìshí. In his book, The Relaxation Response, Dr. Herbert Benson, professor of mind/body medicine at the Harvard Medical School and Director Emeritus of the Benson-Henry Institute at Massachusetts General Hospital in Boston, described his research on the effects of meditation (Yìshí activity) and how it can alter the metabolic rate and the expression of genes.

All external/environmental information can interact with the body's sensory organs. However, whether a certain amount of stimulation can cause sensations and how strong those sensations are depended on the state of a person's Yìshí. The stimulation one receives may not be consistent with the intensity of the stimulus. Whether one pays attention to the stimulation or not can increase or decrease the sensitivity to the stimulus. For example, a highly attentive person might feel the anticipatory pain of a doctor's needle but a highly distracted person could cut a finger without knowing it while chopping vegetables. The condition of one's mental state (Yìshí) can also increase or decrease the sensitivity to the stimulus. For example, an elite soldier can endure high levels of pain by using will power and prior mental conditioning. Conversely, if a person is very afraid of a knife, the pain would be experienced as severe, even if it is from a dull knife that barely grazes the hand.

B. The effects of Yìshí on external substances

Once Yìshí selects and concentrates on an external substance, it can affect the substance's structure directly. But during the interactive process, Qì must be presented and normally will be accompanied by changes in energy. There are two ways Yìshí converts Hùn Yuán Qì into energy. It can concentrate the Primal Hùn Yuán Qì first, then change it, or it can change the substance's Hùn Yuán Qì to create changes in energy. The Princeton Engineering Anomalies Research (PEAR) and International Consciousness Research Laboratories have conducted many studies on the effects of Yìshí (consciousness) on physical matter. The most substantial portion of the PEAR experimental program examined anomalies arising in human/machine interactions. In these studies, human operators attempted to bias the output of a variety of mechanical, electronic, optical, acoustical, and fluid devices to conform to pre-stated intentions, without recourse to any known physical influences. In unattended calibrations, these sophisticated machines produced strictly random data, but the experimental results displayed increases in information content that could only be attributed to the consciousness of their human operators. Over the laboratory's twenty-eight-year history, thousands of such experiments, involving many millions of trials, were performed by several hundred operators. The observed effects were usually quite small, on the order of a few parts in ten thousand on average, but they still resulted in highly significant statistical deviations from chance expectations.

In Qìgōng, Qì healing uses Yìshí to affect external substances to achieve wellness. A person with extraordinary abilities, either inborn or learned, can use Yìshí to affect external substances such as moving objects without touching them, tearing objects apart and reconnecting them, reconnecting broken bones, and making a seed sprout. Some advanced practitioners can concentrate Hùn Yuán Qì into physical substances, manufacture something from nothing, and can change their physical appearance to look like someone else.

C. How Yìshí affects external substances

Yìshí affects the life functions primarily through Yì Yuán Tǐ. Yìshí utilizes the concentrating-dispersing movements of Yì Yuán Tǐ to change the Body Hùn Yuán Qì functions. Yìshí affects external substances in two major ways.

1. **Yìshí activity facilitates Hùn Yuán Qì change to a specific energy form to interact/affect the external substances**

   Because Hùn Yuán Qì is a transmuted state of many forms of energy, Yìshí can direct Hùn Yuán Qì to change toward a specific physical property or energy property of an external substance. For example, Yìshí can direct Hùn Yuán Qì to change to electricity, magnetism, sound, light and heat. Because energy can interact with and can affect physical substances, Yìshí can be used to direct Hùn Yuán Qì to change into energy—then the energy can interact with and can affect the related substance. This is a process in which Yìshí changes Hùn Yuán Qì into energy that is expressed in physical or energetic form.

2. **Yìshí activity interacts directly with the space/time structure of an external object to cause changes**

   Yìshí does not change Hùn Yuán Qì into energy, it interacts directly with the space/time structure of an external object to cause changes. Every substance's feature/characteristic is its unique space and time structure. Yìshí activity is conceptual; it is a special kind of space and time structure that contains wholistic information. When Yì Yuán Tǐ interacts/merges with a substance, it will acquire/contain the wholistic information of the substance. For example, when one looks at a coffee cup, their Yì Yuán Tǐ will capture the cup's wholistic information. Later, when thinking of the cup, Yìshí (the thinking) will direct the Hùn Yuán Qì that contains that wholistic information to merge with the image of the cup. During the process, the information that Yìshí focuses on will be strengthened; if the focus is positive, then the wholistic structure (information) will change in a positive direction, and if negative, then the change will be negative. The focus is to use the biased information of Yìshí to change the substance's time-space structure. Then the new structure concentrates Hùn Yuán Qì which will lead to the change in the substance. In other words, once the substance's time-space structure changes, Hùn Yuán Qì changes, and then the substance changes.

Whether it is one's life function or external substances, Yìshí mainly uses these two methods to interact with the substances and to affect its outcome. The two methods are not completely separated, but are processes within Yìshí that depend on how Yìshí commands the change. For example, when we want a certain substance to become hot, it becomes hot. Where does the heat come from? The heat occurs because Hùn Yuán Qì has changed into heat energy. How does Hùn Yuán Qì change to heat energy? The change occurs because heat has its own space-time structure and thermal radiation (heat) is a form of an electromagnetic wave that is primarily in the infrared wavelength that cannot be seen by the eyes but can be felt by the skin. Infrared radiation is the expression of energy and has its own space-time structure. Heat will occur when Yìshí activity (intend to heat up the substance) changes Hùn Yuán Qì into heat energy, and merges with the substance (space-time structure), as long as the new resulting space time structure is in the infrared wavelength.

How does Yì Yuán Tǐ acquire the heat energy information? Although most people may not know the effects of electromagnetic waves, the body can sense the difference between cold and hot. Moving from cold to hot is a process. People may not know the details of this process and how the infrared radiation works but all of that information is reflected on Yì Yuán Tǐ and becomes reference points. Some people have studied physics and are aware of the infrared radiation and how it works. During the learning process, the information is gradually reflected on Yì Yuán Tǐ and becomes a reference point. When Yìshí gives the command to heat up a substance, Yì Yuán Tǐ will retract the information and change Hùn Yuán Qì into the heat energy.

D. The elements in Yìshí affecting external substances

There are four elements that determine the outcome of Yìshí affecting external substances.

1. The degree of concentration

In order to affect the external substance, one must concentrate mental activities. The degree of effectiveness is proportional to the degree of concentration; the higher the concentration, the better the result. When the mind is focused, Yì Yuán Tǐ can better concentrate the information. In turn, the functions of transforming Hùn Yuán Qì into energy and the merging the space-time structures will be strengthened; consequently, the results are much better.

Yì Yuán Tǐ has many layers such as the logical thinking layer, the emotional layer, and the reference layer—each layer has many activities. If one cannot unite most if not all the activities, Yìshí will be weak. Of all the layers, the "I" (self) Yìshí Layer is the most fundamental (Fig. 5-1), and it is within the Reference System Layer. A mental activity (thought) needs to connect with "I" (self) Yì Yuán Tǐ. The formation of thoughts goes through many layers of adding and subtracting information, and finally concentrates as one inside Yì Yuán Tǐ.

Because information in Yì Yuán Tǐ is scattered among different layers, it is not that easy for most people to concentrate it. Normally, when thinking about one thing, some other thing always comes to mind. Or, instead of focusing on one thing, thoughts about two or more things may occur at the same time. With distractions, the strength of concentrated information will be weak. Only with concentration, can the full strength of Yì Yuán Tǐ be brought forth. In addition, if there are distractions in the layers when the thought goes out, the mental activity will get distracted and the strength of the activity will be weakened. If one can concentrate, the thought will remain intact and the strength of concentrated information will be strong.

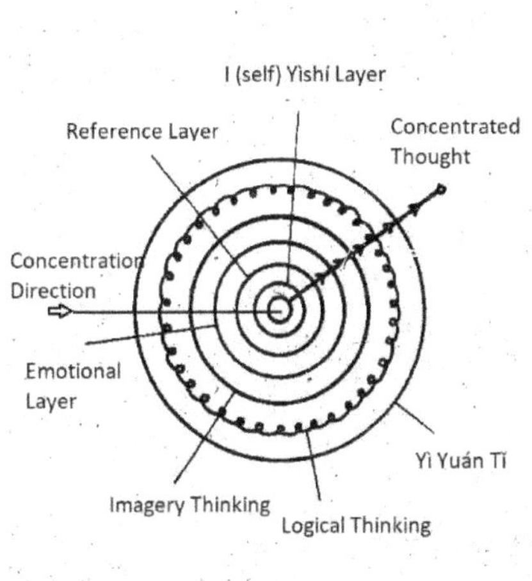

Fig. 5-1 The Yì Yuán Tǐ Layers

2. The degree of accuracy/details in selecting a target

Once a person's ability to concentrate is established, the degree of accuracy in selecting a target becomes important. The degree of accuracy/details determines the effectiveness of Yìshí activity, the more detailed and precise the selection, the better the results. The precise selection can help the connections between the Yìshí activity and the target; therefore, it will improve the effectiveness of their transmutation. For example, in order to wish someone good health, one might say, "I wish John Doe good health;" however, this expression is not effective because the selection is not precise enough. There are many John Does but which John Doe is referenced? It is also not effective to say — "let's heal XYZ Country"— because the selection is too vague, and that kind of ability does not exist in anyone. If one says — "let's heal my dog"— it would work because the target is clear. But if one says — "let's heal my dog's broken leg"— this statement is better because it is more precise.

3. The clarity of Yì Yuán Tǐ

There are many factors that affect the clarity of Yì Yuán Tǐ. One factor is the innate quality of Yì Yuán Tǐ. The more brain cells that one has, the wider and better the connections between the dendrites. With better connections, Yì Yuán Tǐ will be more thorough/accurate and more detailed, and in turn, the volume of information will increase. With more information, Yì Yuán Tǐ will be more thorough and more detailed. Thoroughness and information will determine the degree of clarity. Yìshí activity also affects Yì Yuán Tǐ's clarity. Yìshí activity behaves like the wind affecting water, the stronger the wind, the muddier the water. Steady and calm Yìshí activities can minimize the interference to Yì Yuán Tǐ, and in turn, will increase the clarity of Yì Yuán Tǐ.

Another factor affecting the clarity is the amount of regular Hùn Yuán Qì in Yì Yuán Tǐ. As mentioned in Yì Yuán Tǐ section, Yì Yuán Tǐ is a special form of Hùn Yuán Qì formed by the brain cell Hùn Yuán Qì. if there is too much Organ Hùn Yuán Qì and/or Body Hùn Yuán Qì in the brain, this will affect the clarity of Yì Yuán Tǐ. For example, after consuming alcohol, blood vessels (capillaries) will expand and the blood flow to the brain will be increased. Inside the blood stream, there are Semi-Body Qì (nutrients) and Body Hùn Yuán Qì; with the increased Semi-Body and Body Qì in the brain, one will feel uncomfortable.

4. Heart's desire

The heart's desire is the driving force for Yìshí to affect external substances. With strong desire, the force/strength comes from the "I" (self) Yìshí will be strong and will have a greater impact on the external substances. It works the same for weak desire; with weak desire, the impact will be weak. Concentration, target selection, and clarity of Yì Yuán Tǐ are all closely related to desire. With strong desire to change oneself, one is able to do extraordinary things to accomplish the goal. Chinese Buddhism says that whether one can achieve enlightenment or not depends on three things: belief 信, willing/desire 願 and action 行. It is also true for Qìgōng, desire leads to belief and action.

Conclusion

A. Yì Yuán Tǐ is a forward evolving movement/process

According to Traditional Qìgōng, the consciousness of human beings belongs to Human Primal Qì, and Human Primal Qì is the expression of Nature Primal Qì (Dào). Therefore, Human Primal Qì and Nature Primal Qì are the same Qì. Qìgōng practice involves returning to the essence/truth (返樸歸真). Because of life activities, Dàoism considers that Yuán Shén (primal/empty consciousness with no mental activity) of human beings becomes Shì Shén (consciousness with mental activities), and Prenatal Jīng and Qì becomes Postnatal Jīng and Qì. Qìgōng practice goes back to the primal state. Chinese Buddhism believes every human being has Fúxìng 佛性 (Buddha-nature or enlightened essence). The difference between a Buddha and an ordinary human being is that a Buddha has realized their Buddha-nature, while an ordinary human being has not. Fúxìng is often called the essence of Buddhahood or enlightened essence. Qìgōng practice in Buddhism is to eliminate delusions to realizing Fúxìng. Traditional Qìgōng, Dàoism Qìgōng and Buddhist Qìgōng all cultivate Qì back to the primal state to complete the circle.

Although Yìshí Theory is based on the theories of Yìshí (consciousness) of Buddhism, Dàoism and Traditional Chinese Medicine, instead of returning to the origin (Dào) and completing a loop (circle), Yìshí Theory is a forward progress theory. It does not return to the origin or complete an enclosed circle, it spirals forward. According to Hùn Yuán Wholistic Theory, substances with form/shape which consist of both physical condensed Qì and non-physical formless Qì are evolved from the formless Primal Hùn Yuán Qì. In human beings, some of the formless Qì will evolve into Yì Yuán Tǐ. The characteristics of Yì Yuán Tǐ are similar to those of Primal Hùn Yuán Qì; they are both exceptionally fine and evenly distributed and can beget complex substances. However, the substances that are begotten through the Hùn Huà (transmutation) process of Primal Hùn Yuán Qì are the ten-thousand things of the objective world. The substances that are begotten through the Hùn Huà (transmutation) process of Yì Yuán Tǐ are the Yìshí activities of the subjective world. In addition, substances that are begotten through Primal Hùn Yuán Qì are natural and passive, and Yìshí activities are active. When Primal Hùn Yuán Qì evolves into Yì Yuán Tǐ, it is not the end of the evolutionary process or a return back to Primal Hùn Yuán Qì. Yì Yuán Tǐ will continue to evolve and will undergo a systematic change—from Beginning Yì Yuán Tǐ to "I" (Self) Yì Yuán Tǐ, to Partial/ Biased Yì Yuán Tǐ, to Complete Yì Yuán Tǐ, and Integrated Yì Yuán Tǐ. Fig. 5-2. According to Yìshí theory, the Yìshí activities of modern human beings are based on Partial Yì Yuán Tǐ. In Zhìnéng Qìgōng, one of the purposes of Qìgōng practice is to eliminate bias and partiality in Yì Yuán Tǐ and improve Yì Yuán Tǐ to Complete Yì Yuán Tǐ and Integrated Yì Yuán Tǐ states.

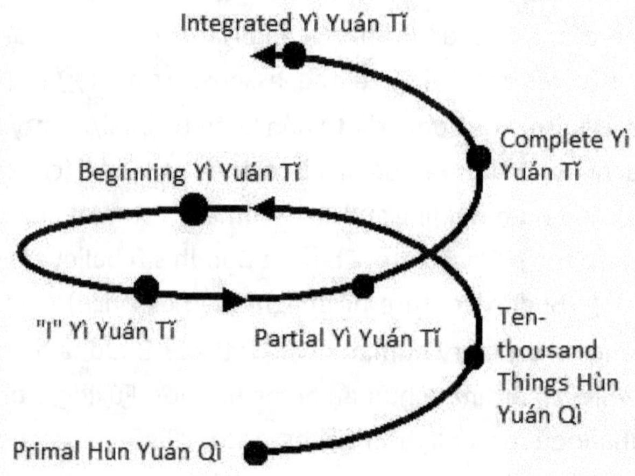

Fig. 5-2 The Evolutionary Process of Hùn Yuán Qì

B. The formation of Yìshí is the result of the transmutation between Prenatal and Postnatal existences

Unlike some philosophical theories that consider the structure of consciousness as Prenatal existence (a priori knowledge) and conscious activities as Postnatal existence (a posteriori knowledge), the Yìshí Theory refers to Yì Yuán Tǐ which only exists in human beings as Prenatal existence and the Nature/External Hùn Yuán Qì as Postnatal existence. Therefore, Yìshí activities are the transmutation processes between human beings and the external environment. According to Yìshí theory, the development period of the brain neurons after a baby is born is the period that the Reference System is formed in Yì Yuán Tǐ. Substances reflected on Yì Yuán Tǐ will become reference points that all Yìshí activities are based upon.

The Beginning Yì Yuán Tǐ of a newborn only has prenatal capacity/condition to carry out the Yìshí activity; Yìshí activity is established in the postnatal period and evolves with the newborn. In other words, the formation of Yìshí in a newborn is the result of transmutation between the Beginning Yì Yuán Tǐ and the Yìshí activities and language of other human beings. Without the influence (transmutation) of the Yìshí activities of other human beings, the newborn will not be able to establish Yìshí activity. Therefore, each individual's Yìshí is the result of Hùn Huà between their Yì Yuán Tǐ and Nature (environment) Hùn Yuán Qì.

C. Yìshí activity is the essence of human nature

Although both human beings and animals have the same basic life activities such as metabolism, searching and consuming food, and reproduction, the difference between human beings and animals is that human beings have Yishi activity. Yìshí activities such as morality, rational and logical reasoning, artistic expression, and language are the characteristics of human beings. Life activities in animals are basically physical with little or no mental activity and are mostly passive. Life activities in human beings consist of physical and mental activities which can be passive or active, and Yìshí commences all active activities. Therefore, Yìshí activity is the essence of human nature and it distinguishes human beings from animals.

第六章：结論

Chapter Six: Conclusion

As mentioned previously, all new knowledge is based on existing knowledge and every new theory has its roots and continuity of history and culture. Hùn Yuán Wholistic Theory is no exception. This chapter explains the difference between Hùn Yuán Wholistic Theory, science, and the Traditional Qì Theories. The role Hùn Yuán Wholistic Theory plays in Qìgōng Medicine is also discussed briefly.

I. The difference between Hùn Yuán Wholistic Entity Theory and science, philosophy and Traditional Qìgōng

A. The difference between Hùn Yuán Wholistic Entity Theory and science and philosophy

Chinese Buddhism considers that the physical realm is the phenomenon of consciousness. Hùn Yuán Wholistic Theory states that the physical realm exists objectively, and all existences are transmuted states of two or more substances. For example, the universe is a transmuted state of physical substances and formless non-physical substances. An organism is a transmuted state of its structure and metabolic functions. An inorganic substance is a transmuted state of its structure and energy. Under normal circumstances, most people would not be able to be aware of the wholistic characteristics of the substance; but if one has developed extraordinary sensory perception ability, they can be aware of the wholistic features.

In science, when describing a substance, it is a standard practice to separate the structure and its functions into two separate entities. Hùn Yuán Wholistic Theory uses the material monism approach that implies reality is one unitary organic whole with no independent parts; therefore, structure and functions cannot be separated, they are partial attributes of the wholistic substance. In observing/understanding substances, science is very precise in its approach which is divided into objective observation and subjective observation. During the observation, there are the observer and the observed; the two cannot be mixed together. To observe the objective world is to understand and distinguish it from the subjective world. The better separation between the observer and the observed, the clearer the objective world. Hùn Yuán Wholistic Theory considers the observation process as the uniting process between the objective and the subjective worlds. For example, in an extremely simplified version, when a beam of light falls on an objective substance such as a picture, according to science, the reflected light reaches the observer's eyes and they become able to see the picture. In Qìgōng, the process of seeing is not just the reflected light received by the eyes. In addition to the light, when the observer looks at the picture, their consciousness, subsequently their energy and Qì, will unite with the picture. When the observer withdraws the vision and receives the information of the picture, they complete the uniting process. It is the observer's Hùn Yuán Qì that merges with the picture's (observed) Hùn Yuán Qì, and only after they are merged can the observer receive the observed information. Remote diagnosis in Qìgōng is the application of this principle. In remote diagnosis, the healer's Yì Yuán Tǐ (consciousness) connects and merges with the patient's Hùn Yuán Qì. When the healer withdraws their consciousness, they will be able to access the patient's information and give a correct diagnosis. This process of remote diagnosis merges the objective world (patient) and subjective world (healer). Another example of how Qìgōng and science are different is in their approach to healing. For example, to treat a tumor, medical science will first give a diagnosis to determine the course of treatment. During the treatment, the tumor exists in an objective world and the doctor is in a subjective world. They are separated and independent from each other. In Qìgōng, the healer's Hùn Yuán Qì unites with the tumor's Hùn Yuán Qì and the healer uses the mind intent to dissolve the tumor. The dissolving of the tumor occurs only after the uniting process is completed.

In science, consciousness is strictly subjective; Hùn Yuán Qì Theory considers consciousness is to be both subjective and objective. Zhìnéng Qìgōng defines Yìshí (consciousness) as a form of brain cell Hùn Yuán Qì movement and is the activity process of Yì Yuán Tǐ. Yìshí is not only able to respond to the information it receives, it can affect the body functions and external environment, and also can dictate the life activities. Therefore, Yìshí is subjective. A substance, whether it is physical or non-physical, is an objective entity. Consciousness is a form of Hùn Yuán Qì; therefore, it is a substance and an objective entity. Since an objective substance should be able to be observed/aware of by others, if consciousness is a substance, then one's consciousness (mental activities) should be observed by others. This concept is opposite to common sense because according to science and philosophy, consciousness is a person's mental state/activity, it is subjective, and no other person can access it. But in Qìgōng, there is a diagnosis technique called Telepathy or Sensing Method 感應法 where the healer can gain access to the patient's consciousness/mind activity. A regular healer can sense the patient's pain (pain is an emotional distress) and discomfort (mental uneasiness). Under certain circumstances, some accomplished Qìgōng practitioners are able to gain access to other person's thoughts.

B. The difference between Hùn Yuán Wholistic Theory and Traditional Qìgōng Theory

The concept of a human being consisting of Jīng, Qì and Shén originates from Dàoist Qìgōng. Nowadays, this concept of a human being is also used by all Qìgōng practices. In Traditional Qìgōng, Jīng and Qì are called Mìng 命, Shén is called Xìng 性. The methods that cultivate Jīng and Qì are called Mìng Gōng 命功, and those that cultivate Shén are called Xìng Gōng 性功. Traditionally, one initially focuses on cultivating either Mìng or Xìng. Once a degree of proficiency is reached, the practitioner will cultivate the second one. Finally, they will cultivate both Xìng and Mìng (性命雙修) at the same time to achieve Xìng and Mìng merged as one. The process is: cultivate/transmute Jīng into Qì, cultivate/transmute Qì to Shén 煉精化氣, 煉氣化神. Since Shén is Xìng (mental) and Jīng and Qì are Mìng (substance), they are different types of entities; this creates contradictions and unknowns in their cultivation. In Dàoist Qìgōng, once Dàdān 大丹 (Dàdān is the dān (Qì ball) that forms by the coherence of Kidney Qì and Heart Qì in the middle Dāntián) is formed, Shén is within Qì and Qì is engulfing Shén 神在氣中, 氣包神外. In theory, it is not possible to transmute Qì into Shén. It is a big question and there are no answers as to how to cultivate/transmute Qì into Shén. This is one of the main reasons that most practitioners cannot advance to a higher level of Qì cultivation after forming the Dàdān. The Hùn Yuán Wholistic Theory considers that Jīng, Qì and Shén are the same Hùn Yuán Qì with different degrees of refinement; Jīng is coarser, Qì is regular, and Shén is finer. According to the Hùn Yuán Wholistic Theory, to cultivate/transmute Jīng into Qì and to cultivate/transmute Qì into Shén are to cultivate the refinement of Hùn Yuán Qì. This approach eliminates the contradictions and confusions in Traditional Qìgōng Wholistic Theory.

Shén is also called Xū Líng 虛靈 in Qìgōng. Xū means nebulous and formless, Líng means intelligent with spirituality overtones. Originally, Xū Líng means the nebulous primeval Qì. Because primeval Qì exists and yet doesn't exist, awareness of it occurs only through consciousness; Xū Líng evolves into Shén. In Chinese writing, Shén 神 can be either consciousness or spirit. Spirit implies God or higher beings, and many Qìgōng practitioners can become superstitious. Hùn Yuán Wholistic Theory defines Shén as Hùn Yuán Qì which is a substance; therefore, this theory prevents superstition and separates Qìgōng from religion.

The traditional Qìgōng concept of wholism states that human beings are evolved from Nature; Nature is also called Dào. Dào begets ten-thousand things, human beings evolve from ten-thousand things, and human beings evolve back to Nature. The process is an enclosed circle, it begins with Dào.

Dào is Xū Wú 虛無 (Xū—nebulous and formless, Wú—nihility), from Xū Wú, it begets Yǒu 有 (existence); Yǒu begets ten-thousand things and human beings evolve from ten-thousand things. Human beings cultivate Qì to become Shén and Shén merges with Dào and back to Dào to repeat the cycle. Some Qìgōng methods bypass Shén and cultivate Qì directly toward Dào. Fig. 6-1

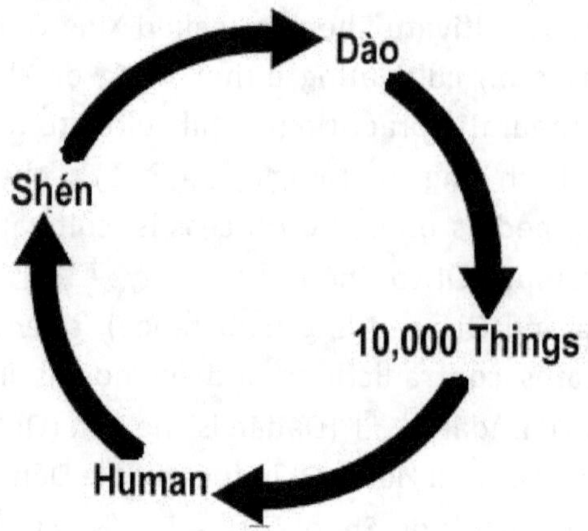

Fig. 6-1 Enclosed Circle

Hùn Yuán Wholistic Theory is different, it states that the evolutionary process is not an enclosed circle, it is an upward spiral. When Primal Qì (Dào) evolves into Yì Yuán Tǐ (Shén), instead of evolving back to Dào, Yì Yuán Tǐ will undergo a systematic change—from Beginning Yì Yuán Tǐ to "I" (Self) Yì Yuán Tǐ, to Partial/Biased Yì Yuán Tǐ, to Complete Yì Yuán Tǐ, and Integrated Yì Yuán Tǐ. According to Yishi theory, the Yishi activities of modern human beings are based on Partial Yì Yuán Tǐ. Human beings are in the middle of the evolutionary process.

Hùn Yuán Wholistic Theory states that changes in substances are caused by the interaction of two factors, one is internal and the other is external. Because a substance constantly interacts with the surrounding environment, the interaction will cause changes in the substance and the environment. Each substance's environment is different; therefore, ten-thousand things are created. Traditional Qìgōng does not have an explanation for how Yuán Qì begets ten-thousand things. There is no concept of evolution in Traditional Qìgōng which leaves how existence is formed to the imagination of individuals. This omission opens the door for religious influence and is the main reason that Buddhist Qìgōng and some Dàoist Qìgōng have religious overtones.

Traditional Qìgōng's theories and methods are not separated, they function as one in guiding the practice and in explaining Nature. Zhìnéng Qìgōng separates theories and practice methods into two systems. Hùn Yuán Wholistic Theory is the foundation theory that explains the relationship between Nature and humans, consciousness and the physical body, and the body and functions. Hùn Yuán Wholistic Theory also explains the functions of Qì that would become the foundation of Zhìnéng Qìgōng practice.

II. Qìgōng and Wellness

Most people practice Qìgōng because of its health benefit. In addition to health benefits, Qìgōng has many healing methods that can be used to treat others. Despite its merits in healing and wellness, Qìgōng has not been able to become established as a branch of medicine on its own. Historically, ancients practiced Qìgōng for enlightenment, healing others was not the focus. After the Hàn Dynasty 漢朝 (25-220 A.D.), religion became part of Qìgōng, and they considered Qì diagnosis and treatment as distractions/sidelines that should not be given any attention. Traditional Chinese Medicine (TCM) and Qìgōng share many theories such as Yīn-Yáng Theory, Five-Element Theory, Jīng Qì Shén Theory and Meridian Theory, and they also share many treatment methods such as Dǎoyǐn 導引 (guiding Qì) and Xíngqì 行氣 (move/activate Qì). Because many TCM doctors use the same treatment methods in their practice, many people have the misconception that Qìgōng is part of TCM. Although treatment methods that TCM and Qìgōng use are the same, their diagnosis is not. Qìgōng Medicine involves Qì diagnosis and Qì treatment. Qì diagnosis requires Qìgōng training and a certain degree of proficiency. Most TCM doctors do not practice Qìgōng or cannot achieve the required proficiency, they only use the treatment methods but not Qì diagnosis. Therefore, it cannot be called Qìgōng Medicine.

Qìgōng Medicine focuses on the body functions. If the functions of Qì and blood are normal, then the person will be healthy. Therefore, Qìgōng treatments begin with the body's internal functions. Although Qìgōng Medicine uses many different techniques in treating ailments, its main focus is on utilizing the normal function of Qì. To be more specific, it is Yuán Qì's (the transmuted Prenatal and Postnatal Qì) functions that Qìgōng Medicine focuses on. Traditional Qìgōng theories guide the practice which emphasizes self cultivation, and practicing Qìgōng is to cultivate Qì for self-healing and wellness. Because Traditional Qìgōng uses Dāntián Qì to heal others, Dāntián Qì takes time and effort to accumulate and is easily depleted; therefore, using Qì to heal others was seldom performed in earlier times. New generation Qìgōng, especially Zhìnéng Qìgōng, uses External Qì instead of Dāntián Qì to heal others. Although most Qì healing does not emphasize precise diagnosis of an illness, whether it is External Qì or Internal Qì healing, one still needs to have a general idea of the cause of an illness and how Qì works to give the correct treatment, and this type of knowledge requires the support of theories.

In order to be recognized as a medical science, Qìgōng Medicine must have theories and methods. There are thousands of practice methods and hundreds of healing techniques that meet this requirement. Although there are many theories about Qì and illness, they are fragmented and cannot be put together as a coherent whole that meets theoretical requirements. Theories such as Yīn-Yáng Theory and Five-Element Theory are not able to clearly define what Qì is, its characteristics, its relationship/interaction with the human body, and how Qì affects the body. One of the most important omissions is the importance of Shén to health. The writings on Shén and health are very vague in classical manuscripts. Zhìnéng Qìgōng's Hùn Yuán Wholistic Theory clearly defines Qì, its formation and characteristics, and its functions and relationship with the human body. More important, Hùn Yuán Wholistic Theory defines Shén and its functions related to the human body and environment. In other words, Hùn Yuán Wholistic Theory meets the theoretical requirement of medical science.

Zhìnéng Qìgōng's Hùn Yuán Wholistic Theory is a new theoretical foundation for Qìgōng Medicine. Instead of following theories such as Yīn-Yáng Theory, Five-Element Theory, Jīng Qì Shén Theory and Meridian Theory that focus on partial characteristics/functions of Qì, Hùn Yuán Wholistic Theory focuses on the function of all four characteristics/movements (Open-Close, In-Out, Concentrate-Disperse and Huà) of Qì. It states that all illnesses are caused by the abnormal function of one or more movements. For example, a tumor is caused by the Concentrate-Disperse function being out of balance, Qì concentrates in an abnormal way and is not able to disperse in a normal way. An infection is caused by improper Huà function—Qì is not able to Huà (transmute) the bacteria that cause the infection. Qì healing in Zhìnéng Qìgōng is to bring the abnormal Qì function back to normal; it can be achieved by either self cultivation (practice Qìgōng) or by receiving Qì adjustment from a healer.

In theory, Qìgōng Medicine can cure all illness. But healing is an art; whether a person can recover from an illness or not depends on mental condition and/or the ability of the healer. The life activities of human beings are the processes of Hùn Yuán Qì movement. Although the human body is divided into Jīng, Qì and Shén, they are the same Hùn Yuán Qì but present in the human body in different ways and expressing their functions differently. Hùn Yuán Qì has different forms of movement; some move and change according to the physiological structure of the human body, and some evolve into Shén. Shén movement is the consciousness movement of a human being and it can dictate their life functions. Zhìnéng Qìgōng focuses on Hùn Yuán Qì, but emphasizes Shén's functions and its ability to direct the body functions. In conclusion, Hùn Yuán Wholistic Theory is the theoretical background for physiological and pathological concepts in Qì healing and guides the development of healing treatments and techniques which will be the subjects of discussion in *Qìgōng Medicine: Theories and Methods*.

Glossary and Index

Bāguà 八卦: The eight trigrams. Space, Lake, Fire, Thunder & Lighting, Wind, Water, Mountain, Land. 9, 11.

Bìgǔ 避谷: Bì means avoid, gǔ means food. 118.

Chilel Qìgōng 氣療氣功: Another name for Zhìnéng Qìgōng. In 1995, in order to introduce Zhìnéng Qìgōng to the non-Chinese, Dr. Páng gave approval for Luke Chan and Frank Chan to teach Zhìnéng Qìgōng as Chilel Qìgōng in the Americas and in Europe.

Dān 丹: Pill or ball. 113, 177.

Dāntián (Dān Tián) 丹田: Qì concentration center. There are three Dāntiáns, Upper Dāntián is located in the center of the head (brain), Middle is located in the Epigastric region, and Lower Dāntián is located in the area between the navel and the Mìngmén. Normally, when Dāntián is mentioned, it refers to Lower Dāntián. 22, 95, 101, 111, 123-124, 163, 177, 179.

Dào 道: Dào is described as "the root of the Universe." All things in the Universe are evolved from Dào. As a substance, the one without form and invisible is call Dào. 6-10, 13, 21, 28, 34, 39, 68-69, 71-72, 177-178.

Dào Dé Jīng 道德經: Common English translation is Tao Te Ching. A philosophical book written by Lǎozi 老子 about 2,600 years ago. It consists of 81 chapters and about 5,000 words with 800 Chinese characters. 7, 33-34, 39, 68, 72.

Eight Octagons 八廓: The areas in the eye that reflect the hollow organs and meridians. 16.

Fǎshēn 法身: The Qì Body (both inside and outside of the body) is called Fǎshēn. 99.

Fèng Shuǐ 風水: One of the Five Arts of Chinese Metaphysics which is a philosophical system of harmonizing everyone with their surrounding environment. 18.

Five Wheels 五輪: The five areas in the eye that reflect the solid organs. 16.

Five-element 五行: Wood (liver), Fire (heart), Earth/Soil (spleen), Metal (lung), Water (kidney). 13, 76, 179-180.

Fúxìng (Fú Xìng) 佛性: Buddha-nature or enlightened essence. 169.

Huà 化: To change or to transmute. 25-26, 50-52, 61.

Huà Qì 化氣: Breaks down the physical substance into Qì. 121-123.

Huángdì Nèijīng 黃帝内經: The Yellow Emperor's Classic of Internal Medicine. 22-23, 25.

Human Hùn Yuán Qì 人的混元氣: Human Hùn Yuán Qì is the result of the transmutation of the Prenatal and Postnatal Qì. It consists of invisible Qì and concentrated Qì (physical substances). 43, 61, 93-97, 99, 104, 107, 114-115, 118, 120-123, 125.

Human Body Hùn Yuán Qì 人體混元氣: The formless and changeable Qì inside Human Hùn Yuán Qì. 99.

Hùn Hé 混合: The process of two or more things transmuting together to form an entity. 34, 52, 61.

Hùn Huà 混化: The process of dissolving (transmuting) a thing into something that can transmute with other things to form a new entity. 34-35, 47, 52-53, 58, 65, 104, 107, 112, 114, 118-125, 152-154, 159, 169-170.

Hùn Yuán 混元: Hùn Yuán means two or more things are transmuted into one. Hùn Yuán (as a concept in Zhìnéng Qìgōng): An awareness of the innate (wholistic) characteristics of an objective substance. In Practice methods, it is transmutation; it is the mind intent and Qì transmuting process. 27-29, 33-35.

Hùn Yuán Element 混元子: The most basic material in the universe. An even and indivisible state. It is the result of the transformation of space, time, mass, energy and information which are all transmuted as an indistinguishable one. 38-40, 44, 50, 61.

Hùn Yuán Qì 混元氣: Two or more things are transmuted together to form an entity, this new entity is called "Hùn Yuán Qì (Entity)." In humans, the transmuted state of prenatal Jīng, Qì and Shén is called Hùn Yuán (Qì). Hùn Yuán Qì is one's genetic marker or DNA. The special existing state of a substance which contains the full unique characteristics of mass, energy and information. 26-29, 33-37. 180

Hùn Yuán Qì Field 混元氣場: The Hùn Yuán Qì surrounding an object is called Hùn Yuán Qì Field. The solid object is the condensed Hùn Yuán Qì; the Hùn Yuán Qì Field is the diffused Hùn Yuán Qì. 36-37, 122.

Hùn Yuán Qìào 混元竅: Qìào is not a physical point and does not exist until one accumulates enough Qì. The Hùn Yuán Qìào is located slightly below the center of the diaphragm. 101-102, 122.

Hùn Yuán Wholistic Entity 混元整體: The relationship between matter inside a substance (structures) and other factors (vitality), where structures and functions are merged/integrated as one: a vitality- structures integrated entity. Also, an entity in which space and time are transmuted as one. 3-5, 175.

Hùn Yuán Wholistic Theory 混元整體理論: A foundation theory of Zhìnéng Qìgōng. This theory describes the Wholistic Entity's formation, characteristics and laws that govern its changes. 3-6, 33, 93, 175, 177, 180.

Jīng 精: Physical body or essence. 7, 9, 12, 15-16, 20, 25-26, 28-29, 34, 93, 96-99, 107-113, 125, 157-158, 177, 179-180.

Liù Qì 六氣: Wind, Fire, Heat, Humidity, Dryness and Cold. 24.

Kōngdòng 空洞: Empty hole, similar to the concept of today's explanation of a Black Hole. 27-28, 34.

Meridian Qì 經絡之氣: Qì in the meridians connects the inner organs with the bones and the extremities to form an entity. Qì regulates the entity's functions. 22.

Mó Luò 膜絡, Mó (膜) means membranes, Luò (絡) means small lateral meridian. Together, the membranes and the small lateral meridians (including tiny blood vessels) are called Mó Luò. 103.

Prenatal Qì 先天之氣 and Postnatal Qì 後天之氣: A fetus is formed by the Qì produced by the merging of sperm and egg; this Qì is called Prenatal Qì, it is the root of all future developments. Once the fetus is formed, the substances (nutrition, air, water, etc.) it absorbs from outside the body is called Postnatal Qì. When Prenatal Qì and Postnatal Qì merge as one, it is called Hùn Yuán Qì. 19, 21-22, 29, 85, 93, 98-102, 105-108, 112, 122.

Primal Hùn Yuán Qì 初始混元氣: Primal Hùn Yuán Qì evolves from the Hùn Yuán Element; its structure is extremely even, and it occupies the whole universe. In this level, space and time are separated and Qì begins to emerge. Primal Hùn Yuán Qì gives birth to the Ten-thousand things (Wànwù). 40-41, 45, 51, 61, 72, 102, 105, 137, 159, 164, 169.

Qì 氣: Broad sense, the building block of the Universe. Narrow sense, air. In living things, the shapeless substance which maintains the physiological functions.

Qì Field 氣場: The uncondensed Qì inside an entity and in its surrounding area. 18, 36-37, 45-46, 52, 79, 96, 99-100, 102, 115-116, 122.

Qìgōng 氣功, also spelled as Chì Kūng, or Chì Gōng. Common modern spelling is Qìgōng. A training process which uses a particular method to meet the goal of improving health and enhancing life functions

Qì Healing 氣療: Uses External Qi and/or Internal Qi to diagnose and treat illness. 37, 116, 160, 165, 179-180.

Qì Huà 氣化: Qì's functions or transmutation or concentrates Qì to give birth to a new physical substance. 12, 20, 23-26, 121, 123-124.

Qì lì 氣立: The exchange and transmutation of Qì between the living thing and Nature. 25, 57-58.

Qìánkūn 乾坤: Another name for Heaven and Earth. 19.

Qìào 竅: Qì's congregation point, it would not show unless one has enough Qì. 100-102, 122.

Remote Healing 遙控治療: Uses External Qi to diagnose and treat illness remotely. 55, 160.

Sāncái 三才: Heaven, Earth and Man. 21, 24, 27.

Sānjiāo 三焦: Three sections of cavity within the trunk of the human body. The upper one is located above the diaphragm. The middle one extends from the diaphragm to the naval. The lower one is located below the diaphragm. 13-14, 21-22, 83, 88.

Shén 神: Mind, the controller of life activities. 9, 12, 15, 22, 24-26, 29-30, 34-35, 43-44, 46, 78-83, 90, 93-95, 97-100, 102, 107-113, 124-125, 145. 147-148, 151-152, 157-158, 169, 177-181.

Shén Jī 神機: The root of life and the life activities controlling mechanism, equivalent to DNA. 25, 57-58.

Shén Jī Qìào 神機竅, Qì concentration point, located at the center of the brain. 100, 102.

Shì Shén 識神: It refers to all mental activities including emotions. Shì Shén is learned behavior. 147-148, 169.

Sìxiàng 四象: Tàiyīn 太陰 (pure Yīn), Tàiyáng 太陽 (pure Yáng), Shǎoyīn 少陰 (more Yīn than Yáng) and Shǎoyáng 少陽 (more Yáng than Yīn). 9, 10.

Tài 太: Extreme, big. 24.

Tàijí (太極): Before it is separated into Heaven and Earth, the transmuted Yuán Qì is called Tàijí. 6, 8-9, 19, 21, 29, 40.

Tàixū (Tài Xū) 太虛: Space, universe. 6.

TCM 中醫: Traditional Chinese Medicine.

The five solid organs 五脏: Heart, spleen, liver, lungs and kidneys. 13, 83.

The six hollow organs 六腑: Stomach, large intestine, small intestine, bladder and Sānjiāo 三焦. 13, 22, 83.

Tiāndì 天地: Heaven and Earth or Universe. 67-68, 76.

Wànwù 萬物: Ten-thousand things. 6, 8, 10, 17-18, 20, 41-43, 45, 51-52, 58, 61, 67-68, 72-73.

Wèi Qì 衛氣: Wèi Qì is a coarse Postnatal Qì (Qì from food we eat). 22-23, 123.

Wholistic Information 整體信息: The complete space and time information of an entity. 34, 46, 6984, 112, 137, 141-142, 150, 159, 165.

Wǔ Xíng 五行: Refers to five shapes: Water is round (•), Wood is straight (I), Fire is point (Λ), Soil is square (L), and Metal is thin surface (ロ). 33, 67.

Wǔ Yùn 五運: Wood, Fire, Soil, Metal and Water. 23-25, 58, 67.

Wú 無: Non-existing or nothing. 10-11, 51, 95, 97, 102, 104, 124.

Wújí 無极: Yīn and Yáng have not been separated; Qì and information are within one another. It is called Wújí. 6-7, 39.

Xī (Qì) 器 and Dào 道: Xī—substance with form (the correct Pīnyīn is Qì). Dào—substance without form. 6, 10-11, 21.

Xīn 心: mind/consciousness with emotion. 12-13, 15, 145-147, 156.

Xíng 形 or Jīng 精: The concentrated Qì has form/shape and is Hùn Yuán Qì's expression of physical substances. 9, 12, 15, 25-26, 28, 33, 35-36, 42-43, 78-83, 90, 93, 97-99, 108-110, 112-113, 152, 163.

Xū 虛: A unique Chinese word. The closest translation is nebulous (existing yet not existing; empty yet not empty). 24, 27, 71, 177.

Yì Yuán Tǐ 意元體: When Hùn Yuán Qì in the brain has evolved to the point that it contains consciousness, logical thinking and abstract concepts activity, it is called Yì Yuán Tǐ. 44, 95, 97-98, 102, 124-125, 129-145, 148-159, 162, 165-170, 176, 178.

Yīn 陰 Yáng 陽: The opposite attributes of a substance. The characteristic of Yīn is static and concentrating, Yáng is dynamic and dispersing. When Yuán Qì changes/evolves, the first outcome is Yīn and Yáng, a fundamental law of the universe. When a substance's Taiji moves/separates, it creates Yīn and Yáng. 7, 9, 14, 18-20, 23-27, 29, 30, 33, 41.

Yíng Qì 營氣: Yíng Qì is finer Postnatal Qì (Qì from food we eat). 22, 123.

Yìshí 意識: Consciousness or mind activity. Yì means thinking, pondering and considering. Shí means differentiating, comprehension and understanding. Yìshí means mental activities and social consciousness. 125, 129, 145-171, 176.

Yǒu 有: Existing or means something. 10-11, 51-52, 95, 97, 102, 104, 124, 178.

Yuán Qì 元氣: Dào and Yuán Qì are the same substance that forms the universe; Yuán Qì is the source material for all existence. As Yuán Qì evolves, the finer Qì becomes Heaven, the coarse Qì becomes Earth and the Heaven and Earth Qì merged to beget humans. In human beings, Yuán Qì is the combination of Prenatal and Postnatal Qì. 8, 20-29, 40.

Yuán Shén 元神: The state in which the mind is empty, and there is no mental activity, no distractions from desire, thinking and reasoning.29-30, 147-148, 169.

Yǔ Zhòu 宇宙: Space and time or the universe. 6

Zhēn Qì 真氣: Prenatal and Postnatal Qì transmuted as one or the combination of Nature Qì and food Qì is called Zhēn Qì. 19, 22-23.

Zhēn Yì 真意: The mental activity following the awareness of Yuán Shén. 147-148.

Zhìnéng Qìgōng 智能氣功, founded in 1980 by Dr. Páng Míng. Zhìnéng Qìgōng has a complete system of methods and special Qìgōng theories. iv, v, ix, x, 3, 35, 61, 97, 101, 103, 116, 129, 148, 152, 157, 176, 179-181.

Zhì 質: Function p. 9, or essence/information p. 28, 29.

Zōng Qì 宗氣: Zōng Qì is the air from Nature that transmutes with Postnatal Qì. 22-23.

ABOUT THE AUTHOR: CHAN (FAMILY NAME) HOU HEE

In the 1990s, Chan Lǎoshī and his brother Luke Chan were among the first teachers to officially introduce Zhìnéng Qìgōng, a medical Qìgōng famous in China for healing thousands with "incurable" diseases, to students in the United States. They named their organization Chilel (meaning Qi Therapy) Qìgōng with the approval of Dr. Páng Míng, founder and grandmaster of Zhìnéng Qìgōng.

Drawing from over 40 years of training and practice in Taiji and Qìgōng and his background as an engineer, the hallmark of Chan Lǎoshī's teaching is his ability to explain to his students HOW and WHY a movement is performed in terms that they are able to understand. Chan Lǎoshī's philosophy is that Qìgōng is not something that is mysterious. He defines Qìgōng as "physical therapy or exercise with mindfulness." Qìgōng is what we practice once we become aware of our body and aware of how we move our body.

To complement the physical forms of Qìgōng, he teamed up with Eva Lew, M.D. who provides insights into the mental and emotional parts of Qìgōng practice as well as the relationship of Qìgōng to Western Medicine. Their collaboration resulted in the release of "Medicine Begins with Me: a Wholism Approach to Healthcare." This program is designed to train healthcare providers as well as the general public in effective, easy to learn Qìgōng techniques.

CHILEL QÌGŌNG TITLES

Guides to Zhìnéng (Chilel) Qìgōng Series:

Book 1: *Zhìnéng Qìgōng: Overview and Foundation Methods*

Book 2: *Zhìnéng Qìgōng: Body and Mind Method*

Book 3: *Qìgōng Theory*

Medicine Begins With Me:
A Holistic Approach to Health Care DVD, by Eva Lew M.D. and Hou Hee Chan

Medicine Begins With Me:
Wellness in Motion DVD, by Eva Lew M.D. and Hou Hee Chan

101 Miracles of Natural Healing Book, by Luke Chan

101 Miracles of Natural Healing DVD, by Luke Chan

Chilel Qìgōng, Body & Mind Method DVD, by Luke Chan

Secrets of Tai Chi Circle: Journey to Enlightenment, by Luke Chan

101 Lessons of Dào, by Luke Chan

For information on workshops, products (DVDs, CDs, books) and practice tips, please visit our website:

www.chilelwellness.com
or
www.chilel.com

www.ingramcontent.com/pod-product-compliance
Lightning Source LLC
LaVergne TN
LVHW080310110826
845155LV00023B/105

* 9 7 8 1 8 9 3 1 0 4 1 6 7 *